Challenging behaviour in schools

The emotional impact of difficult and challenging behaviour in schools has never made it easy for professionals to respond in a calm and considered manner. This applies equally to teachers, senior staff in schools, support services and administrators. Yet the pressure to respond effectively continues to grow.

Challenging Behaviour in Schools describes effective practical approaches which have been developed by schools and support services. It acknowledges that, in dealing with difficult behaviour, it is necessary not only to consider techniques but also the support processes that accompany them.

The editors have each had extensive professional experience in this field, and are the organisers of the annual 'New Directions in Behaviour Support' courses at the University of Nottingham, which have encouraged and disseminated new practice over recent years. All the contributors have led seminars and workshops at these courses and their accounts will be of direct value to senior staff, special needs coordinators and governors in schools, educational psychologists, support teachers and all those involved in policy and planning.

Peter Gray is Principal Educational Psychologist for Nottinghamshire, and has been the editor of the journal *Educational and Child Psychology*. **Andy Miller** is Course Director in Educational Psychology at the University of Nottingham. **Jim Noakes** is Head Teacher of the Northern Area Education Support Service, Warwickshire. All three editors have been classroom teachers, covering between them both primary and secondary mainstream schools and special schools for pupils with moderate learning difficulties, and emotional and behavioural difficulties.

14.99

Challenging behaviour in schools

Teacher support, practical techniques and policy development

Edited by
Peter Gray, Andy Miller and Jim Noakes

London and New York

First published 1994
by Routledge
11 New Fetter Lane, London EC4P 4EE

Simultaneously published in the USA and Canada
by Routledge
29 West 35th Street, New York, NY 10001

Reprinted in 1996

© 1994 Selection and editorial matter, Peter Gray, Andy Miller and Jim Noakes;
individual chapters, the contributors

Typeset in Times by Florencetype Ltd, Kewstoke, Avon
Printed and bound in Great Britain by
Biddles Ltd, Guildford and King's Lynn

British Library Cataloguing in Publication Data
A catalogue record for this book is available from the British Library

Library of Congress Cataloguing in Publication Data
A catalogue record for this book is available from the Library of Congress

ISBN 0–415–09973–0 (hbk)
ISBN 0–415–09974–9 (pbk)

Contents

Illustrations

FIGURES

TABLES

Contributors

Barry Chisholm, Senior Educational Psychologist, Bradford.

David Coombs, Team Coordinator, Northern Area Education Support Service, Warwickshire.

Peter Costa, Educational Psychologist, Leeds.

Jackie Dearden, Deputy Head Teacher, Cantrell Primary School, Nottinghamshire.

Pauline Fell, Team Coordinator, Northern Area Education Support Service, Warwickshire.

Peter Galvin, Educational Psychologist, Leeds.

Peter Gray, Principal Educational Psychologist, Nottinghamshire.

Phil Hamerton, Team Leader (North) Special Needs Support Service (EBD), Nottinghamshire.

Chris Hevey, Deputy Head Teacher, Northern Area Education Support Service, Warwickshire.

Andrea Higgins, Educational Psychologist, Derbyshire.

Penny Holland, Educational Psychologist, Nottinghamshire.

Andre Imich, Senior Educational Psychologist, Essex.

Kath Jefferies, Behaviour Support Teacher, Essex.

David Lane, Director, Professional Development Foundation, London.

Andy Miller, Educational Psychology Course Director, University of Nottingham.

Jim Noakes, Head Teacher, Northern Area Education Support Service, Warwickshire.

Peter Olsen, Team Leader, Behaviour Support Service, Sandwell.

Tim Pickles, Freelance Consultant, Trainer and Writer, Framework, Glasgow.

Michael Pitchford, Senior Educational Psychologist, Derbyshire.

Simon Priest, Educational Psychologist, Derbyshire.

David Prior, Head Teacher, Etone School, Warwickshire.

Carol Stewart-Evans, Educational Psychologist, Nottinghamshire.

Dave Traxson, Senior Educational Psychologist, Wolverhampton.

Phil Watts, Principal Educational Psychologist, Sandwell.

Jayne Wilson, Deputy Head Teacher, Etone School, Warwickshire.

Chapter 1

Challenging behaviour in schools: an introduction

Peter Gray, Andy Miller and Jim Noakes

Ask any teacher what makes their job so difficult and they will point to the problems presented by pupils with challenging behaviour. They will of course also identify other causes, such as increasing curriculum demands, expectations from parents and increasing pupil–teacher ratios. However, challenging behaviour has a particular salience. Why?

By contrast to other problems faced by teachers in schools, challenging behaviour tends to be perceived as a direct and personal threat to the teacher's authority. And the greater the sense of threat, the more likely it is for a number of things to happen. First, it becomes more difficult for teachers (without support) to maintain a dispassionate perspective. Second, teachers can become defensive of their own position and develop negative attitudes towards the pupil, parents or others (including outside agencies). Finally, attitudes can become more hardened, with a loss of flexibility or willingness on the part of teachers to consider alternative approaches (on the basis that flexibility might imply a weakening of their own position or an admission of fault).

All of these emotions are natural enough and arise from the fact that teaching is an intensely *human* profession. These kinds of emotions have always been there, as long as challenging behaviour has existed. We sometimes tend to hold a romantic view of a 'golden age' in education when such problems did not exist and teachers were able to respond, without distraction, to pupils' enthusiastic search for knowledge. This view is not supported by history. The Hadow Report (Board of Education 1927), for example, was, like Elton (DES 1989), initiated as a response to rising concerns about declining standards of behaviour in schools. Humphries (1981), in his oral history of education in the 1920s and 1930s, also provides evidence of incidents comparable to if not worse than some of the more extreme difficulties that teachers currently experience.

Yet, there is no denying the level of current concern among teachers and schools about challenging behaviour. This is evidenced by the rising numbers of exclusions from schools reported nationally. While these may result in part from increases in the level and intensity of difficult behaviour presented in some schools, arising from changes in social conditions, other factors are also relevant.

First, teachers' traditional professional autonomy has been challenged by the developing climate of educational consumerism. Government and media coverage of the teachers' industrial action in the early 1980s has also contributed to an erosion of teachers' public credibility. The political thrust of the National Curriculum has been to give further credence to the view that teachers cannot be trusted to teach effectively unless methods and content are centrally prescribed. In this context, challenging behaviour poses an additional threat to teachers' professional self-confidence and morale.

There has also been a shift in public attitude during the last two decades, away from a therapeutic and tolerant approach to difficult pupil behaviour towards a more retributive and punitive stance. The public outrage that followed the murder of Jamie Bulger, for example, revealed a reluctance among many to accept the legal *status quo* on the age of criminal responsibility. There is a current tendency to see even young children as 'witting offenders' rather than vulnerable individuals in need of planned and caring support.

Teachers' professional responsibility is *educational* not penal in character. However, as members of the public at large, teachers are not immune to influence from a predominantly punitive climate and negative beliefs can emerge when they feel most under threat and least able to achieve a *professional* resolution to the problem.

Another factor that makes challenging behaviour particularly difficult at the present time is the danger of teachers and schools becoming more and more isolated professionally. This leads to a potential lack of awareness of the broader picture. What happens to excluded pupils when they leave and who cares? How far are needs actually met in off-site or specialist provision? Local Education Authorities have traditionally held the responsibility for ensuring a *corporate* view (through policy, planning of provision and specification of professional development opportunities). However, these are very much under threat from new legislation. Schools have been actively encouraged by government to compete and the notion of 'good' and 'bad' schools has extended to 'good' and 'bad' teachers through the development of appraisal and the threat of performance-related pay. This encourages an individualistic as opposed to a mutually supportive culture.

In this context, teachers and schools are bound to be more defensive in the face of challenging behaviour, with schools feeling under pressure to reject difficult pupils in order to improve their competitive image and teachers seeing less value in achieving success with such pupils, as this has relatively low 'market-value'.

Finally, the flexibility that teachers have always needed in order to improvise and develop ways of meeting individual pupil need has been reduced by the narrower view of education imposed by the National Curriculum. While this may have broadened the range of subjects offered formally (e.g. primary school science and technology), it has diminished the importance of personal and social education. It has also reduced the flexibility in organisation of the school day, which has helped many schools lower the incidence of behaviour difficulties overall.

Teachers and schools now face potentially more difficult problems in a context which is less supportive than in the past. The *need* therefore for effective support both from within schools and from outside agencies is greater than ever. However, the task of *providing* support is beset by the same contextual factors that teachers and schools themselves are facing. Support services find it equally difficult to focus their attention on the most troublesome youngsters when they are under pressure to secure their own professional survival (services which are complex in client orientation and potentially challenging to schools are not easily marketable). In this context, a major emphasis within both schools and support services on professional and ethical values is called for to ensure that good practice can occur.

Teachers and schools need a number of things: opportunities to develop skills where appropriate, without having existing skills devalued (and morale further diminished!); opportunities for reassurance that, despite possible slow and painful progress, they are doing the best they can and that, at least professionally, their efforts with difficult pupils are valued; opportunities to have their beliefs challenged where appropriate, together with support and guidance to assist them in making a professional response.

The chapters in this book offer a number of strategies and ways of thinking to help schools and support staff in this process. Several were first presented as sessions at a series of conferences organised by the editors over the last few years, under the general heading 'New Directions in Behaviour Support Work', which have been attended by delegates from both mainstream schools and support services.

A major emphasis within the book (and within the conferences that have led up to it) has been the need to assert a *professional* response in this area of educational support, rather than letting market forces operate for children and young people whose behaviour may be provocative but whose needs for high-quality planned intervention are as great as many others with more 'acceptable' special educational needs. Support in this area is more prone to both professional and personal tensions, and the direct needs of the 'customer' (teacher/school/parent/LEA) and the individual needs of the 'client' (pupil) may sometimes start from opposite extremes. The aim of this book is to consider ways in which both pupil *and* teacher achievements in the resolution of challenging behaviour can be encouraged, supported and valued.

REFERENCES

Board of Education (1927) *The Education of the Adolescent*. Report of the Consultative Committee (The Hadow Report). London: Board of Education.

Department of Education and Science (1989) *Behaviour in Schools* (The Elton Report). London: HMSO.

Humphries, S. (1981) *Hooligans or Rebels? An Oral History of Working-Class Childhood and Youth, 1889–1939*. Oxford: Blackwell.

Chapter 2

Supporting effective responses to challenging behaviour: from theory to practice

David Lane

NOTHING WORKS!

There have been increasing demands in recent years for special provision for children and adolescents who present behaviour difficulties in school or in the community. The impact on the public of the visual images of young children defying the authority of the police, racing cars, killing the innocent, has been dramatic. There is an increasing sense of outrage at the thought that there is nothing that anyone can do. In part the outrage is directed at those in the caring professions who seem to refuse to do anything.

This sense of hopelessness in the face of the onslaught on the public conscience is aggravated by the competing concerns that appear when stories surface of the outrages perpetrated on some young vulnerable people in care. Scandals give way to concern, and then a new story of a child's defiance of accepted conventions washes over the concern and converts it back to outrage. Many people have been left confused, seeking answers to a situation they simply cannot understand. In that set of circumstances, someone is sought to blame, and solutions, the more instant the better, are demanded and funded.

Yet this situation is not new. Each generation expresses shock at the unreasonable 'immorality' of the young. Since the 1950s, new schemes to work with difficult children have emerged. The 1970s in particular saw a dramatic increase in the number of services for 'disruptive pupils'. (ILEA 1978; HMI 1978). Gillham (1981) has argued that there 'was a point in the early seventies when it seemed as if many secondary schools in the major urban areas were heading for breakdown'. Current concerns about exclusions from school and the evidence that disruptivebehaviour is a major reason given for exclusions reflect very closely the issues raised during the 1970s (ACE 1992; NUT 1992)

Various theoretical perspectives have been brought to bear on the problem, and not inconsiderable levels of funding have been devoted to politically popular projects. Yet in many ways, the sense of hopelessness felt by the public was shared by the professionals. The optimism of the 1950s and 1960s that psychology had the answers began to wilt under the impact of an increasing number of studies which seemed to indicate that children improved or did not, and that the psychological interventions to which they were exposed had very little influence on the outcome. The idea that nothing works became the theme of a number of key literature reviews during the 1970s and 1980s (McGuire and Priestley 1992).

The public and professionals it seemed, shared the view that we had no answers.

SOME THINGS DO WORK, SOMETIMES!

There was, however, something missing from the literature reviews, something that is always missing. This was the work of those practitioners, striving to provide high-quality services, who were not writing papers for scientific journals but who were concentrating on the needs of the client groups. Their ideas were not unknown and were being shared as a number of groups began to emerge to help practitioners to look at each other's work and learn from that experience. Groups such as the Association for Behavioural Approaches with Children grew up to meet that need, faded and then died. The Islington Seminar series from the mid-1970s brought many hundreds of practitioners together and encouraged networking activities (eventually transmuting into the Professional Development Foundation) to spread good practice. The Behaviour Support Conference, as an informal grouping of practitioners working in similar fields, enabled many ideas to emerge and helped people to question their own practice. Little of this work ever found its way into print and, therefore, into the literature reviews. Some of this practitioner-based work has, of course, always found its way into the literature (Lane and Miller 1992; Miller and Lane 1993), but the trend towards publications which recognise this experience is reflected in this current volume.

It was possible that something might work. Certainly, reviewers in the UK began to see evidence of effective programmes (Topping 1983) and a revision of the earlier 'nothing works' philosophy emerged. Partly this was in response to new, more hopeful studies, and partly it was from a re-evaluation of the earlier work. There was, it was argued, too crude a grouping of the research in earlier 'meta-analytic' studies. Buried within the general negative findings were examples of projects that did have an impact. With careful selection of client, problem and technique, it now seemed possible to be a little more optimistic (Callias 1992).

Some things did work, sometimes. Not by throwing money at the problem, not by massively increasing one type of provision, be it a child guidance clinic or school for the maladjusted, but through the judicious use of carefully focused ideas children's lives could be turned around.

WHAT ARE THESE THINGS THAT WORK?

Now that is the question that this author dreads. It is, of course, a perfectly legitimate question, but unfortunately it implies that because something works that there is an answer. There is not. There are many different answers, each of which has worked in different situations. Making sense of them is not easy. Recently there has been a move towards the careful evaluation of ideas and the selection on interventions which can draw upon research support. However, traditionally this has not been the method by which programmes have been selected. Interventions for challenging behaviours have been driven by considerations outside the specific service demands of the client group. Programmes have tended to emerge from two traditions: those driven by theoretical concerns, and those focused on specific problem categories. A more focused service-oriented approach was supposed to be the outcome of the Individualised Plans in the USA from 1974, and the Statementing procedures in the UK from 1981. As Widlake (1993) has pointed out, resource availability rather than need has often been the determining factor in the content of the plans. The varying traditions have produced distinct approaches, which still impact on service provision today. A sense of these traditions, therefore, is useful. The analytical tradition, being the oldest, will be considered initially.

Ideas adapted from analytical theories

The child confronts us with unacceptable behaviour, but for the analytically-oriented practitioner that behaviour is not itself the focus of interest. Unconscious anxieties, conflicts and fantasies are believed to provide the key to understanding. Behaviour is seen as the manifestation of the underlying processes and therefore is open to modification only through exploring the child's inner world and the relationships between that inner world and the child's interaction with significant factors in the external world (Callias *et al.* 1992). The theories of Sigmund Freud provided the initial impetus to the development of the understanding of childhood, but it was primarily the work of Melanie Klein (1932) and Anna Freud (1966) that led to the application of analytic ideas to the treatment of children's behaviour problems.

For Klein the first year of life was critical; the psychological processes that arose for the child during that period were crucial to understanding later development. Anna Freud disagreed, stressing the resolution of the Oedipus complex, between the ages of three and five, as the key determinant of the emotional health of the individual. In spite of these fundamental differences, both theorists emphasised the importance of early experience. These ideas greatly influenced the development and provision of child guidance services as a mechanism for resolving conflicts within the child. Prior to the Second World War the main influence on the provision of services came from Melanie Klein and Anna Freud. The settings for therapy have changed, and the child guidance clinics which provided the home for much of the individual therapy offered to children have adapted to the criticisms levelled at them, but key concepts from those theorists remain (Howarth 1992).

The most fundamental of the concepts relate to the provision of a safe setting in which the intervention takes place, the transference relationship between client and practitioner, the use of interpretation to bring about change in the client's inner world, and the containment of anxiety. Following the Second World War, evidence on the effect of separation on children led to an evolution of these ideas. Bowlby (1951, 1969), in particular, contributed a perspective in which he placed attachments at the centre of the clinical considerations when dealing with a child. The traumatic effects of earlier separations on later development were described. These ideas were later challenged (Rutter 1971) and amended (Bowlby 1988) but have remained influential.

One example of the influence of these ideas was the development of part-time provision for 'maladjusted' children in the form of tutorial classes (Rabinowitz 1981). This provision attempted to create a safe place in which anxieties could be contained. In part, that safety was expressed through careful systems for referral and discharge. Tutorial classes focused on educational issues, but it was the emotional issues behind the educational difficulties that marked the distinguishing feature of this, compared with a remedial class, which might deal with difficulties through analysis of the learning itself or neurological process.

Ideas adapted from developmental theories

Analytical theories contained specific developmental phases, but the impact of work from developmental psychology has been slow to generate interventions for problematic behaviour. Recently, developmental theories have begun to influence other perspectives (Yule 1990; Herbert 1991) and specific models have also emerged. (Christie et al. 1992; Newson 1992). Developmental theories have a long history and have influenced thinking in the fields of learning disorders. Similarly, some phase-based ideas of development have impacted on work for emotional disorders. Herbert (1991) has made the important point that some problematic behaviours are characteristic of a particular developmental stage and are often transient, while others may be exaggerations of age-appropriate behaviours, or transitions between stages. Given the reality of this position, any attempt to understand childhood problems that does not take account of developmental ideas seems overly narrow.

Yet it is only in the last fifteen years or so that the call for a more active consideration of developmental ideas has emerged (Achenbach 1974,

1982; Cicchetti 1984; Herbert 1974; Lane 1978, 1990; Sroufe and Rutter 1984). The child is faced with developmental tasks which emerge at different stages and these remain influential, or critical, as the child adapts to them and then faces new issues. The resolutions adopted at one point may structure the resolutions available at a later point. The balance of resources that the child can bring to bear on any problem is thereby tilted.

Models for intervention that build upon understanding of the developmental status of the child, or which explicitly use developmental theory, have been demonstrated to be successful in dealing with a wide range of difficulties. Christie *et al.* (1992) have used such an approach in work with non-speaking children. Newson's work with multiple problems in the context of play therapy (Newson 1992) and programmes for children with severely challenging behaviours (Jones 1993) make use of a mixture of ideas including developmental frameworks. Early attempts to work within a structure informed by this framework were found in the 'nurture groups' run by the ILEA (Boxall 1976). These programmes carefully assisted the child to face key tasks. A programme of supported learning enabled the child to progress through various developmental tasks.

Ideas adapted from behavioural theories

The application of behavioural approaches within education stems largely from a classic study by Madsen, Becker and Thomas (1968). As Burden and Miller (1993) point out, a number of demonstration projects followed, and in the UK during the 1970s several applications were reported (Lane 1973, 1974; Harrop 1974; Presland 1974). By 1977, Yule, in a review of behaviour modification in education, was able to point to a wide variety of applications focused on specific problems or settings. Merrett (1981) was able to add several further examples. McNamara (1988), however, added the criticism that in the UK, like the USA, many studies were carried out under circumstances which were most favourable to a successful outcome. This applied to a number of the published demonstration projects, but could not be said to apply to those which emerged as service-led interventions (see Lane 1990; Gray and Noakes 1993). As behavioural approaches became more prominent during the 1980s a number of elaborated packages for the application of behavioural ideas came onto the market place. The most important of these included *The Behavioural Approach to Teaching Package – Batpac* (Wheldall and Merrett 1985) and *Preventative Approaches to Disruption – PAD* (Chisholm *et al.* 1986). Some practitioners avoided the packaged approach and argued that a more individualised analysis was necessary (Lister 1993).

The analytic, developmental and behavioural have been the most influential of the theoretical frameworks, but there have been others (Callias *et al.* 1992).

A problem-oriented focus on challenging behaviours

Criticism of the models influencing provision for problem behaviour developed from the 1950s onward. Eysenck's (1952) initial attack on the effectiveness of adult psychotherapy, was extended to interventions for children by Levitt (1963). By the 1980s the child guidance movement was under attack (Tizard 1973), but there was an increasing awareness that remission from problems varied between types of behaviour (see Lane 1990 for a review) This led to increased interest in issues of causation because, as Rutter (1972) has argued, family features do significantly differentiate types of disorder. Subsequently, a broad range of additional features have been found to correlate with difficulties. Thus, if we are able to group behaviours and identify features which relate to their occurrence, we might be able to design interventions which take account of them. The search for such features has been very active.

There is now a vast literature devoted to explanations of why individuals develop behaviour disorders. Explanations available tend to fall into broad divisions, which see behaviour in terms of either cultural or individual difference.

Delinquent neighbourhoods

The assumption that delinquent behaviour relates to the existence of poverty and neighbourhoods that generate anti-social behaviour is one of the earliest of cultural theories. The studies of Burt (1925), Thrasler (1935), and Shaw and McKay (1942) consistently emphasised the relationship. Unfortunately, inroads into dealing with poverty have not resulted in a reduction in deviance. Indeed, the rising trend of delinquency noted by Durkheim has continued and delinquent behaviour is very widespread among the young (Rutter and Giller 1982).

Cohen (1955), Merton (1949) and Cloward and Ohlin (1961) in different ways saw juvenile crime both as a reaction to working-class youths' frustration and as a part of a working-class sub-culture, thereby serving an adaptive function. Halleck (1967), however, has argued that while the delinquent behaviour of adolescents is certainly incongruent with the goals of middle-class adults, they are also alien to the working classes, who are similarly disturbed by the unreasonable nature of juvenile crime. Robbins (1966) has pointed out that anti-social behaviour in childhood is equally predictive of adult disturbance in all classes, and therefore its so-called adaptive function must be questioned. The fact that in the long term most working-class youths do not remain delinquent, and the remarkable similarity in the type of offences committed by working-class and middle-class youths (Nye 1958; Herskowitz et al. 1959) makes cultural transmission theories less tenable than they used to be.

However, this is not to say that poverty does not lead to deprivation, only that the cultural infection theory lacks support. In a major report based on ten years of accumulated research, Brown and Madge (1982) concluded that all the evidence suggested that cultural values are not important for the development and transmission of deprivation. They also quote West's (1979) research for the same project as concluding that the role of delinquent sub-cultures can be largely discounted.

Cultural theories probably have little to offer as potential models for the design of intervention programmes, in spite of the popularity of the idea. A number of early intervention projects did operate with the idea that it was important to take the child out of the delinquent sub-culture. The problem has always been that a return to that culture followed any intervention. (Similar problems have influenced thinking in areas such as drug abuse; see Lane 1972, 1973.) However, research into bullying behaviour has pointed to the role of peer groups and power/affiliation issues (Askew 1988; Roland 1988). A narrower focus on such factors rather than the broader cultural theories may be fruitful.

Delinquent families and socialisation

Alternative theories are those which see anti-social behaviour as arising from patterns within families. The early pioneering study was that of the Gluecks (1950), in which they compared 500 delinquent youths with 500 non-delinquent youths. There were a number of problems with the study but many of their conclusions were reflected in later studies. Argyle (1964), reviewing the main results of a number of studies, pointed to the role of parental discipline, the absence of a parent or parental conflict and delin- quency in the parents as important. A major emphasis on the role of the mother in early studies (Bowlby 1951) gave way to consideration of the role of the father. Andry (1960) implicated the inadequacy of role relation- ships between father and son in delinquency. Family pathology models represent, in part, a recognition of the importance of the models to which an individual is exposed in shaping behaviour patterns. Extensive reviews (Ellis 1988) have lent credence to the idea that a range of features of family/social construction do impact on behaviour.

Trasler (1964) attempted to integrate sociological and psychological models. He argued that experience within the family constitutes the oppor- tunity to learn skills and confidence in interpersonal relationships and is also a means of acquiring social and moral training. Individuals whose early experience is unsatisfactory, inconsistent or unrewarding will be deprived of opportunities for acquiring either social anxiety and other motives or the techniques of social interaction. An individual whose social skill learning has been deficient will be comparatively invulnerable to social pressure and therefore will remain under-socialised.

The impact of ideas from family therapy (Burnham 1986) on work with challenging behaviour is increasing. Much has been restricted to the confines of clinical settings, but more recently has in adapted forms found its way into the practice of social workers, teachers and psychologists based in the community. The emphasis in family therapy on the patterns of interaction within natural groupings does provide a potential framework for behaviour support teachers. However, some of the pioneers of the family therapy movement have recently recanted much of the theoretical framework and now propose models which have more in common with cognitive and social interactionist approaches.

These newer models concentrate on the 'stories' used to explain events, and the construction and reconstruction of explanations as the model of behaviour change (McNamee and Gergen 1992). They are likely to have greater appeal to many working in the field of behaviour support than the more dominant family therapy ideas. Taken together with Trasler's earlier work a combined model seems viable, one which explores the views of the world that influence the child's response and involves a process to help the child acquire social skills in which there is a deficiency.

Many working with challenging behaviour would argue that their practice already reflects such a combined position. Within a number of settings the emphasis has been to help the child to restructure the way they view events and to provide the skills to act differently in respect of those events. This is an area in which practice precedes theory.

Delinquent schools

During the 1960s there was an increasing emphasis on the role of the school in promoting anti-social behaviour or low expectations in pupils (Willmott 1958; Musgrove 1964; Partridge 1966; Hargreaves 1967). Power and his associates (Power *et al.* 1969) pointed to differences between schools in fostering delinquent attitudes. This study in particular was influential and led to a spate of interest in the role of the school. Schools, in the way they are organised, through conflicts of role, the weight placed on achievement, attitudes of teachers in promoting conflict or cooperation, the content of lessons and the operation of rewards, can greatly influence behaviour, attendance and the learning that takes place (Lane 1973, 1976, 1978).

The role of the school has recently received far more attention. The work of Reynolds (1982), Rutter *et al.* (1979), and Mortimore *et al.* (1988) has been very important in refocusing the debate on the role of the school. From our perspective, however, the studies by Galloway and his associates (Galloway *et al.* 1982) are highly relevant in their concentration on disruptive pupils. They point among other things to the way in which organisational problems in the school contribute to disruptive behaviour and how some forms of support for the child may actually increase difficulties.

Support groups may function as ways of removing the evidence of tension within a school. The relationship between schools, disruptive behaviour and delinquency is a complex one worthy of attention, but much of the data is difficult to interpret. It does appear, as a Home Office research review indicates, that some practices in schools influence the progression from minor misbehaviour to delinquency (Graham 1988).

Thus it is not just the school attended which matters, but patterns of interaction within it. Understanding those patterns may be essential if long-term impact from any intervention is to take place. The recognition of the importance of those patterns has greatly influenced 'school-focused' behaviour support work (Lane 1975, 1978, 1990; Coulby and Harper 1983; Gray and Noakes 1992; Lister 1993). The struggle to balance the impact of the role of the school and that of the individual referred is central to many intervention projects.

Discrimination and language

Discrimination in society is clear and obvious, and whole groups can receive adverse treatment (Brown and Madge 1982). However, the possibility of selective labelling of children from different ethnic minorities, and the consequent placement of them in special education, has concentrated attention. A number of suggestions that black children were over-represented in units for disruptive children did raise questions about differences between groups in levels of difficulty (ACE 1992).

That language can have a powerful effect on how children are seen and labelled in schools was clearly established by Eggleston et al. (1986). The level of representation of pupils in groups labelled as especially difficult requires consideration in spite of the sensitivity of the issue. The possibility of pupils being referred for special education on grounds of racial differences rather than any objective difference in behaviour cannot be ignored. West et al. (1986) referred to the over-representation of pupils classified as Caribbean in centres for pupils with difficulties, and an under-representation of Asian pupils. Surveys by the Inner London Education Authority (1988) confirm this pattern. They argue for greater vigilance by teachers in referral. There is a wide range of ways in which cultural factors influence therapeutic services, and practitioners have learned to become more vigilant in recent years.

Intervention projects in many parts of the UK were faced with uncomfortable dilemmas when confronted by racially biased referral patterns. The argument that such services act as agents of social control has received less attention (Keise et al. 1993). Attempts to deal with the issue have found their way into the work of a number of practitioners, as Keise indicates.

The labelling of the child

As Becker (1963) pointed out, 'Social groups create deviance by making the rules whose infraction constitutes deviance and by applying those rules to particular people and labelling them as outsiders'.

If we apply this thinking to our consideration of those referred to behaviour support services, it becomes clear that whatever it is that counts as challenging behaviour is not a simple quality present in the act of deviance itself, but rather the end product of a process of response by others to the act, which results in the gradual development of conflict between the child and the referring agent and the alienation of the individual from sources of support. Coser (1956) refers to the positive function of such conflict for the in group. Attempts to bring the individual back have the effect of strengthening existing bonds and values, but where the attempt fails the individual's exclusion serves as a restatement of the in-group values. A number of behaviour support teachers have seen this pattern when they have attempted reintegration from an off-site provision back into the school. Such reintegration needs very careful structuring (Gray and Noakes 1993).

Social learning explanations: aggression and anti-social behaviour

Traditional formulations of aggression focus on concepts such as inhibition, drive or guilt deficit: for example, the view of Dollard *et al.* (1939) that frustration leads to aggression. An alternative position (Bandura and Walters 1959) sees aggressive behaviour as normal behaviour that has been negatively labelled by some person in authority. Aggressive behaviour can be placed in such a view within the larger category of assertive behaviour (Patterson *et al.* 1967). So defined, it is normally occurring behaviour that may or may not receive a negative response. It is nevertheless governed by standard principles of learning and no elaborate pathological theories are needed to explain it. An individual learns to behave aggressively because it is reinforcing to do so.

There are numerous experimental studies supporting the value of such learning principles applied to behaviour problems (Ullman and Krasner 1975). For example, the experience of the individual might be one of severe punishment or punishment based on the adults' shifting moods rather than on consistent objective principles related to the child's behaviour. The result is that the individual learns that people are sources of punishment, to be avoided, rather than sources of reinforcement to be sought. The use of the personal relationship between the teacher and the child as the mechanism for promoting behaviour change is very difficult in such circumstances. A more pragmatic set of external reinforcers may need to precede the development of the relationship. 'What's in it for me?', the child asks.

Services operating within a behavioural model have attempted to address such concerns and have frequently turned to the use of external reinforcers as part of their response.

Genetic, individual difference and congenital explanations

Although the learning principles discussed above are well established, it is necessary to explain why some individuals respond more readily than others to some learning situations. There does appear to be some evidence to support the idea that individuals vary constitutionally in responsiveness to conditioning.

Theories of causation also include genetic and constitutional concepts. The early ideas that physical characteristics were important concomitants of deviant behaviours (Sheldon *et al*. 1949; Lombroso 1917) have largely disappeared. A modern variant, the concept of minor physical abnormalities, has appeared instead. High rates of MPAs have been found in various groups of children presenting behaviour problems, and these features are usually evident from birth (Quinn and Rappaport 1974). Genetic studies also point to inheritance factors playing a part in determining the level of disturbance (Shields and Slater 1960).

It is also commonly argued that there is a relationship between gender and aggression. Physical aggression (for example, bullying) is more common in boys (Roland and Munthe 1989). This is partly the result of learned sex roles, but, since even young children vary on this dimension (Sears *et al*. 1957) and since animal research has indicated that injecting male sex hormones into animals makes them more aggressive (Suhl 1961), it may be partly constitutional. Nevertheless, it is apparent that aggressive fathers will serve as models to their sons. Parents who do not generally permit aggression, but who also do not punish it when it occurs, produce less aggressive children than parents who do punish aggression (Sears *et al*. 1957).

More sophisticated studies, based on brain-wave activity, have shown that delinquents in general do not differ from non-delinquents, but certain groups who often commit offences do differ on such measures (Michaels 1955; Volavka 1987). Of interest are the increasing number of studies which link arousal levels in the brain with response to punishment (Hare 1971). It is argued that some individuals do not change their behaviour in anticipation of punishment in the way that other individuals do, and thus the threat of punishment has no impact. Ellis (1987), in a review of numerous studies in this field, argues strongly for the link with arousal. Studies of the relationship between congenital factors and behaviour problems such as Stott's data (Stott *et al*. 1975), make it difficult to ignore the possibility of some congenital explanation and therefore the health of the pupils becomes a factor to take into account.

These factors may be ignored in a programme focused specifically on behaviour problems, but, where differences in patterns of arousal or neurological factors are present, effective programmes will need to take account of them. There have been few attempts to take account of individual difference factors in the design of interventions, but calls for such an approach have appeared in work for bullying (see Tattum and Lane 1988; Roland and Munthe 1989) and delinquency (see Eysenck and Gudjonsson 1989). Specific attempts to adapt programmes to deal with the influence of individual differences were illustrated in the early Islington Series in work for learning programmes (Lane 1976), truancy (Lane 1974) and behaviour problems (Lane 1978).

Service perspectives on challenging behaviours

During the 1970s a few voices were heard appealing for a more service-oriented approach. It was argued that a focus on the individual problem or a single theoretical perspective was ineffective or less efficient. The impact of the context within which problems occurred, school–community–family, and the rights of the client had been neglected. These criticisms emerged from a number of sources and with different targets. Thus Tizard (1973) pointed to the ineffectiveness of the child guidance clinics (see Howarth 1992 for a more recent discussion). Others (Lane 1973; Lawrence 1973; Hart 1979; Miller 1980) pointed to the impact of context and argued for a more systems-oriented approach, in which not the individual but rather the context might be the focus for a programme of change. These views slowly gained credence during the 1980s, helped substantially by the publication of the work of Rutter and his associates (Rutter *et al.* 1979). The impact of this later report was made possible by the gradual change in climate that preceded it. The ideas within it, that schools matter, had been flagged in a pioneering study by Power and his colleagues in 1969 (Power *et al.* 1969). Power had argued that schools might create delinquency, and pointed to possible features of the way a school might be managed. That research was cut short by its sponsors, the message being too radical for the times. Only later was the team led by Rutter allowed by the same sponsors to answer some of the questions first raised by Power. However, in the interim, the Warnock Report (DES 1978) had appeared, and the categorical approach to labelling the child was in the process of being abandoned. Those practitioners who were struggling to present a service orientation with the emphasis on a flexible approach incorporating clients' rights, in the years prior to Rutter and Warnock, were relieved to have powerful allies (see Lane 1990).

Three important themes emerged in the 1980s:

1 *The emergence of a focus on the context in which difficulties occurred*

Several practitioners were working towards the development of services which placed the emphasis on understanding behaviour in context. The earliest full service which combined a range of provision – from programmes specifically with the individual child to attempts at whole-school policy – was the Islington Educational Guidance Centre (Lane 1974, 1975). This scheme under the auspices of the Inner London Education Authority was widely copied, although it remained controversial. The ideas were shared by many practitioners and, increasingly, service provisions based on these and complementary ideas appeared throughout the UK. In Southwark and Tower Hamlets in Inner London and Waltham Forest, and Barking and Dagenham in Outer London, services appeared that embodied a flexible approach to individual and system change. Outside London, important services developed in Manchester, Hampshire, Knowsley, and under the influence of Exeter University in the South-west. By the mid-1980s a new professional began to appear, 'the Behaviour Support Teacher', and a regular series of programmes to share ideas emerged, based at Nottingham University.

The ideas influencing these provisions were varied, but the emphasis on looking at the behaviour in context was shared. Many had a behavioural orientation, but it was a more flexible approach than had marked the earlier experiments with behaviourism in education (Yule 1977).

2 *The move towards statements of need*

The 1981 Education Act and the 1989 Children Act share an emphasis on the idea that it is possible to devise an individual plan to meet identified need. The advantage of both lay in the move away from categorical labels. The disadvantage lay in a philosophy which equated with 'children in need' rather than 'contexts which generate problems'. Thus the child or family has the problem, to which professionals (in partnership!) have the solution. That the professionals might be contributors to the problem, or may even be the primary source of the problem does not feature sufficiently in either piece of legislation. Some very elaborate manuals designed to take practitioners step by step through an assessment of need have emerged to support the Children Act. The contrast between a philosophy which purports to value partnership, with assessment models which dictate the questions, pace and structure of the data-gathering exercise seems to have passed by the exponents of the models. Systems of assessment are now in vogue that depart from everything the last decade has taught us about listening to children, helping them to assert their own position and have it respected. A move back to referral-led systems is perhaps inevitable. It will be ironic if legislation intended to take us forward to partnership in fact provides the mechanism for the re-emergence of the professional's power to 'place'.

Lip-service is paid to the impact of culture and there is no recognition of the power imbalance in the process of assessment. Keise *et al*. (1993) argue that we must: (a) learn about our clients' experience; (b) learn about the processes which underline that experience; (c) learn to listen to children in a way that respects their experience; (d) learn that experience is embedded in culture; (e) learn to identify the links between sexism, racism, and disabling therapy; (f) learn to empower our clients.

Some of the structured assessment models appearing in official publications fail to take full account of the fact (Keise *et al*. 1993) that the context is one in which someone in a position of power is able to apply a prescriptive label to another, direct them to change and apply consequences if they do not. Power is an inevitable part of our role – pretending otherwise does not make it go away; recognising the nature of that power and how it operates does help the client to understand the limits and potentials of their own position and hence their rights. Widlake (1993) has argued that we find 'professionals deciding what should be taught in ways decided by professionals just as if there had been no legislation, nor any tradition of parental involvement'.

3 *The emergence of the rights of clients*

A recently published method for classifying services (Callias *et al*. 1992) places the nature of the power relationships at the centre of the exercise. It is suggested that the assignment of services is based on three systems underpinned by three notions of causation. The child might be 'placed' in an off-site unit, on the basis of a professional decision, and the child is seen as the focus for change. The child might be 'referred' through a gatekeeper to a suitable provision. They may be allowed to influence this decision but power remains primarily with the professional. Or an 'assessment' based on partnership might happen with a joint decision emerging. These three models for structuring the decision process are matched by three models of service intervention, with the individual, a natural system such as the family or the peer group, being the main focus. The third approach has an ecological focus in which the service may be directed at a range of groupings, including the school.

Careful analysis of these different methods does reveal shortcomings in service provision. For example, the behaviour support teacher may prefer a partnership approach, but if the service model is based on 'placement' then establishing the partnership will be very difficult.

The increasing emphasis on the idea of partnerships has been fuelled by two features stressed in the Education Reform Act 1988. The local management of schools has introduced a market economy into provision of services. Parental rights and the role of governors have shifted the power balance within schools, a little or a lot! The ERA has, as Widlake (1993) pointed out, been a watershed in educational history. The market is now firmly and perhaps permanently a part of our thinking. Provision for children presenting with behaviour difficulties will now have to be justified in economic not just educational terms. The Act does emphasise that the feelings of the child must be taken into account when provision is suggested. There is, in principle at least, a move away from placement and referral towards assessment models. How far, in practice, the structures of statementing will generate the continuance of referral models remains to be seen. Widlake (1993) argues that there remain good and bad practices, with some educational psychologists receiving full marks from parents for their careful attempts fully to involve them and the child in the process. However, as comments from parents to the ILEA indicate (ILEA 1985), there is still a sense among many that professionals will do what they want anyway.

Some services have grasped the ERA philosophy firmly and have introduced charging for off-site services. Schools have to be prepared to spend part of their own budget on any places required. Some schools and specialist services taking the market seriously have added the pursuit of quality systems from industry to their agenda. They have sought and been awarded the British Standard for quality management (BS 5750). (See Woodgate 1993 for a discussion.)

Although it is certainly the case that the ERA appears to threaten many of the gains made during the last two decades towards a more integrated service (Widlake 1993), there are features that behaviour support teachers might welcome. The stress that quality systems and market forces place on effective work undertaken within the framework of a service agreement does favour those practitioners who are prepared to state the case for their service and deliver it. Clear aims, backed by a systematic implementation process do fit within the idea of a quality service.

Miller and Lane (1993) have argued that key quality questions are worth considering as we strive to provide services to our clients.

The clients' right to know

Do our clients have a right to know the basis on which the service provided operates?

Are they entitled to see evidence that the service is designed to satisfy their needs?

Is someone responsible for ensuring that a quality service is provided?

Are the principles on which the service is based made explicit?

Is there an appropriate system to document the service provided, open to the client, or even created with the client?

Is there a method to ensure that those providing a service do stay up to date with developments in the field and research into effective provision?

The new service-led agenda will force consideration of these issues. But, many practitioners have been focusing on such issues for many years. Those who regularly attend the meetings of such groups as the Behaviour Support Conference are concerned with current developments in practice. Those practitioners working with the most difficult problems within the educational system are able to learn from each other.

They will, I believe, answer the questions above in the affirmative and strive to turn the questions into answers.

REFERENCES

Achenbach, T.M. (1974) (1st edn) and (1982) (2nd edn) *Developmental Psychopathology*. New York: Ronald Press.

Advisory Centre for Education (1992) *Exclusions*. ACE Bulletin No. 47, London: ACE.

Andry, R.G. (1960) *Delinquency and Parental Pathology*. London: Methuen.

Argyle, M. (1964) *Psychology and Social Problems*. London: Methuen.

Askew, S. (1988) 'Aggressive behaviour in boys: to what extent is it institutionalised?' in Tattum, D.P. and Lane, D.A. (1989) *Bullying in Schools*. Stoke-on-Trent: Trentham Books.

Bandura, A. and Walters, R.H. (1959) *Adolescent Aggression*. New York: Ronald.

Becker, H.S. (1963) *Outsiders: Studies in the Sociology of Deviance*. Glencoe, Minn.: Free Press.

Bowlby, J. (1951) *Maternal Care and Mental Health*. New York: World Health Organisation.

Bowlby, J. (1969) *Attachment and Loss*. Vol 1. London: Hogarth Press.

Bowlby, J. (1988) *A Secure Base*. London: Routledge & Kegan Paul.

Boxall, M. (1976) *The Nurture Group in the Primary School*. London: Inner London Education Authority.

Brown, M. and Madge, N. (1982) *Despite the Welfare State*. London: Heinemann.

Burden, R. and Miller, A. (1993) 'Intervention or prevention; applying educational psychology to therapeutic issues', in A. Miller and D.A. Lane (eds) *Silent Conspiracies*. Stoke-on-Trent: Trentham Books.

Burnham, J.B. (1986) *Family Therapy*. London: Routledge & Kegan Paul.

Burt, C. (1925). *The Sub-normal School-child. 1. The Young Delinquent*. London: University of London Press.

Callias, M. (1992) 'Evaluation of therapy with children and adolescents'. In D.A. Lane and A. Miller (eds) *Child and Adolescent Therapy*. Milton Keynes: Open University Press.

Callias, M., Miller, A., Lane, D.A. and Lanyado, M. (1992) 'Child and adult therapy: a changing agenda', in D.A. Lane and A. Miller (eds) *Child and Adolescent Therapy*. Milton Keynes: Open University Press.

Chisholm, B., Kearney, D., Knight, G., Little, H., Morris, S. and Tweddle, D. (1986) *Preventative Approaches to Disruption*. Basingstoke: Macmillan.

Christie, P., Newson, E., Newson, J. and Prevezer, W. (1992) 'An interactive approach to language and communication for non-speaking children', in D.A. Lane and A. Miller (eds) *Child and Adolescent Therapy: A Handbook*. Milton Keynes: Open University Press.

Cicchetti, D. (1984) 'The emergence of developmental psychopathology', *Child Development*, 55: 1–7.

Cloward, R.A. and Ohlin, L.E. (1961) *Delinquency and Opportunity*. London: Routledge & Kegan Paul

Cohen, A.K. (1955) *Delinquent Boys: The Culture of the Gang*. New York: Free Press.

Coser, L.A. (1956) *The Functions of Social Conflict*. Glencoe, Minn.: Free Press.

Coulby, D. and Harper, T. (1983) *D.O.5. Schools Support Unit. Evaluation: Phase 2*. London: Croom Helm.

Department of Education and Science (1978) *Special Educational Needs*. Report of the Committee of Enquiry into the educational needs of handicapped children and young people (The Warnock Report). London: HMSO.

Dollard, J., Doob, L.W., Miller, N.E., Mowrer, O.H. and Sears, R.R. (1939) *Frustration and Aggression*. New Haven, Conn.: Yale University Press.

Eggleston, J. (1975) *Ecology of the School*. London: Methuen.

Eggleston, J., Dunn, D. and Anjali, M. (1986) *Education for Some*. Stoke-on-Trent: Trentham Books.

Ellis, L. (1987) 'Evidence of neuroendrogenic etiology of sex roles from a combined analysis of human, nonhuman, primate and nonprimate mammalian studies.' (Discussed in H.J. Eysenck and G.H. Gudjonsson (1989) *The Causes and Cures of Criminality*. New York: Plenum Press.)

Ellis, L. (1988) The victimful-victimless crime distinction, and seven universal correlates of victimful behaviour', *Personality & Individual Differences*, 9: 524–548.

Eysenck, H.J. (1952) 'The effects of psychotherapy, an evaluation', *Journal of Consulting Psychology*, 16: 319–324.

Eysenck H.J. and Gudjonnson, G.H. (1989) *The Causes and Cures of Criminality*. New York: Plenum Press.

Freud, A. (1966) *Normality and Pathology in Childhood*. London: Hogarth Press.

Galloway, D. (1982) 'Persistent absence from school', *Educational Research*, 24: 188–196.

Galloway, D., Ball, T., Bloomfield, D. and Seyd, R. (1982) *Schools and Disruptive Pupils*. London: Longman.

Gillham, W. (1981) *Problem Behaviour in the Secondary School*. London: Croom Helm.

Glueck, S. and Glueck, E. (1950) *Unravelling Juvenile Delinquency*. New York: Commonwealth.

Gray, P.J. and Noakes, J.S. (1992) 'Multidisciplinary work', in D.A. Lane and A. Miller (eds) *Child and Adolescent Therapy: A Handbook*. Milton Keynes: Open University Press.

Gray, P.J. and Noakes, J.S. (1993) 'Reintegration of children with challenging behaviour into the mainstream community', in A. Miller and D.A. Lane (eds) *Silent Conspiracies*. Stoke-on-Trent: Trentham Books.

Halleck, S.L. (1967) *Psychiatry and the Dilemmas of Crime*. New York: Harper & Row.

Hare, R.D. (1971) 'Psychopathic behaviour: some recent theory and research', in H.E. Adams and W.K. Boardman, *Advances in Experimental Clinical Psychology*. New York: Pergamon.

Hargreaves, D.H. (1967) *Social Relations in a Secondary School*. London: Routledge & Kegan Paul.

Harrop, L.A. (1974) 'A behavioural workshop for the management of classroom problems', *British Journal of In-Service Education*. 1.1: 47–50.

Hart, D. (1979) 'More business as usual: implications of an individual referral', *Association of Educational Psychologists Journal*, 4, 10: 30–33.

Herbert, M. (1974) *Emotional Problems of Development in Children*. London: Academic Press.

Herbert, M. (1991) *Clinical Child Psychology: Social Learning Theory, Development and Behaviour*. Chichester: Wiley.

Her Majesty's Inspectorate (1978) *Behavioural Units: A Survey of Special Units for Pupils with Behavioural Problems*. London: Department of Education and Science.

Herskowitz, H.H., Levine, M. and Spivak, G. (1959) 'Anti-social behaviour of adolescents from higher socioeconomic groups', *Journal of Nervous and Mental Diseases*, 125: 1–9.

Howarth, R. (1992) 'The child guidance clinic', in D.A. Lane and A. Miller (eds) *Child and Adolescent Therapy: A Handbook*. Milton Keynes: Open University Press.

Inner London Education Authority (1978) *Programmes for Disruptive Pupils*. London: ILEA.

Inner London Education Authority (1985) *Response to Fish Report*. London: ILEA.

Inner London Education Authority (1988) *Report Survey on Ethnic Monitoring*. London: ILEA.

Jones, M. (1993) 'Children with special educational needs compounded by severe challenging behaviour', in A. Miller and D.A. Lane (eds) *Silent Conspiracies*. Stoke-on-Trent: Trentham Books.

Keise, C., Kelly, E., King, O. & Lane, D.A. (1993) 'Culture and child services', in A. Miller and D.A. Lane (eds) *Silent Conspiracies*. Stoke-on-Trent: Trentham Books.

Klein, M. (1932) *The Psycho-analysis of Children*. London: Hogarth Press.

Lane, D.A. (1972) 'Contract therapy'. Conference paper. Islington, London: IEGC.

Lane, D.A. (1973) 'The problem of order', *Remedial Education*, 8, 3: 9–11.

Lane, D.A. (1974) 'The behavioural analysis of complex cases'. Conference paper. Islington, London: IEGC.

Lane, D.A. (1975) *The Educational Guidance Centre: A New Approach to Children's Problems*. London: Kings Fund Centres.

Lane, D.A. (1976) *Persistent Failure and Potential Success*. Research Monograph, London: IEGC.

Lane, D.A. (1978) *The Impossible Child*. Vols 1 & 2. London: Inner London Education Authority.

Lane, D.A. (1990) *The Impossible Child*. Stoke-on-Trent: Trentham Books.

Lane, D.A. and Miller, A. (eds) (1992) *Child & Adolescent Therapy: A Handbook*. Milton Keynes: Open University Press.

Lawrence, J. (1973) 'Comment on "The problem child . . .," vol. 2 no. 2'. *London Educational Review*, vol. 2 no. 3: Autumn. *Aims of Education: an Interdisciplinary Inquiry*. London: Institute of Education, University of London.

Levitt, E. (1963) 'Psychotherapy with children: a further evaluation', *Behaviour Research and Therapy*, 1: 45–51.

Lister, P. (1993) 'Maintaining the child in the school and in the community', in A. Miller and D.A. Lane (eds) *Silent Conspiracies*. Stoke-on-Trent: Trentham Books.

Lombrosco, C. (1917) *Crime, its Causes and Remedies*. Boston: Little Brown.

McGuire, R.J. and Priestley, P. (1992) 'Some things do work: psychological interventions with offenders and the effectiveness debate,' in F. Losel, D. Bender, and T. Bliesener (1992) (eds) *Psychology and Law*. Berlin; New York: Walter de Gruyter.

McNamara, E. (1988) 'Behavioural contracting with secondary aged pupils', *Educational Psychology in Practice*, 2,4: 21–26.

McNamee, S. and Gergen, K. (1992) *Therapy of Social Construction*. London: Sage.

Madsen, C.H., Becker, W.C. and Thomas, D.R. (1968) 'Rules, praise and ignoring elements of elementary classroom control', *Journal of Applied Behaviour Analysis*. 5,1: 131–150.

Merrett, F.E. (1981) 'Studies in behaviour modification in British educational settings', *Educational Psychology*, 1,1: 13–28.

Merton, R.K. (1949) *Social Theory and Social Structure*. New York: Free Press.

Michaels, J.J. (1955) *Disorders of Character*. Chicago: Thomas.

Miller, A. (1990) 'Systems theory applied to the work of an educational psychologist', *Association of Educational Psychologists Journal*, 5,3: 11–15.

Miller, A. and Lane, D.A. (eds) (1993) *Silent Conspiracies: Scandals and Successes in the Care and Education of Vulnerable Young People*. Stoke-on-Trent: Trentham Books, in association with the Professional Development Foundation, London.

Mortimore, P., Sammons, P., Stoll, L., Lewis, D. and Ecob, R. (1988) *School Matters: The Junior Years*. Wells: Open Books.

Musgrove, F. (1964) *Youth and the Social Order*. London: Routledge & Kegan Paul.

National Union of Teachers (1992) *NUT Survey of Pupils' Exclusion: Information from LEAs*. London: NUT.

Newson, E. (1992) 'The barefoot play therapist: adapting skills for a time in need', in D.A. Lane and A. Miller (eds) *Child and Adolescent Therapy*. Milton Keynes: Open University Press.

Nye, F.I. (1958) *Family Relationships and Delinquent Behaviour*. New York: Wiley.

Partridge, J. (1966) *Life in a Secondary Modern School*. Hardmondsworth: Penguin.

Patterson, G.R., Littman, R.A. and Bricker, W. (1967) 'Assertive behaviour in children: a step toward a theory of aggression', *Monograph Social Research on Child Development*, 32, no. 5. (Serial No. 113).

Power, M.S., *et al.* (1969) 'Delinquent schools', in *Crime, Deviance and Social Sickness*. London: New Society Publications.

Presland, J. (1974) 'Modifying behaviour now', *Special Education Forward Trends*, 1: 20–22.

Quinn, P.O. and Rappaport, J.L. (1974) 'Minor physical anomalies and neurologic status in hyperactive boys', *Pediatrics*, 53: 742–747.

Rabinowitz, A. (1981) 'The range of solutions, a critical analysis', in B. Gillham (ed.) *Problem Behaviour in the Secondary School*. London: Croom Helm.

Reynolds, D. (1982) 'A state of ignorance', *Education for Development*, 7, 2: 4–35.

Robbins, L.N. (1966) *Deviant Children Growing Up*. Baltimore: Williams & Wilkins.

Roland, E. (1988) 'Bullying: the Scandanavian research tradition', in D.P. Tattum and D.A. Lane, *Bullying in Schools*. Stoke-on-Trent: Trentham Books.

Roland, E. and Munthe, E. (eds) (1989) *Bullying, an International Perspective*. London: David Fulton, in association with the Professional Development Foundation.

Rutter, M. (1972). 'Critical notice', in B. Oppenheim and S. Mitchell *Childhood Behaviour and Mental Health*. London: University of London Press.

Rutter, M. and Giller, H. (1982) *Juvenile Delinquency: Trends and Perspectives*. Harmondsworth: Penguin.

Rutter, M., Maughan, B., Mortimore, P. and Ouston, J. (1979) *Fifteen Thousand Hours*. London: Open Books.

Sears, R.R., Maccoby, J.E. and Leven, H. (1957) *Patterns of Child Rearing*. Patterson, Illinois: Row.

Shaw, C.R. and McKay, H.D. (1942) *Juvenile Delinquency and Urban Areas*. Chicago: University of Chicago Press.

Sheldon, W.H., Hartl, E.M. and McDermott, E. (1949) *Varieties of Delinquent Youth*. New York: Harper.

Shields, J. and Slater, E. (1960) 'Heredity and physical abnormality', in H.J. Eysenck *Handbook of Abnormal Psychology*. London: Pitman.

Sroufe, L.A. and Rutter, M. (1984) 'The domain of developmental psychpathology', *Child Development*, 55: 17–29.

Stott, D.H., Marston, M.C. and Neill, S.J. (1975) *Taxonomy of Behaviour Disturbance*. London: London University Press.

Suhl, A.M. (1961) 'Gonadal hormones and social behaviour in infrahuman vertebrates', in W.C. Young, *Sex and Internal Secretions*. Baltimore: Williams & Wilkins.

Tattum, D.P. and Lane, D.A. (1988) 'Violence and aggression in schools', in D. Tattum, and D.A. Lane, *Bullying in Schools*. Stoke-on-Trent: Trentham Books, in association with the Professional Development Foundation.

Thrasler, F. (1935) *The Gang*. Chicago, Ill.: Chicago University Press.

Tizard, J. (1973) 'Maladjusted children and the Child Guidance Service', *London Educational Review*, 2,2: 22–37

Topping, K.J (1983) *Educational Systems for Disruptive Adults*. London: Croom Helm.

Trasler, G.B. (1964) 'Socialisation, a new approach', *Cambridge Opinion*, 38: 17–22.

Ullman, L.P. and Krasner, L. (1975) *A Psychological Approach to Abnormal Behaviour*. Englewood Cliffs, NJ: Prentice-Hall.

Volavka, J. (1987) 'Electroencephalogram among criminals', in S.A. Mednick, T.E. Moffitt and S.A. Stack (eds) *The Causes of Crime*. Cambridge: Cambridge University Press, pp. 137–145.

West, A., Davies, J. and Varlaam, A. (1986) 'The management of behaviour problems: a local authority response', in D.P. Tattum (ed.) *Management of Disruptive Pupil Behaviour in Schools*. New York: Wiley.

West, D.J. (1979) 'The distribution of young adult delinquency and other social problems in relating to early social deprivation and family background', in N. Brown and N. Madge (1982) *Despite the Welfare State*. London: Heinemann.

Wheldall, K. and Merrett, F. (1985) *The Behavioural Approach to Teaching Package*. Birmingham: Positive Products.

Widlake, P. (1993) 'Parents as partners: involving parents in the education of children with special educational needs', in A. Miller and D.A. Lane (eds) *Silent Conspiracies*. Stoke-on-Trent: Trentham Books.

Willmott, P. (1958) *Adolescent Boys in East London*. London: Routledge Paul & Kegan.

Woodgate, R. (1993) 'Applying quality standards to child care and education', in A. Miller and D.A. Lane (eds) *Silent Conspiracies*. Stoke-on-Trent: Trentham Books.

Yule, W. (1977) 'Behavioural treatment of children and adolescents with conduct disorders', in L. Hersov, M. Berger and D. Shaffer (eds) (1978) *Aggression and Anti-social Behaviour in Childhood and Adolescence*. New York: Pergamon.

Yule, W. (1990) 'The psychological sequelae of disasters and resulting compensation', *Practical Reviews in Psychiatry*, Series 2 (No. 9), pp. 6–8, 12.

Part I

Schools, parents and support services

Section A

Schools and support services

Chapter 3

Mainstream teachers talking about successful behaviour support

Andy Miller

In addition to the volume and ferocity of rhetoric that often surrounds the issue of difficult behaviour in schools, there also exists a slowly accumulating body of research evidence concerning effective interventions. Often this perspective only seems to contribute to the public debate in a still, small voice.

This research, the experiments or the case studies, if it is published, is almost always written by external personnel such as educational psychologists, behaviour support teachers or professional researchers. Very seldom do we hear from the front-line professionals themselves – the classroom teachers who are on the receiving end of all these recommendations. Unless I have moved in very untypical circles, I suspect there is, among teachers, a widely shared set of anecdotal accounts of time-consuming and wildly unrealistic suggestions that have been made by professionals external to the school. If there is a growing body of successful practice in behaviour support, where are the accounts from those classroom teachers who have been its fortunate recipients?

This chapter describes some of the results from a larger research study that set out to collect a set of just such accounts.

WHO TOOK PART?

Several Educational Psychology Services in the Midlands and North of England were contacted. They were asked if they could nominate any primary-level teachers with whom they had carried out a successful intervention aimed at improving the difficult behaviour of particular pupils. Primary teachers were chosen because this is where the bulk of the existing research by external personnel has taken place. By this means, 24 teachers from 23 different schools in 8 local education authorities, ranging from the East and West Midlands to the Scottish border, were contacted. Because my work is in the area of training educational psychologists, I restricted the study to this particular professional group rather than also including behaviour support teachers.

These teachers had worked with primary-aged children for between 2 and 25 years, the mean being 11.6 years. All were women except one, and there was one teaching head, one deputy head, three special needs coordinators, with the rest being class teachers.

The schools in which these teachers worked ranged in size from 71 to 484 pupils, excluding any nursery places, with a mean of 218. The percentage of the school population eligible for free school meals in these schools was between 3 and 67 with a mean of 21 per cent. National figures for a similar period were average primary school sizes of 193 pupils and a take-up rate for free school meals of 13 per cent, suggesting that the teachers interviewed were not untypical of the national picture, at least in terms of these criteria.

THE RESEARCH METHOD

The teachers who agreed to take part were interviewed either in their schools at the end of the day, in their homes or in the researcher's office. The conversations were tape-recorded and subsequently transcribed. The style of the interview was such that the teachers were encouraged to talk widely about the particular pupil they had been concerned about and the strategy that had been devised with the educational psychologist. Participants were assured about the confidentiality of their replies, and the quotes used in this chapter have all been given anonymity by the use of false names for pupils, teachers and others.

The transcripts were analysed by means of a technique known as 'grounded theory' (Strauss and Corbin 1990). This is basically a method that attempts to derive explanations of events, and eventually build theories, from data such as interview transcripts, by laying aside the preconceptions of the researcher and analysing data in minute detail.

THE PUPILS

The pupils represented the full primary age range with a bias towards the younger group, the mean age being 7.1 years. Of the 24 children, only one was a girl. Ten teachers said the pupil was the most difficult they had ever encountered and eight said he or she was among the most difficult half dozen. Quotes from the first and last three interviews give a flavour of the types of difficulties being experienced and are typical of the whole sample:

> I've been teaching twelve years and I've never met such destructive, such wanton – . . . under tables – attacking other children under tables (Boy aged 5, Interview 1)

> . . . aggressive and disruptive and he didn't cooperate in a group, anti-social with his peers (Boy aged 10 – Teaching head, Interview 2)

He's very destructive, very aggressive, spitting, bad language and so on (Boy aged 6 – Deputy head, Interview 3)

Quite aggressive to teachers as well as children . . . if you refused a request of his . . . he'd be throwing chairs and leave the classroom, leave the school quite frequently as well (Boy aged 10, Interview 22)

A lot of physical abuse on teachers and people that were supporting him . . . an incident of arson and various other things outside school (Boy aged 6, Interview 23)

He was causing a lot of problems for her [his mother] at home in that he was having tantrums, refusing to do whatever she told him, throwing things, swearing, kicking, generally uncontrollable for her (Boy aged 5, Interview 24)

THE EMOTIONAL IMPACT OF DIFFICULT BEHAVIOUR

Teachers and non-teachers alike will not be surprised to discover that behaviour such as this had a profound emotional impact upon many of the teachers in the sample. For most it was having a significant impact upon their stress levels and for some this was also transferring to their out-of-school lives:

Quite honestly, never having met a child like this in twelve years of teaching, I would go home some days and say 'I don't know what to do next' (Interview 1)

I just felt 'Well it's not doing the other children any good, and it's not doing me any good and it's not doing my family any good'. I came home at night and I was so wound up . . . (Interview 3)

Additionally, these stresses provoked doubt among some of the teachers about their professional competence in general:

I really was upset because I felt that I was failing, and I mean I've taught for a long time and I can honestly say I've never felt like that before. I just felt that I couldn't cope (Interview 3)

You sometimes think 'Will they [colleagues] think it's me, that I'm inadequate?' (Interview 21)

A third emotional component, experienced by most of the teachers, was a sense of feeling alone and solely responsible for the pupil's behaviour, even in schools where colleagues were seen as generally friendly and supportive. This feeling was conveyed strongly in ten instances and in a more mixed fashion in another nine:

It's a fairly strong feeling, you know, you keep your problems in your classroom (Interview 10)

I don't think anyone else was that interested to be honest . . . he's my problem, Lee. And I don't think anyone thought that much about it (Interview 14)

There was a lot of feeling from other [staff] that he shouldn't be [in our school] . . . When he was naughty in assembly I was the one who always had to fetch him out . . . I always had to have him. Nobody ever said to me 'Look I'll take him for you while you get on with what you're supposed to be doing' (Interview 17)

I was very aware that the rest of the staff . . . would blame Darren for anything because they always have done . . . I was having a lot – no, a fair amount of opposition from the head . . . any kind of misdemeanour on Darren's part was just jumped on . . . you can feel quite isolated in a school (Interview 18)

It is worth noting that this pervasive sense of shouldering the burden of difficult behaviour alone existed despite the fact that, of the 23 schools in this sample, 14 were said to have a written policy concerning behaviour, 6 were in the process of developing one, and only 3 were without such plans as far as the interviewees were aware.

THE INTERVENTION STRATEGIES

The intervention stategies devised for these pupils could be said to derive to a greater or lesser extent from behavioural psychology. The usual content of such interventions has been determined from a national survey of educational psychologists and is described in detail elsewhere (Miller 1989). However, these plans frequently contain elements to be found in many of the other chapters in this book, such as:

— rules being presented to the pupil more explicitly
— the identification of behavioural targets
— the splitting of these down into smaller steps
— an emphasis on praise for accomplishments
— some ignoring of behaviour on the teacher's part
— involvement of parents.

Outcomes of the intervention strategies

The sample was of course made up of teachers who had experienced successful outcomes. A selection of comments, however, the first and last three interviewees again, gives an additional flavour to these outcomes;

Quite honestly I can say I was knocked for six because it had worked and it has worked ever since (Interview 1)

I think it's now that he's found that it's easier for him if he cooperates in school (Interview 2)

I can honestly say he's not like the same child (Interview 3)

I think he was finally motivated to do something about it [behaviour] and it was quite evident he was very involved in this (Interview 22)

Towards the end of last of last term I felt very positive about what had been achieved . . . but this term the last couple of weeks for some reason have been awful . . . I'm hoping it was just Christmas . . . and yesterday was a very good day (Interview 23)

It was one of those wonderful 'Aah, this is great' – one of those wonderful success stories (Interview 24)

In total, six interviewees expressed the view that the intervention had been successful but had some reservations, such as that there might be a deterioration again in the future (as in Interview 23), eleven saw a definite improvement with no qualifications (as in Interview 22) and seven saw such a degree of success that it had made a strong emotional impact on them (as in Interview 24)

Making sense of the outcomes

The argument so far suggests that, in a selection of schools across a wide geographical area, a similar phenomenon has taken place. Challenging pupil behaviour, intense enough often to cause strong emotional reactions, has been improved to a highly significant degree. The most difficult pupil, or one of the most difficult that these teachers have ever taught, has made considerable improvements. How has this happened? What factors have been implicated in this dramatic reversal?

There is a substantial body of research to show that behavioural approaches can be highly effective. There is also, however, a dearth of systematic information about how these approaches can best be implemented with teachers on a casework basis, at a time when feelings are running as strongly as in the interviews quoted.

By looking closely at what the teachers in this study have to say about the psychologists who worked with them, it may be possible to draw conclusions about what is required from external personnel in order to ensure that teachers benefit fully from such consultations. Consequently, the grounded analysis paid particular attention to all the comments within the interviews concerning the manner and behaviour of the psychologists.

Four broad categories emerged from the analysis of the teacher interviews: (a) knowledge base; (b) skills; (c) personal qualities; (d) aspects of role. The rest of this chapter will examine these categories in detail in order to focus on the specific aspects of each one that the teachers considered particularly pertinent. It will conclude with a summary table that puts together for the first time teachers' views on the significant components of successful behavioural consultations in British primary schools.

The knowledge base

Many of the teachers felt that the psychologist had had *experience of successful interventions with other pupils*:

> She gave some examples of how she'd tried it with other children and they had been very successful (Interview 11)

> She's seen it so many times in so many different places. I mean she's drawing on all her resources, isn't she, from previous experiences? (Interview 7)

One also expressed the view that this experience would be much broader than could be gained by a teacher, even one working in a specialist capacity within a school:

> It was quite obvious that Carol had come across the situation, had lots of information at her fingertips and could actually cheer you up with the news that this child wasn't the worst behaved one in the world. Whereas a member of staff may not have come across the same situation, [even if] they were the special needs expert (Interview 20)

There was a more mixed view, however, among those who commented upon the exact nature of this *specialist knowledge*. A few felt critical that this knowledge did not seem to be any more technical than their own:

> I thought perhaps she was looking at it a bit too simplistically. I was expecting something – I don't know how to say it – perhaps a little bit more technical. I didn't expect it to be quite so simple. I think I expected a lot more hype – perhaps something that she would have from her research or whatever (Interview 18)

The majority, however, saw the knowledge that informed the strategy as characterised by a sense of timing and appropriateness:

> He was a professional so he knew what to do . . . he was very specific about exactly what I should be doing, the length of time I should be doing it, and so therefore I felt that must be the right thing to do (Interview 8)

An area of practical knowledge that many of the teachers appreciated seeing in their psychologists was a recognition of the *constraints* that were imposed upon their time by the realities of classroom teaching. This was a subject that sometimes elicited accounts of other much less successful encounters with psychologists, or stories about the experiences of other teachers they had known:

> It was very simple what she did. Because there was no way I could keep reams and reams of notes (Interview 16)

> I think she was very realistic about the programme. I know I have dealt on several occasions with educational psychologists who have a rather rosy view sometimes of classroom existence . . . I have been given tick sheets for how many times they do this or that – quite honestly it's impossible to do in a class of that size. There was no way I could note down the time they did something or how long they did it (Interview 20)

The main way in which these constraints could be appreciated was by the psychologist spending some *time actually in the classroom*:

> He'd been in, he'd watched them, he'd seen me working with them (Interview 3)

> I was quite cross that she was talking about this child on a piece of paper, that she hadn't actually got to know Brian and come to work with him in the classroom. I can remember going home feeling quite angry about that. And that's when I actually asked her if she would come in and see him (Interview 15)

In general, although there are some indications that teachers perceive psychologists as having a knowledge base that may prove helpful, their comments are hedged in with enough qualifications and reservations to suggest that actual specialist knowledge *per se* is not seen as the main contributor to these very successful interventions. If it is not what psychologists know, might it be what they are able to do?

The skills

Three main skill areas emerge from the interviews – listening, questioning and problem-solving – and all are commented upon in far more unequivocal and positive terms than aspects of the knowledge base. *Listening* was seen as an active process, sometimes akin to a counselling procedure, that aided problem-solving:

> The most valuable thing for us is for somebody to listen to our problems, like talking it through and trying to help us see one thing at a time (Interview 6)

> She listened. Teachers have an awful habit of chipping in, don't they?

. . . She listens and I'm sure she picks up lots of vibes [with parents] just by listening, whereas we don't because we're thinking of the answers to the next question (Interview 15)

Intimately linked to an active listening approach is the use of *questioning*:

She's had training in listening as well as talking and in the sort of questions she wanted to ask (Interview 4)

I think the way she questioned me, she got that information and the way she spoke to me, she encouraged me to talk . . . I think I almost discovered something of what I was doing myself, and probably I didn't even know I was doing it (Interview 18)

Both of these skills feed into the *joint problem-solving* that subsequently takes place:

There was that kind of emphasis of looking and exploring ways of developing strategies . . . there was sort of a tone of careful step-building . . . it was more analytical I think than the way a teacher would handle it and perhaps more objective. Less waffly, perhaps (Interview 23)

Many of the teachers in the sample commented favourably on the fact that, during this planning procedure, the psychologist had *avoided adopting a dogmatic stance*. This point was often made with a sense of relief, as if there had been an expectation of a different type of approach:

She doesn't dictate, she doesn't say 'Do this' (Interview 7)

I'm delighted to say that I've never been in a situation where I've been told what to do, you know, just like a child (Interview 6)

I don't think she was trying to teach me my job or whatever (Interview 13)

Another closely related aspect that emerged from the interviews was that many of the teachers appreciated the working relationship being one in which they could feel at *liberty to challenge* the psychologist's suggestions:

One thing she said that encouraged me was . . . 'Some of the things that I'm going to suggest to you will really get up your nose as a teacher'. She said 'I will tell you that now' and she said 'I want you to say . . . "it won't work for me"'. So that was really good because we had the relationship and I then felt the freedom to say to her 'No, I can't do that' (Interview 1)

On one occasion I think I just said to him 'It's all right you saying this, that and the other, but it's different when I'm in there and I've got the parents queuing up outside the door complaining . . .' We just talked round it, we didn't – we always got on very well (Interview 17)

Personal qualities

The interviews revealed a complex interaction between what might be termed the personal qualities of the psychologist and the skills already considered above. Although no definite dividing line can be drawn between the two (or between any of the factors discussed in this chapter, for that matter) it is possible to add some clarity to the understanding of successful consultative behaviour by attempting to make finer distinctions.

The most frequently occurring and the most widely appreciated of these qualities was the psychologist's *encouraging approach*:

> She didn't quiz me. She was lovely, she would just sit there and I could ask her questions like 'I'm trying this particular thing, is that all right?' . . . She would sort of say 'You're doing well, yes you are doing the right sort of thing' (Interview 15)

> The first thing she did for me, if nothing else, she made me feel that I was worthy and she made me feel that I was doing the right thing. She made me feel that all was not lost and she gave me more confidence to go on and to persevere . . . she was really sort of heartening and she sort of spurred you on to do more (Interview 18)

Another feature identified by a number of the teachers was the psychologist's *empathy* with the emotional reactions produced in the teacher by the pupil's behaviour:

> He said he would have it all on to cope with these two. I mean he'd been in, he'd watched them, he'd seen me working with them and he said 'It's enough to drive anybody round the bend, you're doing well' . . . Obviously, as a psychologist he was boosting my morale but it's still nice to be told (Interview 3)

> The feeling that there's somebody else who knows . . . If you got so desperate, there's somebody else in the authority who knows what's going on (Interview 17)

A slighty different aspect was the ability to act as a *facilitator of social interactions*, especially in meetings that also involved parents:

> She smiled a lot . . . she was just a very calm, collected person (Interview 16)

> She seemed calm and always positive . . . she would never get cross. When we had the small group [of staff] she wouldn't get cross with

people and everything she said brought the positive side out of them (Interview 19)

Aspects of role

In addition to the knowledge, skills and qualities that the teachers identified as being important, there was also a range of comments alluding to aspects of the role of the psychologist. Some teachers referred to the psychologist as an *'authority figure'* although the nature of this authority was variously construed:

He had the authority to make suggestions and he also in a way was taking some of the responsibility (Interview 3)

Because it was an outside agency perhaps one feels that you have to respond a little bit more positively to what they are going to be saying (Interview 22)

By being external to the everyday life of the school, the psychologists were also seen to be more *detatched from the emotional effects* of the difficult behaviour:

He was more detached, he didn't obviously have the same level of panic that I was getting into (Interview 5)

It's nice to meet and talk to someone who's not involved with the day-to-day turmoil, or can look at it in a detached manner (Interview 21)

Another characteristic of this more detached position is that it *allows basic information-seeking questions to be asked.* A special educational needs coordinator explained how it was far less easy for her to ask the same questions about a pupil of whom she will have at least a fleeting knowledge:

It takes somebody out of the situation. You see if I went in and said to a member of staff, who might be much more mature than me and have a lot more experience . . . 'Now what do you mean by badly behaved?', if I said that, it could come over as me saying 'You don't know what badly behaved means' or taken another way. But because it's coming from an objective situation, not having seen the child, and trying to get a clear comprehensive picture, then it's taken in the manner in which it's intended (Interview 6)

The external position was also seen to contribute to the psychologist being able to act as an *arbiter*, especially between school and parents:

Mum and dad sat over there, Sandra sat there, and I sat there and Miss Jones sat here . . . It was an 'us and them' situation. She was very quiet, she listened a lot . . . [and] acted as a judge and jury in a way (Interview 15)

Quite often if you've got an interview between a parent and a teacher, it starts off at an aggressive level . . . If an interview is set up with a psychologist, because they are obviously not to blame, there's no element of blame there. It's somebody removed from the situation . . . We still get a starting off by accusing the school to a certain extent, but then it breaks down and you get to look more into the home side of things because the psychologist is there . . . and delves into it (Interview 24)

The issue of 'arbitration' and others implicated in work with parents will be considered in more detail in Chapter 8.

CONCLUSION

The teachers in this study gave extensive interviews in their own time, so that a greater understanding could be gained of how external support agencies can work effectively with schools. It might have been possible to approach this task by seeking out examples of support work that had not led to positive outcomes and attempting to analyse the reasons for this. The chapters in this book certainly do not propose that there are simplistic solutions to the problems of difficult behaviour. However, dwelling upon instances of unsuccessful work may have led to a sense of despondency and despair, and the choice was made to pursue and analyse those possibly under-reported success stories and accentuate the positive.

It has only been possible in this chapter to give very brief and selected quotes from the transcripts. Table 3.1 is an attempt both to summarise the argument and judge, on the basis of the whole set of transcripts, the features considered to be most implicated in these successful outcomes.

By participating in this research, the teachers whose views are represented here have, it is hoped, pointed the way towards more effective collaboration between schools and support personnel. The list of features should be of benefit to behaviour support teachers and educational psychologists in helping them deliver the type of service that is seen as positive and effective by mainstream teachers. It should also, conversely, enable mainstream staff to be more clear about the types of services they might legitimately request, with the ultimate result of maximising the professional effectiveness of all concerned and diverting more troubled and troubling pupils away from a spiral of increasing failure and disruption and into a positive educational experience.

Table 3.1 Features of the psychologist's contribution as identified by interviewees

A *Knowledge base*	***	Experience of other difficult pupils
	*	Specialist research-based knowledge
	***	Constraints on teacher
	**	Pupil in class
B *Skills*	***	Listening skills
	*	Questioning skills
	**	Problem-solving
	**	Avoiding dogmatic stance
	**	Legitimising challenge
C *Personal qualities*	*	Empathy with emotional reactions
	***	Approval/encouragement
	**	Facilitating social interaction
D *Aspects of role*	*	Authority figure
	**	Detached from emotional effects
	*	Need for information about the obvious
	***	Arbitration

Key * = useful   ** = especially valued   *** = seen as essential

REFERENCES

Miller, A. (1989) 'Behavioural approaches and classroom realities: how educational psychologists and teachers devise and implement behavioural interventions', in K. Reid (ed.) *Helping Troubled Pupils in Secondary Schools*. Oxford: Blackwell.

Strauss, A.L. and Corbin, J. (1990) *Basics of Qualitative Research: Grounded Theory Procedures and Techniques*. London: Sage.

Chapter 4

Using support effectively at primary level

Jackie Dearden

'I'd like to talk to someone, please. We've just moved in down the road. My daughter is six. She was in the nursery at her last school because of her behaviour. She's been through a lot. When can she start?' [No eye contact is received from the child and the photocopier is at risk of being rendered even more unreliable than it is already.]

'Do you think we could have a chat? Sean is really causing problems. The rest of the class are missing out and it's not fair. I want to manage this before it gets out of hand. Can I see you at lunch time?'

'We need to talk to someone. Our Peter's started burning things again. What should we do? What time should he go to bed? Should we let his friends come round and play?'

'Help! Anthony just hit Mark and has disappeared. What do I do?'

'I tell you what, Jessica has him taped better than any of us. You want to watch her ignore him. She just talks to the wall. That soon lets him know he's not going to get attention by misbehaving.'

'She will not tell the truth. Even when I've seen her do something she still denies it. I can't accept blatant lying. What are you going to do about it?'

How do we attempt to respond to the wide range of needs of children, parents and teachers in a large primary school with approximately 450 children on roll (15 classes and a 40-place nursery)?

What methods of support can we adapt and adopt to meet the needs encountered in a school with an active policy of integration of children experiencing learning and behavioural difficulties into mainstream education?

I shall discuss how my present school has attempted to develop a system of support which promotes meeting the needs of all individuals. I have found it useful to distinguish between whole-school and individual support systems:

1 *Whole-school support systems*
  philosophy
  communication
  training and development of behaviour initiatives
2 *Individual support systems*
  responding to specific needs

WHOLE-SCHOOL SUPPORT SYSTEMS

Philosophy

I believe that support begins with the head teacher and philosophy of a school. Support for each other is vital and achievable through establishing agreed and negotiated aims. This is no easy task. How many groups do you know where everyone is working to the same philosophy and with common aims? Aims are not merely printed statements in a school brochure. They have to be actively promoted and constantly reinforced if they are not to become statements that sound wonderful but which nobody really believes can be attained.

Within our school individuality is accepted and valued. There is a constant challenge to understand and meet the needs of all individuals, with the emphasis being strongly in favour of inclusion as opposed to exclusion. Every opportunity is seized to emphasise what I like to call the 'It's OK to be different' approach.

Andrew experiences difficulties with speech, language and behaviour. He has a statement of educational need and has been in our school for four years. When he began to join in singing the hymns in whole-school assembly he could be heard singing at the top of his voice completely out of tune. The staff and children smiled and continued. At the end of the hymn the person leading the assembly would acknowledge his efforts by thanking him and the rest of the school for joining in. The general feeling of acceptance was intrinsically rewarding for everyone.

On another occasion I was taking an assembly on the theme of greed. I was attempting to make the point that the most important things in life can't be bought with money and asked the children what they would like if they could have anything in the world. After the usual responses of bikes, computers, etc., I decided to listen to what Andrew wanted – encouraging him to speak in front of so many other children was also in the back of my mind. His reply was one word – 'Talk'. There was a stunned silence from the whole school as it hit home how very lucky we all were. We then discussed how we could help Andrew by being patient and giving more time to listen and try to understand him when he spoke to us.

Open acceptance of each other and each other's needs can become a very powerful system of support, which is self-perpetuating, especially when a school actively accepts children who are experiencing difficulties in behaviour and/or learning. This policy directly challenges attitudes and raises questions which have to be addressed if appropriate responses are to be reached in meeting the needs of these children. Further, I believe, this also has a beneficial effect in meeting the needs of all pupils within a school.

Communication

If support for parents and teachers is to be established and maintained then honest, open communication is essential. Opening the dialogue can be rewarding and painful. Establishing open communication not only opens the door to positive attitudes but also means that you have to be prepared to receive and respond to negative attitudes.

Discussion between teachers, parents and children about acceptable and unacceptable behaviour and our expectations of each other was initiated by the head teacher. Here is a selection of the types of positive and negative comments that were made:

'Children should be made to do what they are told.'

'I'm here to teach not to be a social worker.'

'Lunchtimes in this place are appalling!'

'Teachers should make you laugh.'

'Bad children shouldn't be rewarded with sweets and stickers.'

'What about those children who are always good. We think they don't get enough recognition. The naughty children get more attention than the good children do.'

'Teachers should tell us when our child has done something wrong. We shouldn't have to find out from other children or other mums.'

'I believe no one should expect too much from children, teachers or parents as everyone is human and no one can be 100 per cent all the time, but a combination of all three working together could create better behaviour all round.'

'There should be more playground games for lonely children. Would it cost so much money for equipment to encourage happier playtimes for all?'

This long and sometimes painful process resulted in a questionnaire to all parents, asking them to indicate their views on what parents, teachers, children and schools should ideally do. The following were the three most commonly agreed statements in each category:

Children should:
  Respect teachers, friends and property
  Enjoy learning
  Be honest, fair and truthful

Teachers should:
  Be firm but fair
  Encourage and praise
  Listen

Parents should:
  Be understanding and patient
  Be encouraging
  Give children time

Schools should:
  Educate children to their full potential
  Have a happy atmosphere
  Be safe

Our 'Behaviour Support Group', to which I shall refer later, had a major input in putting together this questionnaire and has now taken on the task of helping to write a 'Good Behaviour Book' for all the families, which will include these expectations of each other and strategies for promoting good behaviour and reducing inappropriate behaviour in children. I believe that this level of open discussion and parental involvement will play a large part in making such initiatives successful and meaningful to the whole school community.

Training

When it comes to behavioural difficulties, parents and teachers become emotionally involved. There are feelings of guilt, authority being threatened, losing face, uncertainty and insecurity, to name but a few. There appears to be much less understanding or sympathy toward behavioural difficulties, and many people still regard behavioural difficulties as the child's fault. It is taking time for research to become general knowledge. The Elton Report (DES 1989) goes a long way towards challenging attitudes, and teachers are becoming more aware of the factors that influence children's behaviour. Understanding children's behaviour can have a very beneficial effect in enabling adults to respond to the behaviour without becoming emotionally involved themselves. There is a need for training in this area for both teachers and parents. Input from our school's educational psychologist was greatly appreciated in beginning this training.

A cold wet November evening – the school hall is filling up with parents, the overhead projector is not cooperating and our guest speaker (the school's educational psychologist) is attempting to improvise. Will he manage to alter the screen without it falling off the wall? The staff are all here, and several of them are extremely nervous at the prospect of taking part in the improvised drama role-play and wish they hadn't volunteered for it!

The projector screen has been adjusted without incident. Approximately seventy parents and governors have arrived. Booklets on 'Positive Behaviour Management' are being flipped through, with extra copies being hastily reproduced – we hadn't expected this many people!

The welcome and introduction is made by the head teacher and every-one is being asked to take part in an activity – talking to the people near them, parents are attempting to write down any behaviour problems they are facing with their children and how they tackle these problems – there is a lot of chatting and laughter. The parents' problems are collected and it is obvious that they are very similar to the problems faced by the teachers.

Why do children behave in this way? What are the needs of children that lead to difficult behaviour to manage? What do we, as adults, do that sometimes reinforces difficult behaviour? What strategies can we use to manage difficult behaviour? These questions are raised by the speaker. The staff join in to help illustrate what he is saying with drama sketches that result in a considerable amount of laughter from everyone.

Parents are signing up to help form a working party on positive behav-iour management!

We had no idea this would be so successful and enjoyable. The working party developed into the 'Parents Behaviour Support Group', who helped put together the questionnaire mentioned above and are currently involved in writing the school's 'Good Behaviour Book'. There was an increase in the number of people wanting to see the educational psychologist to talk through their problems, many of them commenting that they felt much better now they knew that they weren't the only people finding behaviour difficult to manage.

Staff training was further developed through INSET. With the help of our educational psychologist we looked more closely at these issues:

— what makes a supporting relationship
— what makes us who we are
— how we can best support each other
— how we might change our own behaviour
— how we could apply the same process to changing children's behaviour
— observing children's behaviour
— activities for promoting personal and social development
— whole-school behaviour policy

This resulted in:

— development of individual behaviour programmes for specific children
— ideas for raising self-esteem through personal and social education
— a whole-school behaviour policy, which contained these main agreements:
    — to negotiate class rules and sanctions with the children
    — to use 'safe havens' in supporting each other with children with challenging behaviour which may be causing repeated disruption of the class
    — to use individual behaviour programmes with children who persistently exhibit unacceptable behaviour, involving the parents, head teacher and deputy head teacher as and when appropriate
    — to place an emphasis on rewarding good behaviour
    — actively to encourage children to accept the decisions of the midday supervisors and ask for their permission and help during the lunch break

Development of behaviour initiatives

One workshop and in-service training event is not enough if initiatives are to be developed into actual practice. A system needs to be developed which will ensure ongoing development and support. One method of maintaining development is through working parties. This is the method that we adopted with working parties of teachers being established to review, evaluate and improve practice in relation to the National Curriculum and the school's Management Plan. The establishment of working parties was also seen as an attempt further to improve open communication between staff, who felt that: 'The curriculum working party strategy has done much to foster the sharing of ideas openly and to promote policy formation which is both manageable and based on a whole-school approach.'

Positive Behaviour Management was identified as a priority for development within the school's Management Plan and a working party accepted the responsibility for developing the initiatives identified in the initial training events.

Establishing clear, negotiated class rules was not as simple as it sounds. Class teachers were asked to supply a copy of their class rules to contribute towards a whole-school code of behaviour. The rules varied dramatically. One class had four positive statements about what they agreed to do in their class; another had a list of twenty-one don'ts. Clearly laid out guidelines from *Building a Better Behaved School* (Galvin *et al.* 1990) facilitated the process of reaching a degree of consensus about the nature of the rules.

Equally difficult to reach agreement on was the type of sanctions that could be used to reduce inappropriate behaviour. We recognised that even though we were concentrating on good behaviour, it was still necessary to have a consistent system for responding to inappropriate behaviour.

George was experiencing difficulties in behaviour. He was aggressive and abusive to other children, parents and midday supervisors. His class teacher had received support from the educational psychologist and was working towards building up George's self-image along with strategies for managing his temper. It was felt that if George was able to feel good about himself then this might effectively reduce his aggressive behaviour towards others. However, another member of staff had taken to deliberately humiliating George in front of others by making him stand on a chair and read something that the teacher knew he was incapable of.

Such inconsistency had to be acknowledged and discussed. Appropriate strategies and sanctions have now been agreed by the staff, who are now working towards consistency in their responses to inappropriate behaviour.

A 'Personal and Social Education' booklet, containing strategies and games for promoting personal and social development through raising the self-image of the child was written and produced by the working party and distributed to the staff as a resource.

Playground organisation and the development of playground games has become a priority for the working party, who are involved in compiling a resource book of playground games, establishing a means of providing playground furniture and equipment, and suggestions for playground organisation.

Records of Achievement have been implemented as a means of recognising and giving a high profile to children's achievements throughout the whole school, including the nursery. These are regularly evaluated and updated and normally sent home at termly intervals. The working party continues to look at ways in which the Record of Achievement can become a more central part of everyday classroom practice.

Working with the 'Behaviour Support Group' has also been the responsibility of the working party, who are currently planning another staff–parent–governor workshop to facilitate the writing of the 'Good Behaviour Book'.

This whole-school system of support is ongoing and responsive to the needs of the school. Many elements will continue to be a priority, while others will become less of a priority as we respond to the ever-changing needs of the children, parents and teachers. For example, I expect that once the 'Good Behaviour Book' has been written and distributed the support group will then run sessions on specific problems, such as bullying, racism or truancy. What is important is that the system is such that it allows for these initiatives to be pursued and it allows for support to be developed where it is needed. However, the support I have described so far is not enough in meeting the needs of some of our children, parents and teachers. It is still necessary to have what I call an 'Individual Support System'.

INDIVIDUAL SUPPORT SYSTEMS

Individual support systems are a further attempt to empower teachers and parents to meet the needs of children who may be experiencing difficulties in learning and/or behaviour. I find it difficult to distinguish between difficulties in learning and behaviour at this individual level, owing to the fact that many of our children who experience difficulties in learning also experience difficulties in behaviour, and the approach used to meet the needs of these children is essentially the same.

Over the last eighteen months we have attempted to devise an individual support system for our 'exceptional' needs children. I would describe these children as experiencing long-term difficulties in learning and/or behaviour, who may previously have attended a special unit or special school as opposed to having their needs met in mainstream schools. We have adopted a joint problem-solving approach which involves the following stages:

1 Clarifying what we know about a child.
2 Identifying specific difficulties that the child may be experiencing.
3 Discussing what factors may be affecting the child's learning/behaviour and why these difficulties may be occurring.
4 Agreeing on what we feel we can do towards improving and developing the child's learning/behaviour.

As the special needs coordinator I made it my task to set up and manage this system of support. I began by arranging meetings for all our 'exceptional' needs children, involving myself, the class teacher and the special needs support assistant. The purpose of the meetings was to follow the problem-solving approach to write a long-term learning/behaviour programme for each child, which would contain achievable objectives for the term. These objectives may cover all areas of development (social, emotional, play, independence, self-discipline, speaking, listening, concentration, reading, writing, fine motor skills, gross motor skills, number) or just one or two, depending on the child's needs and ability. Here is an example of an individual programme:

SPEECH: singular and plural (which plate has none, one, lots); symbols – to continue and extend to positions – what, where, who, behind, in front, etc. – refer to speech therapy programme for ideas.

READING: continue with colour words – green, red, yellow, blue. Recognise mummy, daddy, Chris, Christopher, dog, cat, without symbols.

Work daily on red, then red and green. Continue to share books and stories.

MOTOR SKILLS – WRITING: independent writing to continue. At the same time continue to copy write and to encourage more detailed pictures through talk. Work on Ch, Chr, Chri, Chris. Continue to encourage colouring within large and small shapes. Scissors – continue cutting exercise with different-sized shapes, paper, scissors, etc.

LISTENING AND CONCENTRATION: extend work on task from 5 to 10 minutes.

MATHS: number recognition 1–5. Counting, matching. Begin with numbers to 3. Work on daily. Use shapes for classification, sorting.

PSE: Tolerance and awareness of others, care for others. Discouraging other children from encouraging him to be rough (e.g. pushing in the playground with older children). Work towards observance of school rules (e.g. not coming in at playtimes, lunchtimes, etc.). Encouraging sharing, turn taking, cooperative play.

These termly objectives were then to be used by the class teacher and special needs support assistant to draw up specific weekly targets. These weekly targets were to be recorded and progress to commented on so that a continual record of activities and progress would be built up into an open file, which would aid review and evaluation of the longer-term objectives. A specific target might be:

TARGET: To take his turn in a group of 6 children.

ACTIVITY: In a circle taking turns to: Say name out loud, clapping name. Saying 'My name is —— and I like ——.'

COMMENT: Began by shouting out, but soon got the idea of waiting for his go. I'll try getting him to repeat other children next so he's aware of what others are saying.

We have gradually improved this system, learning how to be specific about learning and behaviour; making our targets observable and achievable. Both the staff and myself have gained in confidence and the review and evaluation process has often become a celebration of achievement. Because we were working towards targets and recording responses, we could see progress was being made. This was reassuring and motivating and led us to develop the system further.

Identifying the needs of nursery-age children was more difficult. I lacked experience with this age-group and found that we were setting targets that were far too difficult to reach. We needed to break targets down into much smaller steps and we needed more information on the children's ability. This led to us adapting the Portage materials (Bluma *et al.* 1976). We purchased our own pack of checklists and activity cards and began to use it with our 'exceptional' needs children as a guideline. We were helped in this by using a teacher parent counsellor who was involved with one of our children and the child's mother. The whole of the nursery staff and special needs support assistant for the child became involved in helping to complete the checklists and development chart and to identify which targets we should concentrate on working towards. Once the targets were identified, we then used the activity cards for ideas, which both the mother and nursery staff used. This was then further extended with the input of speech therapists, who suggested adaptations to the activities and identified further stages of development to be included. Anyone who worked with the child on a targeted activity would date and comment on any progress. An example of a behaviour target is given below.

TARGET AIM: To respond to 'No' 50 per cent of the time.

SUGGESTED ACTIVITIES: When the child is engaged in an undesirable activity, ensure that they are looking at you, maintain eye contact, say and sign 'No'. If the child stops, then praise with a smile and say and sign 'Good girl/boy'. If the child does not respond to 'No', remove object, redirect activity, or remove child from situation.

Date	Comment
18.12.92	Jane was pulling Judy's hair – I turned Jane's face towards me and signed and said 'No'. Jane took no notice so I removed Judy, leaving Jane to sit on her own.
19.12.92	Jane was again pulling Judy's hair – I did the same as yesterday and Jane let go. I smiled and signed and said 'Good girl' and read a story to Jane and Judy with no more hair pulling.

Régular review meetings were established with the parents and any outside support agencies (speech therapists, support teachers for visually-impaired or hearing-impaired children, physiotherapists, occupational therapists, parent counsellor, educational psychologist, etc.). The system of recording developed for individual targets was extended to the individual programmes of other children. Involving parents to this extent and working with them gave us much more confidence, and we are now beginning to invite parents along to all our review meetings and to involve them in setting targets for their children. Involvement of outside support agencies with nursery children extended to older children too, so that now, rather than try to implement a speech therapy report, the speech therapist comes along to the review meetings and offers direct advice.

The development of this support system was, to a certain extent, made easy by having children with 'exceptional' needs within the school. Staff were needing and asking for support and reassurance. Also, being the deputy head teacher in a senior management position facilitated the implementation of this support system, as I was able to follow through individual programmes with a system of recording which might otherwise have been difficult to maintain. Input from our educational psychologist was also instrumental in achieving a workable system: he was able to reinforce these initiatives in full review meetings, reassuring myself, class teachers, special needs support assistants and parents that the methods we were adopting were relevant and appropriate. Further support was also received from our Outreach support teacher from a local special school. She responded to the need for further reinforcement of teaching specific targets and provided a six-week programme of training for all our special needs support assistants.

I have described the individual support system established for 'exceptional' needs children, but they are not the only children in need of individual support. There also needs to be a system capable of responding to the needs of children who experience difficulties that are not necessarily long-term or easily defined: the children who begin to reject authority; whose behaviour is becoming increasingly aggressive; who are not responding to their parents and/or teacher; who are not adapting to a change in the home/school situation; whose difficulties in learning can no longer be attributed to lack of concentration or effort, etc.

There are several options open to class teachers attempting to meet the needs of children:

1 Devising their own behaviour/learning programme for the child.
2 Discussing the child with another colleague (previous teacher, special needs coordinator, head teacher).
3 Contacting the parents to try to understand what is happening and developing strategies with the parents.
4 Requesting to talk with the educational psychologist to gain another perspective.
5 Requesting a full review of the problems with the educational psychologist, parents and special needs coordinator and/or head teacher.

Parents also have several options open to them within the school if they become concerned about their children's behaviour and/or learning:

1 Discussing their concerns with the class teacher.
2 Discussing their concerns with the special needs coordinator and/or the head teacher.
3 Requesting a meeting with the educational psychologist.

Whichever option is followed, an attempt is made to follow the same problem-solving approach described earlier.

The mother of a nursery child approached the nursery staff for advice about problems she was having in managing the behaviour of her child. The nursery staff gave time to listening to and supporting the mother, but found themselves unable to offer the level of support the mother needed. The child was becoming increasingly difficult to handle at home, and there was considerable concern on the part of the nursery staff that the mother needed immediate support if the situation was going to improve. As deputy head teacher and special needs coordinator, I discussed with the mother the problems she was experiencing. She described her child's behaviour as being resentful of her, kicking out at her, thumping her, answering back, wanting his own way all the time, being argumentative, harping on all day and having major tantrums. I agreed with the nursery staff that she was in need of further support and arranged a meeting for her with the school's educational psychologist.

During this meeting the mother was open and honest about the difficulties she was experiencing and acknowledged that she often 'gave in' to her child and recognised the need to exert more control over some situations. Several strategies were suggested, including time out, praising good behaviour, establishing support for these management strategies from the child's grandparents, and meeting me on a weekly basis for further support if needed.

After several weeks of support from myself, which involved listening and restating the use of the strategies agreed upon, the mother began to report an improvement in her child's behaviour. It certainly hadn't been easy for her and I do not believe she would have achieved success without support. It was very rewarding when she arrived one morning with her husband and described to me and the educational psychologist how grateful they both were for the advice and support she had received.

This is just one example of how support can be successful. It also served to illustrate, to me, the effectiveness of empowering parents to take control of a situation themselves, and how this could be achieved. I learnt a great deal from observing an educational psychologist facilitate this process by establishing an unthreatening atmosphere in which the parent was able to clarify the problems she was having, reflect on why they might be occurring, and then suggest and adopt strategies to reduce these difficulties.

I believe that in many cases we, as teachers, are capable of supporting each other and parents in identifying and working towards reducing difficulties experienced by children in learning and behaviour. We need to be increasingly aware that it is necessary to make the time to identify what a child's specific learning/behaviour problems really are; to consider our own behaviour in response to a child as a significant factor in determining how a child is going to react; to be ready and willing to change our behaviour towards a child in an attempt to change their responses effectively; to create a situation in which we can openly discuss learning and behaviour with parents on an equal non-threatening basis with neither party being made to feel guilt or blame; to stop blaming someone else for the difficulties, whether it be the parent, child or school management; to emphasise the positive and do everything we can to make children feel good about themselves; to be very clear about rewards and consequences and stick to them; not to expect that difficult behaviour will just go away on its own (it won't!); to recognise when we are becoming too closely involved and ask for help from other professionals to facilitate the problem-solving process.

This is a personal account of the development and management of support for children experiencing difficulties in learning and/or behaviour within one school. I strongly believe that a policy of integration does enhance the provision for all children as we are continually challenged to question our own attitudes and methods of working. How often have you found yourself saying that a child's behaviour is not fair on the other children? I would ask you to stop and ask yourself 'How fair is it on the child experiencing the difficulties?' Is our initial response not laying the blame squarely on the shoulders of the child and absolving ourselves from the responsibility to respond to their needs? The provision of learning and/or behaviour support cannot be left to chance. It is every teacher's responsibility to support every child effectively, every school's responsibility to support every teacher effectively and every Local Education Authority's responsibility to support schools effectively.

ACKNOWLEDGEMENTS

I would like to acknowledge the support I have received from Mr Brian Crossman (head teacher of Cantrell Primary School), Mr Colin Newton (senior educational psychologist in Nottinghamshire and our school's educational psychologist) and the pupils, staff and parents of Cantrell Primary School.

REFERENCES

Bluma, S., Shearer, M., Frohman, A. and Hilliard, J. (1976) *Portage Guide to Early Education: Checklist*. Windsor: NFER–Nelson.
Department of Education and Science (1989) *Discipline in Schools*, Report of the Committee of Enquiry chaired by Lord Elton (The Elton Report). London: HMSO.
Galvin, P., Mercer, S. and Costa, P. (1990) *Building a Better Behaved School: A Development Manual for Primary Schools*. Harlow: Longman.

Chapter 5

Support in secondary schools: a complex problem

David Prior and Jayne Wilson

The following case study describes the discipline problems faced by a 12–16 years comprehensive school and how these problems were addressed both at an individual school level and also through the school working with external agencies.

Etone School was built in 1911 as a girls' high school with a selective intake and is situated in a Labour-controlled borough in the Midlands. The town in which it is located had close connections with coalmining in the past but all of the local pits have now been closed and many of the former larger industrial employers have disappeared. These major employers have been replaced by many smaller service industries and the best description of the area's present status would be of a light industrial conurbation centred around a market town. The school site is very close to the town centre and, with additional extensions to its buildings in the late 1950s and the 1960s, the school remained an all-girls (11–18 years) selective school until comprehensive reorganisation within the area in 1974. This change of status had at least four major effects upon the future development of the school and the discipline problems that were encountered.

First, when boys were taken into the school in 1974, for the first time, very few of the staff had had any experience of teaching boys.

Second, few of the staff had had any experience of teaching students other than those of above-average academic ability who were well motivated and from families who valued education.

Third, reorganisation within the area also saw the introduction of a tertiary college system, which meant the school no longer had any sixth-form students.

Finally, the school was no longer able to select its students on academic performance from throughout the town but was required to take the whole range of ability from a defined catchment area, principally from within the town centre.

WHAT WAS THE PROBLEM?

By the mid-1980s, the school found itself with few clear aims or objectives, many demoralised staff (the majority of whom had been in the school prior to comprehensive reorganisation), no clear code of conduct for student behaviour, a sanctions system but no rewards system, poorly motivated students and a poor reputation with many parents and the community at large.

From this background, at a school staff meeting in 1985 one or two new teachers to the school voiced their concern about the increasing indiscipline of students. This view was generally supported, with anecdotal evidence, by most of the more established members of staff. The feeling was that someone (meaning the school's senior management) should do something about the situation. Following discussion, it was agreed that this was a problem that affected all staff and therefore the solution lay with the whole staff not just the school's senior management. So what was actually happening in the school at this time with regard to student behaviour and how was it being dealt with?

First, the relationships between students themselves and between students and staff were good in the majority of cases, but there was a significant hardcore of students who seemed to be continually at loggerheads with staff.

Second, the school had a system of sanctions that was being employed for these students, but apparently without bringing about any desired behavioural changes.

Third, there was no formal rewards system in the school through which the achievements of children could be recognised, nor was there any way in which appropriate behaviour could be rewarded.

Fourth, the traditional academic curriculum as operated by the school was unsuited to a significant proportion of the school cohort. Furthermore, strict streaming of classes led to a lowering of self-esteem in the students and increasing cases of disaffection in the bottom group.

All of these factors meant that there seemed to be a downward spiral of behaviour, with the level of sanction imposed being increased in an attempt to maintain the *status quo*. This was a very reactive strategy and did not deal with the real problems that existed.

HOW COULD THE SCHOOL MOVE FORWARD?

As outlined above, the 'need for something to be done' about the discipline problem came from the grass-roots members of staff. This fact is very important as it led to greater staff participation in solving the problem and a large amount of the success that has been achieved in the school can be attributed to staff ownership of the subsequent developments.

And so, a well-balanced staff working party, in terms of age and gender, was set up to look at the whole question of discipline within the school. Unfortunately, one of the major dangers of setting up such a working party within the climate of deteriorating school discipline is that such a working party will be quite negative in their attitude from the outset. This leads members to think initially of possible further sanctions that can be imposed to rectify the situation which is seen to be deteriorating.

At the first meeting these very negative opinions were voiced and the temptation was to look at why the current sanctions available to staff were not working and how we could make these sanctions work better. The working party was therefore instructed that, first, they should consider the kind of behaviour that we wanted to see from the students, and then explore ways in which we might be able to bring about these desired changes. It was felt that this would involve structuring a rewards system within the school as well as reviewing and modifying the sanctions system that was already in existence.

After much deliberation the working party agreed upon a code of student conduct to cover everyday situations that occurred in school. This code of student conduct was then discussed by staff in the pastoral year team meetings that are held within the school so that everyone has the opportunity to comment on the suggestions and make recommendations for amendments.

Possible problems to be faced when moving forward

Within the school, at that particular time, there was a great deal of urgency for change to be brought about, and the initiative for that change rested with the staff. Staff were not generally used to being involved in consultation and decision-making exercises, and they were certainly not used to involving students in the consultation. However, it would seem far more sensible to involve the students in this process of setting the ground rules for the school if there is a genuine desire for shared owner-ship. That is certainly the pattern of working that would be used at the school now, but it would have been inappropriate in the mid-1980s. Just as every school has its own particular ethos, so it is that each school will have its own different starting place when change is being initiated. It is very important for the senior managers in a school to remember that change usually works best if it is started from the point at which the staff and students actually are, rather than from where the managers would like the participants to be.

It was agreed that it would be useful to both students and staff if all school rules could be encapsulated in a single behaviour code statement. The one overriding school rule, therefore, is that: 'At no time should anyone do anything that causes harm, offence, inconvenience or unnecessary work for any other member of the school community. Always be polite and considerate to others.'

An expected code of student conduct was drawn up that was based on this one school rule. The code of conduct was divided into sections to cover the main areas of school life, such as general behaviour, classroom behaviour, appearance and movement around the school. Having decided upon this wide-ranging code of expected behaviour, the next stage of the working party's deliberations centred on positive ways of encouraging this desired behaviour in the students. Perhaps not surprisingly, some members of the working party viewed this approach with suspicion as it was something completely new to their way of thinking. A commonly held view was that if you told students how you wanted them to behave then they would automatically behave in that fashion. If they didn't do as you wanted, then the solution was quite simple – you punished them! After a good deal of discussion it was pointed out that this is exactly what had been happening in the school in the past and it had not brought about the desired behaviour in the students. If this route was pursued further, it was suggested that the only kind of sanctions that would work, and then only for a relatively short time, would be ones that were even more draconian than those already in existence. This would lead to a downward spiral of behaviour in which the students would eventually rebel completely against the imposed authority.

Concentrate on positive aspects but be realistic

It was decided, therefore, to concentrate on finding suitable rewards that would encourage the desired behavioural characteristics in the students. It was agreed that a good school climate, or ethos, could best be produced by emphasising the good things that the students do, and that it should be remembered that the vast majority of the school's students are well-behaved and responsible members of the school community. It was realised that, unfortunately, there will always be a minority of students who, on occasions, fail to respond to encouragement and reward and who will need to be punished for failing to conform to the expected code of behaviour. The working party examined the various sanctions that were in existence in the school and modified these where it was thought to be necessary. Additionally, the working party decided to band the sanctions into various levels to discourage staff from using high-level sanctions as a first answer to inappropriate behaviour.

Then a series of questions was posed for the consideration of the whole staff with regard to the academic curriculum: How highly does the school value its students? Is the development of a disaffected group of students a necessary consequence of the pursuit of excellence? What messages does the content of the curriculum convey to the students, first, in terms of subjects offered and, second, in terms of syllabus content and teaching methods employed?

To summarise, do the academic curriculum of the school and the teaching methods employed tend to reinforce the students' successes, on which they can build, or do they reinforce the students' feelings of failure, so that they lose interest in school?

It was when questions like this were posed that staff began to realise the enormity of the task that they had started when a fairly casual comment had been made a few months previously in a staff meeting about deteriorating discipline. What was required was much more than a tinkering with systems that already existed. What was required was a fundamental review of the working of the school. Such a review takes time to carry out and it takes even longer to implement any changes that are perceived as necessary. The main reason that the change is relatively slow is that in many cases we are talking about changing the behaviour of staff and the attitudes of students.

Building effective partnerships

It is perhaps appropriate at this point to refer to the important tripartite relationship that must exist between the school, the students and the parents if success is going to be achieved. We believe the quality of this three-way relationship to be instrumental in helping to bring about behavioural change.

Every school has a major responsibility for communicating its ethos and modus operandi to its students, their parents and to other members of the community at every possible opportunity. Having a set of aims and objectives or a mission statement which can be readily quoted is simply not good enough. Often the difference between a good school and a bad school is that, in a good school, its mission statement is explicit in everything that it does and especially in the way in which it deals with each member of the educational partnership. Rhetoric must be translated into reality and quality must pervade everything that happens within the organisation. Parents must feel welcomed by the school. They must be made to feel equal partners whose views, opinions and ideas are valued by the staff. To achieve this, home–school communications should be efficient and regular. Parents should be invited into school on frequent occasions to meet and talk with staff, and these invitations should start even before their child joins the school.

In this respect, perhaps, smaller schools have some distinct advantages in being able to come to a corporate agreement with all partners having shared values.

Translating the rhetoric into reality

Having agreed on a policy for desired student behaviour, the next major consideration was how to put it into practice. The cause of undesirable student behaviour in a secondary school can rarely, if ever, be ascribed to one individual factor. Therefore, the plan of action, through necessity, must often be multi-faceted with several issues being tackled concurrently. It is this that makes support in the secondary school such a complex matter.

Curriculum change was addressed initially (a) through the provision of a wider range of courses, with some options specifically designed to cater for the children with less academic talents, (b) by the choice of new syllabuses, and (c) by the removal of streaming and the introduction of broad banding throughout the school.

The pastoral issues were tackled through the introduction of timetabled tutor periods and the involvement of all staff in the production of the pastoral scheme of work. The development and refinement of these programmes is still continuing.

But the major change that was still required was that of changing staff attitudes and teaching methods. This required a major programme of whole-school INSET, which was initially introduced during a residential training weekend and subsequently followed up with work on staff training days.

The publication of the Elton Report (DES 1989) led to a re-evaluation of the whole-school discipline policy. This impetus brought about a further change in staff attitudes and methodology, and led to the more widespread use of positive behavioural strategies within the school.

Key performance indicators for student behaviour were established during this period of time and these are used to report to the governing body on a termly basis. Statistics have shown a considerable improvement in school attendance, behaviour in lessons and a substantial reduction in the number of exclusions of students. These improvements were only achieved because over the period of a number of years changes in staff attitudes were accomplished.

This change in climate, or ethos, from a negative approach to a more positive one in which students are valued more highly as individuals, is perhaps the key factor in bringing about an improvement in student behaviour in the school. Following staff discussion, a school mission statement was agreed: 'Etone School aims to put each child first.' We do not believe that this is just rhetoric and we use this on a day-to-day basis as the main criterion when taking any school management decision.

Steps towards establishing good school discipline

It is our belief that good school discipline is established by:

(a) having clear educational aims and objectives which are known and shared by all staff;
(b) having clear guidelines on acceptable behaviour;
(c) having a positive system of rewards and privileges, which are valued by the students;
(d) having a system of sanctions that are seen to be firm but fair;
(e) providing high-quality experiences for students both in and out of the classroom;
(f) working in close partnership with parents and keeping them informed of good as well as poor behaviour;
(g) involving the governing body in the day-to-day working of the school;
(h) but, above all, we believe that the quality of the relationships that exist within the school are crucial to the school's success.

It is only when this point has been reached, when staff are working in a positive way with students and their parents, and when students are valued as individuals, that you can really move forward as a school. It is then that a school can consider other methods of offering support for students who are displaying emotional and behavioural difficulties outside the normal range of acceptability for a mainstream school. Achieving the desired working practice within your own school builds staff confidence, and moving further forward definitely demands a confident whole-school approach!

Isn't this a risky business?

In the climate of competition between schools, a senior management team and their governors might well consider that it is indeed a risky business to accept students who have emotional and behavioural difficulties. Saunders (1971) expressed some concerns in his work in the early 1970s that might seem to be even more relevant now. How will the school be viewed by the local community? Will there be a detrimental effect upon recruitment of other, possibly brighter, students who would reflect well upon the school in league tables? These and many other considerations will possibly exercise the team's thoughts and decision-making. After all, isn't it better for a school to get rid of its own problem students through the use of exclusion procedures, rather than take in students who have been other people's problems? Apart from the financial penalties that are now attached when students are removed through permanent exclusion there are other legal obligations placed upon schools, not the least of which is the opportunity for parental choice of school. However, at the end of the day the debate really centres on how the educational philosophy relates to a school's own aims and objectives. If a school claims to be a 'caring society', does it really mean that it cares for all categories of students or just for a selected range? But if a school does take the positive decision that it wishes to accommodate the whole range of aptitudes, abilities and behaviours, then it must be sure that it has prepared itself thoroughly to do so.

Whose job is it anyway?

Under the terms of the 1981 Education Act, governors of all schools are required to use their best endeavours to secure for any pupil registered with special educational needs the special provision that is required. The Warnock Report (DES 1978) had indicated that some 20 per cent of children had some form of special educational need, and so a considerable onus was placed upon individual schools to identify and meet the needs of these children. It was further recognised that a large percentage of these children with special educational needs would fall into the category of being 'emotionally and behaviourally disturbed'.

In spite of the Warnock Report, the 1981 Education Act and other publications relating to children with special educational needs, many teachers in ordinary schools still don't see coping with behaviourally disturbed children as part of their job. It must be acknowledged by senior managers in schools that the management of children with emotional and behavioural problems demands a high level of skill and training, and very few teachers have had any preparation for this role in their initial teacher training. The acceptance by staff that when we are dealing with children with emotional and behavioural problems we are dealing with children with special educational needs, rather than with children who are maladjusted, is a major step forward for any school to achieve and presents a far more positive concept of this area of concern.

The Wallasey Joint Council for the Education of Handicapped Children, in their pamphlet *Needs of the Emotionally Disturbed Child* (1972), highlighted the fact that these children are causing an increasing anxiety for both their parents and teachers.

The Joint Council made several recommendations on how these special needs should be met, but primarily they suggested that every education authority should offer a wide range of provision to meet the differing degrees of need. We feel that several of their recommendations are pertinent to mainstream schools and that they are also reflected in recommendations made in both the Warnock Report and the Elton Report (DES 1989). Therefore they have been included in our own working practice. However, these arrangements do bring with them associated management challenges.

Restructuring and extending the partnership

Two of the recommendations made were that mainstream schools should adopt special management structures to cater for children with special educational needs and also that better liaison should exist between schools and other external agencies.

Within our school this has led to the appointment of a learning support co-ordinator upon the retirement of the previous head of special needs. This different title for the post was chosen quite deliberately, as it was felt that it made an explicit statement to all of the staff within the school: that the responsibility for children with special needs lies not with one member of staff alone, but is the responsibility of every teacher within the school. If it was only the title of the job that changed, however, it would not have been sufficient. What happened was that a different way of working evolved. Teacher support was provided for identified students in the normal classroom situation, and very little withdrawal of students took place when compared with previous practice. Teachers were encouraged to produce appropriately differentiated work for all students within their groups, and they were also given first-hand guidance on how to deal effectively with students with emotional and behavioural problems. Positive behavioural schemes became a standard part of the working repertoire of staff across all subject areas.

In addition to the new role adopted by the learning support coordinator, the role of the heads of year groups took on an extra significance as they became more directly involved in the academic side of the students' school lives. This has now been developed even further with the replacement of heads of year groups by the introduction of keystage team leaders and assistant team leaders at both National Curriculum keystages three and four. These new posts combine both pastoral and academic responsibilities and provide a more pro-active approach than the largely reactive approach seen in the past. These are key middle-management posts within the school and provide convenient and effective means for liaison with external agencies.

The keystage team leaders and their assistants, together with the learning support coordinator, have regular meetings with the educational social worker and the educational psychologist attached to the school. A further recommendation was that psychologists should be able to offer consultative help for class teachers. This advice was reiterated in the work of Wheldall and Congrieve (1980), who also suggested that courses for teachers in applying behaviour modification in the classroom would be useful. Although this has not been entirely achieved at Etone, we have started to make use of the services of the educational psychologist attached to the school in slightly different ways from our previous practice. Formerly, the educational psychologist only dealt with nominated cases.

More recently, she has been used to provide in-service training for staff, with advice on referral procedures and the prioritising of individual cases. Additional advice has been suggested for strategies to try with students for whom it has not been possible to allocate specific educational psychologist time. Students may also be referred by this middle-management group for counselling by the school nurse, who also accepts appointments from students by self-referral.

One significant area where cooperative working has developed is between members of school staff and members of staff from a local area support service. Staff from this support service, who are primarily involved with students with emotional and behavioural difficulties, have worked together with our own staff both in delivering in-service training and on individual student cases. One of these cases is discussed in detail later as an indication of the kind of cooperative working that it is possible to achieve between a mainstream school and a support agency. The delicate balancing act that seems to be performed between the academic and pastoral areas in many schools is gradually being broken down and rationalised within our school. All teachers are expected to be concerned with the education of the whole child.

This networking of school staff with support agencies, both internal and external to the school, provides a stimulating management challenge, but one which is worth solving for the benefits that can be gained by the students. However, our experiences suggest that successful integration of emotionally and behaviourally disturbed students in mainstream schools cannot be achieved without (a) quality training for mainstream teachers, (b) special intervention, often involving the home, and (c) back-up support for the mainstream schools through a variety of external agencies.

How can this happen in practice?

Mary had been in a residential special school for two years. Through parental pressure and her continuing progress, it was decided after consultation between the local behaviour support service and Etone School to integrate Mary into the mainstream school.

As argued elsewhere (Gray and Noakes 1993), no reintegration is possible unless the mainstream school is receptive to the individual special needs of children and the school also fosters positive attitudes in general.

An initial meeting between the behavioural support service's case worker and the deputy head was arranged to discuss in detail all information relevant to Mary's case. Mary's levels of attainment were discussed, and possible strategies that might be adopted for her induction. There is a need for a system that operates when the child is successful as well as when there may be problems. Staff need to be fully briefed and informed as each stage is successfully completed or repeated.

At this early point, it is vital that all parties have complete professional trust and regard for each other. Honesty is vital. We have been very fortunate to work with only two case workers from our local behaviour support service, as the agency is structured on a team-per-area basis. Dealing with such a small number of contacts helps to develop professional trust and mutual support. Team work with external agencies is as important as team work within schools.

Mary's case worker and the deputy head looked at developing a plan of action that had clear targets for Mary and was easy to implement for staff. Any strategies, or procedures, that a support agency suggests for implementation must fit into a school's existing structure.

Schools do not enter into reintegration without some trepidation. Having confidence in the case worker's expertise in designing a behavioural programme that matches with the school's existing rewards/sanctions framework and overall knowledge of the staff within the school, however, helps to provide a programme that suits all parties and removes any doubts that they might have. This should be, after all, a joint project and the ultimate aim is for the external agency eventually to withdraw.

It was decided that Mary would join the mainstream school in several stages. Stage one involved Mary coming into school for two subjects. Every time Mary came into school she would be accompanied by a 'monitor', who would observe her on/off-task behaviour in class. If she met her targets in each subject then stage two would be implemented, where another subject would be assessed. The monitor would move from one of the successful subjects in order to pick up a new one. If Mary did not achieve her targets, the programme had the facility to repeat the stage. It was envisaged that this programme would operate until Mary was fully integrated with all subjects in place.

Only when the framework for the programme had been discussed fully did the deputy head arrange a meeting with Mary and her parents. Every effort was made to make Mary feel at ease in the school. Both Mary's mother and her case worker were initially present, but once Mary was more relaxed both her mother and the case worker left. The deputy head showed Mary around the school, pointing out places that she would be visiting in her first few days. Mary was very enthusiastic and asked a lot of questions, particularly about what would happen in certain subjects and what happens to students who misbehave in class. Where clear boundaries are set for the student, the more secure they feel.

After this initial visit, the support service spent time with Mary and her parents, negotiating the targets she would work towards in her positive report sheet. This daily sheet provides the opportunity for all staff who teach Mary to record where she has successfully met her targets during the lesson. Only positive comments can be recorded on the report. A warning slip is issued to Mary if she is not meeting a target successfully. The number of that target would be entered on her report sheet, without further comment. Staff would be given a file containing all the relevant information at the start of each lesson. Enclosed in the file would be a copy of Mary's targets for the day/week, her warning slips and exclusion slips (for use if Mary continued to break a target). Exclusion slips are included in the system principally to avoid confrontation. Should Mary be given either a warning slip or an exclusion slip there is no arguing. She must not confront the member of staff. Although the monitor would be specifically observing Mary's behaviour in the lesson, the classroom teacher is still the person who is in control of the class and, should Mary consistently break a target, she would be dealt with by using the agreed procedures of the programme. This is the normal practice for all of our students, and Mary should be part of that system.

Staff were informed of Mary's reintegration programme during a staff meeting. Mary's case worker spoke to the staff, about Mary's background and the programme that had been planned for her. Staff concerns were acknowledged and dealt with seriously. The school management team reaffirmed at this point the procedures that we already operated in school and how Mary's programme had been designed to fit into our existing programme, as well as being special to Mary. Likewise, it was important for staff to see that, while Mary had a rewards system built into her special programme, she was still a student at our school and therefore part of our own rewards system.

Once Mary had begun in the mainstream school, her pastoral tutor monitored her progress and met regularly with Mary's case worker. Together they decided if it was desirable to commence the next stage of the programme. Normal pastoral procedures are followed, the aim being for the child to move off the special programme into normal school. During Mary's reintegration, school frequently contacted Mary's parents directly with positive news. It is a shame that many schools only contact parents when they have something negative to say.

It must be acknowledged that reintegration can sometimes be slow if success is to be achieved, but this is no different from any other learning process. If the programme appears to be unsuccessful, steps can be taken to renegotiate more realistic targets, as well as repeating stages of integration until all parties, particularly the child, are happy to proceed.

As the school grows in confidence and the child is phased successfully into the school programme, the external agency can gradually withdraw. Following the reintegration of a difficult student through to a satisfactory conclusion can give the school confidence to take on other more complicated cases in the future and to be able to incorporate even more sophisticated programmes into their day-to-day working.

The concept of educating children with emotional and behavioural difficulties in the ordinary classroom, whenever possible, reverses the trend of removing them at the first opportunity to a special unit or 'anywhere else as long as it's not here!' It has advantages from a social viewpoint in so far as these children are not treated differently from their peers. It also makes financial sense, because LEAs no longer have to provide the same level of increasingly expensive specialist facilities. Finally, it makes educational sense in that such children still have access to the whole curriculum. Similarly, there are also benefits to the staff in the individual school concerned. School staff can benefit through their own professional development, through the shared expertise of working with staff from an external support service and from in-house in-service training. Also, working with an external support service in the way outlined provides the school's management team with the opportunity to examine critically their own existing working structures and practice.

Establishing successful partnerships with external agencies

The following guidelines are suggested as an aid to establishing successful partnerships between mainstream schools and external agencies when managing students with emotional and behavioural problems:

1 The agreement of common goals.
2 A positive climate within the mainstream school, in which the staff look to reward desired behaviour.
3 An acceptance by the support agency of the ethos and discipline systems which exist within a school, and a willingness to operate within these constraints.
4 The establishment of clear functions for the workers in the different agencies so that each understands the role of the others.
5 Well-organised channels of communication and regular professional meetings between all partners.
6 Having key individuals from the support agency linked to specific schools.
7 Trust between the different partners, based upon the belief that all partners desire the same successful outcomes.
8 An acceptance that neither partner knows all the answers and that on occasions we will fail to bring about the desired changes.

THE MANAGEMENT CHALLENGE – IS IT WORTH IT?

In summary, secondary schools are complex institutions. Where pastoral and academic divisions exist within a school, and are reinforced by the idea that children with special educational needs are the responsibility of a small group of specialised staff, then conflicting ideologies and differing educational objectives are also likely to exist. It is quite likely that these internal conflicts could prevent a school from working effectively with external agencies. Our experience suggests that success comes through (a) creating a school ethos in which parents are welcomed as equal partners and where the needs of the individual student are paramount; (b) establishing a coherent approach to the management of students with special educational needs within the school; (c) showing a willingness to share expertise with fellow professionals from other agencies.

The management of these overlapping boundaries can be difficult, but the rewards for the individual student make it a management challenge that no caring school can afford to ignore.

REFERENCES

Aspey, D.N. and Roebuck, F.N. (1971) 'An investigation of the relationship between students' levels of cognitive functioning and the teacher's classroom behaviour', *Journal of Educational Research*, 65, 3: 365–368.

Cowen, E., Lorion, E.P., Dorr, D., Clarfield, S.P. and Wilson, A.B. (1975) 'Evaluation of a preventively oriented school-based mental health program', *Psychology in the Schools*, 12, 2: 161–166.

Department of Education and Science (1978) Special Educational *Needs*. Report of the committee of enquiry into the education of handicapped children and young people (The Warnock Report). London: HMSO.

Department of Education and Science (1989) *Discipline in Schools* (The Elton Report). London: HMSO.

Gray, P.J. and Noakes, J.S. (1993) 'Reintegration of children with challenging behaviours into the mainstream school community', in D.A. Lane and A. Miller (eds) *Silent Conspiracies*. Stoke-on-Trent: Trentham Books.

Grunsell, R. (1980) *Beyond Control? Schools and Suspension*. London: Writers and Readers with Chameleon Books.

Sassoon, D. (1992) 'The exclusion of pupils: is it the most appropriate way of dealing with indiscipline?' *Education and the Law*, 4, 2: 55–59.

Saunders, B.T. (1971) 'The effect of the emotionally disturbed child in the public school classroom', *Psychology in the Schools*, 8, 1: 23–26

Wallasey Joint Council for the Education of Handicapped Children (1972) *Needs of the Emotionally Disturbed Child*. Pamphlet.

Wheldall, K. and Congrieve, S. (1980) *The Attitudes of British Teachers Towards Behavioural Modification*. Birmingham: Department of Educational Psychology, University of Birmingham.

Chapter 6

Teachers and social workers working together

Tim Pickles

The problem of working with school students who exhibit difficult or challenging behaviour so often turns into a game of pass-the-parcel. Our memory of this time-honoured childhood game provides a number of parallels to this area of work. The game itself holds interest as we wait with anticipation to receive the parcel – but are then only too eager to pass it on. During out brief ownership of the parcel, we struggle to make a small impression on stripping off the wrappings. Eventually, someone else (never us) succeeds in removing the final wrapping and revealing the hidden contents – which so frequently turn out to be disappointing and quickly forgotten as we move on to another, and potentially more interesting, game.

How often in our schools and classrooms do individual students feel themselves to be that helpless, hapless and ultimately hopeless parcel?

The difficulties in responding to the needs and problems of behaviourally disturbed students cannot be solved by focusing exclusively on the individual student as both the cause and the consequence of the matter. To treat the student merely as the parcel, to be passed from one person or agency to another in the vain hope that someone, somewhere, will come up with a better answer, is to belittle and trivialise the issues which that student presents for his or her school, family and community. Other contributors to this book have explored in some detail the respective contributions which individual teachers, support programmes, school peers and whole-school policies can make to the effective support of difficult students. I have argued in another book (Pickles 1992), that disaffection within schools can only be satisfactorily dealt with in the long term by means of coordinated attention to all three players in the game – the student, the teacher and the school itself. It is insufficient to expect the student alone to be responsible for the difficulty and to make all the effort to change, although there is an increasing range of methods and practical approaches which can be employed to help the student understand his or her difficulties and take more responsibility for personal actions. The starting point must involve equal attention on the teacher as the other contributing player, whose responses, comments, approach to authority and teaching style all have an impact on the situation. Finally – and arguably of greatest significance – the school itself, as an institution in its own right, must examine the contribution which it makes to both the creation and reduction of behavioural problems; if such difficulties are not to be transferred from one generation of students to the next, those causes which lie within the school's own functioning must be detected and changed. The method for doing this rests on the analysis of a systems approach to the school – a technique which has been shown to be of increasing effectiveness in other related contexts, and to which we will return later in this chapter.

At this point we should remember that students, teachers and schools, while centrally involved in responding to challenging behaviour, are not the only players involved in the pass-the-parcel game. All too often we hear the cries of 'I blame the parents', 'If only TV was not as violent', and 'What do you expect in a neighbourhood like this'. Such comments are a useful device for externalising the problem and placing the blame for it somewhere else – in this case outside the school. Of course the problem of difficult behaviour is a complex one, and there are contributing factors both within and outside the school. It is only in our simplistic game of pass-the-parcel that we lay all the blame and responsibility on just one agency or individual. However, if responsibility is to be shared, is there not also something to be learned within the school from looking at how those operating outside the school gates also attempt to respond to similar – frequently the same – problems?

The experience and contribution of other agencies, and the ways in which this can be tapped into by the school through a multidisciplinary approach, form the subject matter of this chapter.

A BROADER VIEW

Many other agencies and organisations work alongside schools in coping with the consequences of troublesome behaviour. The result is frequently a continuum of inter-agency collaboration extending across several fields. Within families there are examples of aggressive and uncooperative behaviour arising from abuse, neglect, poor or inconsistent parenting and inadequate control. Among the statutory services, it is the Social Services and Social Work (in Scotland) Departments which are expected to assess these difficulties and make appropriate interventions. Out on the streets of any housing estate or town, there are instances of juvenile graffiti, petty vandalism, and anti-social activity generally classified as 'hanging around'. Youth work agencies, both statutory and voluntary, respond by offering not only youth clubs but an increasing range of Outreach services, designed to establish contact with such young people and to start to work with them on their terms and on their issues. Juvenile and youth crime is consistently perceived as 'on the increase' (despite the fact that in recent years the number of convictions has actually decreased); there is a real fear of youth crime among victims – both young people and adults. Youth crime ranges from a lot of petty and irritating vandalism, through theft and burglary, to physical attacks and assault. With the trend towards finding community-based sentencing options for convicted young offenders, there is a growing number of professionals in both social work and probation engaged in the design and delivery of suitable and effective response programmes.

Research has shown that it is often the same young person, who truants or is disruptive in school, who also is out of control at home, hangs around aimlessly on the street, or is engaged in criminal activities. The correlation is far from exact and the one is a false predictor of the other; nevertheless, there is a common core of problem behaviours here, from which we should be able to derive some common solutions. A multidisciplinary approach, in which social work or youth and community agencies work in partnership with teachers across a whole range of issues, is increasingly regarded as a creative way forward. As with other agencies, teachers cannot and need not operate in isolation. There is much to be gained by combining forces to tackle the same problems simultaneously through a pooling of ideas, skills and techniques.

MULTIDISCIPLINARY WORK IN SCHOOLS

Multidisciplinary working is not a new idea, of course. During the past twenty years there has been a growing number of examples of collaborative practice. At its most basic, collaboration is concerned with liaison – informing other people of what is going on and comparing notes. But liaison is merely the simplest form of collaboration, because it leaves intact the autonomy and discretion of each participant. Rather more sophisticated forms of collaboration have arisen as a result of child protection procedures, which are now standard in every authority. Although varying in detail, most procedures rely on a multidisciplinary case conference at their core. This case conference is a joint assessment and planning forum in which professionals from different agencies – school, social services, medical services, police and others – meet together to share their information and decide together on what action, if any, to take.

A second example relates more directly to the school's response to difficult students. In social work, the use of groupwork approaches to young people, rather than one-to-one casework, has long been recognised as an effective method of both communicating with young people and of helping them to focus on their own difficulties. Teachers are practised experts in groupwork, although they may not recognise the term: their everyday handling of students in a classroom employs many techniques drawn from group dynamics theory. The more deliberate use of group-work methods, combined with a smaller group size, has been used as a format in many schools to tackle specific behavioural problems on a multidisciplinary basis.

In one high school, a group of second and third-year students were identified as increasingly disaffected and likely to pose further behavioural and truancy problems as they progressed through the school. Pastoral staff were concerned to intervene now to support the students, rather than to pick up the consequences through the discipline system later. Through collaboration with the local area social services team it was decided to run a 12-week groupwork programme for ten of these students. The group was introduced as part of the pastoral care network of the school and as a positive way in which the students could look at their own difficulties in school and learn and rehearse ways of coping better within the school. The students were released from normal classes for three hours each week, with the consent of their parents. A teacher and a social worker worked together to run the group. They met for an hour each week to plan the programme and review progress, and from this meeting both went away to prepare materials for the group. The 12-week programme started with a range of self-assessment materials in which the students were able to both explore and talk about their experience of school. This included their primary as well as secondary schooling careers. The largest part of the programme was devoted to social skills' training about the issues and difficulties identified by the students – handling authority, responding to conflict without resorting to aggression, asking for help when unsure of what to do. Methods involved recreating difficult situations, exploring the options available, role-plays, identifying support people in the school, and devising less destructive ways of 'letting off steam'. Part of this programme also involved the students in explaining which aspects of their schooling they found unhelpful, and this resulted in some changes to their time-tabling and in proposals for changing playground arrangements at break-times. Throughout the group's life, students were asked to keep a personal log of positive and negative incidents involving them in school, and this was regularly reviewed by the group leaders. Towards the end of the group's life, students and leaders awarded themselves a simple treat in recognition of the progress they had made.

This is a simple example of a school-based group founded upon the sharing of multidisciplinary skills and staffing. Its largest cost is not financial but staff time released from other duties; the school concerned took the view that three to four hours per week of one teacher's time to work as a group leader was likely to be the same as the amount of time spent less fruitlessly chasing these individual students over the next few months.

MULTIDISCIPLINARY PROJECTS

At a larger scale, the value of collaborative working is now recognised by the number of specialist multidisciplinary projects being established to provide an integrated response to challenging behaviour in schools.

One such example is a joint teacher and social work initiative to provide a community-based assessment service. As we have discussed, difficulties in school are frequently mirrored by difficulties in the family, but to get a more complete picture of the situation we require information from both sources. For particularly difficult young people, a common response from youth courts has been to request a formal assessment report. Some years ago, such assessments were frequently prepared over four to six weeks by residential assessment centres. It was long recognised that, while such centres may be able to provide a very comprehensive report, and also give young person and family a breathing space apart, the removal of the young person to a residential setting could also change the dynamics of what was really happening. Community-based assessment panels were developed as a more local response, collating information about the student's attitude, behaviour and difficulties while he or she remained in touch with conventional resources in the community. The assessment panel began its work as a multidisciplinary case conference, identifying what needed to be assessed. It then went on to devise a programme of activities and methods which would generate this information by using the various skills of members of the multidisciplinary panel. There was no standard assessment programme: each was uniquely devised to provide the information required.

In practice, the teaching members continued to involve the student in normal classes but provided access to psychologists and assessing social workers to meet the student within the school context. Both social worker and teacher were involved in meetings with the parents both at school and in the family home. A joint youth worker and social worker assessment group was run on a continuous weekly basis, with a flow of young people joining and leaving the group. The group's programme included a range of formal and informal assessment exercises combined with observation of the young person's behaviour with peers in a mix of settings. After several weeks, the information from all these sources was pooled on a multidisciplinary basis by the community assessment panel, to be sifted and presented in the final assessment report.

Day-care projects for students with behavioural difficulties represent another example of a multidisciplinary project approach to the problem. The range of day-care programmes is almost as great as the number of such projects, so we must look at one as illustrative of many, while recognising that each differs in funding, staffing and programme procedures.

This day-care project offers a time-limited resource for working with students outside the conventional school. Based in a converted house, it can accommodate up to fourteen secondary students at a time with four staff – two teachers and two social workers who, while having different remits, tend to work interchangeably with each other. During term time, students attend the project during normal school hours. They receive a limited part of the national school curriculum, but the emphasis is on developing and preparing a range of 'school survival skills' tailored to the needs of each individual student. These survival skills are explored, refined and rehearsed so that each student is better equipped to cope with the demands of ordinary school. At the same time, social work staff are engaging with each student's parents, both at the project and at home through family-based work, to support the parents in providing effective control over their child. Further work is being carried out by the teaching staff with both student and his or her original school, to find out what factors within the school contributed to the breakdown – timetable factors, peer influences, excessive movement around the school, specific forms of discipline, etc. The teacher's role is then to act as advocate and negotiator between student and school to achieve change and reconciliation on both sides. This, of course, is a delicate process and mirrors the work of the social worker in affecting change between young person and parents. It is the way in which the work is done – the process of achieving change – rather than any specific technique or method which achieves results. A significant amount of effort must inevitably be spent on encouraging and sustaining motivation for change on the part of students, family and school.

This day-care approach is not intended as a permanent alternative to conventional schooling. It is about teachers and social workers working together to achieve change and reconciliation in both student and school, so that the student can make best use of the facilities and opportunities of the school, and the school is better able to accommodate a diverse range of students within its population without resorting to exclusions or the use of such projects. The day-care approach as described here is failing in this function if it allows itself to become a substitute for school. Its programme has to be short-term, multidisciplinary and focused on achieving the return to mainstream school. In practice, this is often achieved by part-time attendance at the day-care project (with the rest of the week spent in school) and by a transitional return to school on an incremental basis. The school holiday periods can then be used to maintain support for the young person at home and enable continued contact if desired between the project and its former students.

MULTIDISCIPLINARY POLICIES

The process of introducing multidisciplinary working practices has been aided in some authorities by the establishment of formal policies agreed jointly between the Social Service and Education Departments. In Scotland, where a range of such initiatives has now become common practice, the resulting policies are widely known as Youth Strategies.

The Lothian youth strategy is founded on five jointly agreed principles:

1 Problems associated with children's behaviour or circumstances should be dealt with wherever possible by keeping the child in his/her local community, using the resources of the family and other local resources in a flexible manner.
2 Children who are at risk of having to leave home or who are at risk of being excluded from school or who have a special educational need should be jointly assessed and in some cases jointly reviewed.
3 Both the education and social work departments will endeavour to contribute day and groupwork provision as an alternative to the residential care of adolescent children where this is appropriate.
4 No child shall be recommended for residential care unless:
   (a) s/he has no home (including substitute home) in the community which can, with appropriate support, provide an adequate degree of control or care, or
   (b) s/he is at risk to herself/himself or others in the community, or
   (c) s/he has a medical, psychiatric or special educational need which can only be dealt with in a residential context, and/or it is in the child's best interest which cannot be met in any other way.
5 No child of primary school age should be sent outside Lothian Region on a List G school placement [residential special school] without the prior specific approval of the education committee.

(Lothian Regional Council 1987)

This joint policy seeks to frame all work with difficult young people and its scope is, of course, far wider than just those young people who present challenging behaviour in schools. Nevertheless, its implementation has had a number of consequences which directly affect every school. The most obvious is the establishment of School Liaison Groups (SLGs) in every secondary school (and now copied by some primary schools). The SLG is a collaborative forum, usually chaired by an assistant head teacher or senior guidance teacher, and attended by local social workers, education welfare staff, and, often, an educational psychologist, youth worker and other community group representatives. Meeting two or three times a term, it considers individual cases of students who are failing to be accommodated satisfactorily within the school. It is open to all those present to share information and put forward constructive ideas for resolving the tensions. Other agencies as well as the school can put forward cases for consideration. Perhaps once a term the SLG will review its work to draw out broader trends and themes from the individual cases, so that changes to the school system or the support services themselves can be considered and introduced. In this way the focus is broadened from that of individual students to the wider school and community environment.

A similar policy within Strathclyde Region establishes common forums for social workers and teachers to meet together on a regular basis in each area to discuss current provision for young people in trouble and the patterns of difficulty and response that are emerging.

The search for, and recognition of, patterns of difficulty in an area is a key aspect of any policy approach. It implies that challenging behaviour is not merely an individual's response to a situation which can be dealt with just by changing the student. Where patterns exist, there may be an underlying factor contributing to the difficulty, and this causal relationship may have more to do with institutional or community issues than individual pathology. One approach to this area is the introduction of systems thinking.

The systems approach has been increasingly used in the analysis of juvenile offending. Data is gathered across an area relating to the nature and location of offences, their frequency, the perpetrator, his or her previous convictions and responses to earlier sentences, etc. A systems approach seeks to relate this information and examine the relationship between 'what goes in' and 'what comes out', i.e. to collate information across the whole range of offences to determine what actually works. If this information is then fed back to the decision-makers in the form of 'You did this, and the results were that', improved decision-making will result in the long term through informed discussion.

In the schools context, when examining responses to difficult behaviour, several schools are beginning to adopt a systems approach, often within the framework of multidisciplinary policy. This involves determining which information is important and then creating procedures for routinely collecting it. Several examples may illustrate this approach.

In one area, data on truancy was collected to show which year groups were involved, which classes were avoided, and what days of the week and times of the day truancy most often occurred. Since the school had attempted a number of different responses, the effect of each was then monitored in both the short and medium term. The results were considered jointly by senior teachers and social workers. As a result the classroom registration procedure was changed, and the discipline system was shifted away from punishing poor attendance to rewarding good attendance. Such changes came about as a result of systems monitoring across a great number of incidents, and not just in response to individual and arbitrary decision-making on single cases.

Another school used a systems approach to tackle its problem of student suspensions for poor behaviour. Data was gathered on those involved, the nature of the incident which led to the suspension, the teacher involved, who took the decision, the process for lifting the suspension, and the subsequent behaviour of the student. This analysis showed a very discretionary approach to suspensions, with some teachers using it far more than others; as a result, the students did not know what the behavioural boundaries actually were. After discussion of these results within the school, a much tighter code was produced regarding the use of suspensions, the autonomy of many teachers was reduced, and the total number of suspensions decreased significantly without any noticeable deterioration in student behaviour.

The use of systems analysis itself does not solve or remove difficult behaviour, but it provides those who work with such students, often on a multidisciplinary basis, with helpful information about both what is happening and what works. This in turn directs energy towards the more effective responses, and encourages a broader thinking about the causes of such behaviour.

TRAINING FOR JOINT WORKING

Preparing staff to work in a multidisciplinary manner requires considerable thought and planning. Most social workers, teachers and youth workers have been brought up almost entirely within their own traditions. These professional boundaries are well defined – they establish the unique culture and ethos of each profession, its norms and working methods. They also tend to carry a mythology about what other people do. In this way 'professional identity' can serve to defend the interests of one group and implicitly criticise those of another. Teachers and social workers are no exception – witness the buck-passing in any staff room!

Most training events which seek to prepare people for multidisciplinary working are centrally concerned with naming these mutual stereotypes – and exposing them for the myths they are. A common way of doing this is to bring a multidisciplinary group together for two or three days (not necessarily consecutive), and involving both managers and front-line staff. A series of exercises can encourage each professional group to set out its views on the others' priorities, and its statement of its own key roles. The resulting comparison is often both revealing and educational, as participants come to see each other as human beings struggling with the same common problems.

Training events then need to capitalise on this interest by encouraging people to share their practical techniques and methods for working with such problems. This can be done through role-plays and simulations, as well as the informal interchanges and trust-building which so frequently occur once the ice has been broken. Finally, the group may identify some long-standing common difficulties in the area and then form task-centred multidisciplinary groups to devise new practical initiatives to tackle them, based upon a sharing of skills and knowledge. Most multidisciplinary training of this nature requires opportunities to review and update the contact, not least because staff may change and fresh problems and joint responses may become possible.

In conclusion, this chapter has sought to illustrate both the benefits and range of methods which can be employed by teachers and social workers collaborating together in practice. Such collaboration is possible at the level of the classroom or year group, of the whole school, or through cross-authority policies. While not offering solutions to all problems of difficult behaviour, multidisciplinary working opens up the opportunity of new and creative approaches and brings the tested skills of one profession into the domain of another. By working together, it is possible to remove the need to 'pass-the-parcel' and create an environment in which both the music and the game stop and the players can sit down together to look creatively at what they have to share.

REFERENCES

Gill, K. and Pickles, T. (1989) *Active Collaboration: Joint Practice and Youth Strategies*. Glasgow: ITRC (now available from Framework, 2 Mill Cottages, Campsie Road, Torrance, Glasgow G64 4BW).

Lloyd, G. (ed.) (1992) *Chosen with Care? Responses to Disturbing and Disruptive Behaviour*. Edinburgh: Moray House Publications.

Lothian Regional Council (1987) *Lothian Regional Council Youth Strategy*. Edinburgh: Lothian Regional Council.

Pickles, T. (1992) *Dealing with Disaffection*. London: Longman.

Chapter 7

Providing effective support to mainstream schools: issues and strategies

Peter Gray and Jim Noakes

This chapter looks at some of the factors that should be taken into account when providing support to teachers in mainstream schools who are experiencing difficult pupil behaviour. A major consideration in this area of support is the challenge that difficult behaviour presents to teachers' basic sense of professionalism. Effective behavioural support work needs to acknowledge this, as well as offering strategies to assist teachers in responding to the particular behaviours presented by the child.

The main part of the chapter outlines some specific 'rules of thumb' which we have found particularly helpful in offering support to teachers and schools over a number of years. By way of introduction, however, the first section describes the context and expectations which characterise those seeking support. Teachers have sets of beliefs about the causes of difficult behaviour. These can affect their degree of optimism about the possibility of change for particular individuals, as well as setting parameters for the kinds of approaches which they consider appropriate. Effective behavioural support requires adequate cognisance of teacher beliefs, feelings and perceptions, as well as successful strategies for going beyond these where they may be inhibiting the possibilities of change.

Supporting teachers experiencing difficult behaviour: the context

'TEACHERS STRESSED BY RISING TIDE OF CLASSROOM VIOLENCE'

'GET RID OF THE BAD APPLES'

These two headlines are typical of recent newspaper coverage of schools' and teachers' concerns about difficult behaviour. The extent of personal threat experienced by some teachers was evidenced at a recent teacher union conference (reported in *Education*: see Pinnell 1993), during which a representative gave a demonstration of a personal alarm.

Many explanations have been suggested for rising teacher concerns in this area. Some have pointed to the increasing social divide between 'haves' and 'have-nots', with a corresponding upward trend in pupil disaffection, youth crime and delinquency (see, for example, Willis 1984). Others have argued that pupils' behaviour has become more difficult as a result of a *moral* decline, with increased family breakdown and parental 'fecklessness'. At the child level, a whole host of possible causes have been proposed, ranging from changes in diet, earlier pubertal thresholds, as well as an increase in capacity to observe violence and anti-social behaviour (through television and video availability).

Many teachers would subscribe to one or more of these hypotheses. This is in line with research evidence (for example, Croll and Moses 1985), which shows an inclination among teachers to attribute pupil difficulty to within-child or home factors. And yet, other studies (for example, Rutter *et al.* 1979; Reynolds *et al.* 1981) have also pointed to *school* factors which contribute to outcomes. Teachers themselves agree that schools and individual staff can and do make a difference to the nature of pupil behaviour.

Research on school effectiveness has been intended to be *enabling* for those involved in school development. In a sense, too, researchers such as Rutter have wished to stress a more optimistic and preventative approach to work with children, in the face of some traditional assumptions about the power of nature over nurture. However, there is no doubt that such evidence has been used in recent years by sections of the right-wing press and some Tory politicians to fuel public concern about educational trends. The weight of political emphasis here has come to rest on a view that pupil misconduct, both in and out of school, is the *product* of ineffective schools and teachers who can no longer be trusted to be professional. This assertion has been used by government in the 1980s and early 1990s to support their view that standards (of work and behaviour) can only be improved with a centrally driven curriculum and publication of 'objective' results.

Difficulties arising from the implementation of the Government's reforms, and some change in the climate of public opinion, have led to a recent softening of attitudes towards schools and teachers as potential causes of their own problems. However, government reforms, both through their explicit demands and their more implicit messages, have no doubt contributed to teachers' stress and lowered self-esteem. In this context, it is perhaps not surprising to see less positive public attitudes towards pupils who present further demands, as well as some direct challenges to teachers' sense of their own competence.

It is difficult to obtain objective evidence of a decline in pupil behaviour (the research linked to the Elton Report, for example, did not support the level of pupil violence in schools which recent teacher trade union discussion might imply). The possibility of a real decline (for any of the reasons given above) must always be set against the strong themes and emotions that difficult pupil behaviour will always elicit from those charged with the care of children (both teachers and parents). These themes include a continuing belief that things were better in previous generations.

They also include a strong tendency to think that, if we are not feeling good about things, it is probably someone else's fault!

It is such themes and emotions that provide a particular context for those offering support to teachers experiencing difficult pupil behaviour.

Supporting teachers experiencing difficult pupil behaviour: teacher beliefs

David Lane (1978) has described elsewhere beliefs held by teachers which are likely to have a bearing on their work with external change agents or support staff. Lane considers that these beliefs serve a number of functions for teachers, who are typically involved in a system where individuals stand or fall on their own with little built-in peer support. These beliefs can best be summarised as follows:

1 *Beliefs that reinforce one's own belief system against external assault*

(a) A belief in a basic good and bad character which is unchangeable.
(b) A lack of respect for external agencies ('they don't have our problems').
(c) A pride in one's own methods, which makes it difficult to accept that someone else could succeed where one's own efforts have failed.
(d) A belief in regression to type: that is, a child might make a temporary change but sooner or later his/her 'real self' will assert itself.

2 *Lack of willingness to accept change because of the possible consequences of doing so*

(a) The history of difficulty can be very long; this causes fixed attitudes where even lengthy improvement (sustained for a year) cannot undo the painful memories.
(b) A fear that, if you comment on improvement, it will disappear (change being down to luck rather than real).
(c) A fear that, if you admit improvement, external agencies will withdraw their support and leave you to it.

3 *Expectations about what outsiders can provide*

(a) A belief that the LEA has or should have infinite resources and that failure to make them available is simply a matter of bureaucratic stubbornness.
(b) A belief that children's behaviour can be changed without any reference to the situation in which it occurs.

Effects of teacher expectations on behaviour support work: considerations for practice

These expectations provide a powerful context within which support teachers must work. In delivering effective support, a number of issues must be considered. The remainder of this chapter outlines these issues and particular strategies that we have found useful in practice.

1 *Find out who is concerned and why*

On arrival at a school to discuss a referred child, the support teacher can often find the atmosphere highly charged. The link person from the school (the special educational needs coordinator, head of year or even head teacher) experiences a feeling of vulnerability on being questioned by an outsider intent on information-gathering. School staff also need to maintain professional credibility in this situation. This can lead them to generalise their own concerns to a range of others. These could be members of the school's governing body, parents of other children and even the parents of the referred child.

Sometimes, such pressures can be real. However, at other times, concern is over-generalised in order to validate the seriousness of the case. Fears about the future can also lead to over-generalisation. For example, a head teacher may be worried about staff and parental attitudes if there is an increase in the number of 'problem' children being placed at the school, even if concern is currently limited in focus to the referred child.

It is useful for the support teacher to appraise the situation by gently teasing out the issues. For example, how did this matter come to the attention of the chairperson of the school's governing body? Which parents have expressed concern? Is this legitimate? It may also be appropriate to arrange to speak directly to those reported as expressing concern in order to verify the situation and reassure them where necessary.

If members of a governing body have an interest in a case, then the support teacher should feel confident in extending them the opportunity to help resolve the difficulties as opposed to just expressing opinions from the sideline. This could mean inviting them to regular review meetings and involving them in programme planning.

2 *Find out what people actually want from you*

Schools have a wide range of expectations when they make a referral to a support service. Support teachers should clarify what is expected before offering an intervention programme based on preconceived assumptions. Possible expectations include the following:

(a) Removing the problem (the 'undertaker' approach!)

The school may wish the child to be removed and placed in 'more appropriate' provision. In this situation, there is little immediate interest in developing an intervention programme within school, as this is seen simply as delaying the inevitable.

Support services should be clear, both with schools and among themselves, about the specific advantages as well as the disadvantages of maintaining children in both mainstream and special education settings. Inclusion in mainstream is assisted where LEAs have a clear and explicit policy. Warwickshire County Council, for example, has stated:

> We are firmly committed to the principle of integration in the delivery of special educational provision. We believe that education should both reflect and enhance the goals of society in which it takes place . . . Thus if we are opposed to discrimination and social segregation in our society we must be opposed to it in our schools.
>
> (Warwickshire County Council 1989)

Support services have a major role to play in working with schools to enable such policies to become part of the prevailing culture. This does not mean that support programmes for children should never include periods of withdrawal or segregation. However, such action should form part of an overall structured plan, as opposed to a 'knee-jerk' response when difficulties arise (Gray and Noakes 1987).

The recent Education Bill supports the view that segregation of pupils with behaviour difficulties should be time-limited. However, reintegration from off-site provision is notoriously difficult (Gray and Noakes 1992a). To be effective, plans should be drawn up *before* off-site arrangements are made.

These should clearly state the circumstances under which a child will be removed from mainstream education and when and how reintegration is to be carried out. Targets should be specified for all stages of the plan and should link strongly to changes that will assist the pupil in returning successfully to mainstream school. Those holding the strongest views that an alternative special educational placement is necessary should be most directly involved in structuring and reviewing such plans.

(b) Validating resource requests (e.g. classroom helper time)

Considerable pressure is sometimes placed on support teachers to validate school requests for additional resources. However, resources are finite, and it is necessary to ensure that any additional support is appropriately targeted to those children presenting the most need across all schools in an area. Such pressures should be resisted by support services: one school's satisfaction with a support service that accedes inappropriately is ultimately at the expense of others, who may have a greater need for scarce resources.

While the available resources should be targeted to the most difficult pupils, it is important too that they should be linked to interventions that have demonstrated even partial success and where additional support is clearly needed to underpin the gains made. Resources alone rarely succeed in situations where no groundwork has been done. It should also be stressed that the focus of any additional resources should be to allow an intervention programme to move forward to a stage where the situation can be normalised by using the school's own resources. This ensures that the additional help can be withdrawn and reallocated to new priorities.

(c) Using the support service to provide ancillary help

This situation often occurs owing to a lack of understanding regarding the role of support services. However, there may be times when it is appropriate for a support teacher to provide such help for a short period of time.

An example of this could be when a support teacher escorts a school refuser into school as part of a reintegration programme. It would be unlikely that such help could be maintained in the long term, and it is vital that the time-scale and the circumstances under which such help will be both provided and withdrawn is made clear from the outset.

(d) Providing assistance to enable the school to tackle the problem

This is how schools should use support services! However, considering the likely nature of the problems presented, it would be naive to assume that schools will automatically share this perspective. A considerable amount of effort is necessary over a period of time to enable schools and support services to forge close and cooperative teamwork approaches where both successes and failures can be equally shared.

Success, when achieved, is rarely publicised. This aspect should be more actively considered and opportunities taken to disseminate particularly positive pieces of joint work. The school and support service should always take equal credit as partners. There is a range of possibilities for celebrating successes (e.g. presentations to meetings or conferences, articles in educational journals).

(e) Auditing the school's good practice

Schools often expect the support teacher to register their successes and the stresses they incur, as well as to validate the work they are doing. In these circumstances, an alternative intervention programme is not needed, and offering one can endanger the relationship between the support service and the schools.

In general terms, support services should always distinguish and clarify expectations held by teachers and schools before offering an intervention.

3 *From start to finish, check what people say*

When gathering information about the problems presented, support teachers tend to be presented with absolutes and generalities. This applies not just to the sources of concern but also to the range of problems experienced. Thus, a head of year in a secondary school may state that all the subject teachers experience considerable difficulties in managing the child. This may or may not be the case. A problem behaviour checklist (Coulby and Harper 1985), sent individually to all subject staff, can prove helpful in measuring teacher perspectives across subject areas. Similar questionnaires can also cover a range of settings outside the classroom.

Direct observation may also be useful, though teachers may not agree with the findings if these are in conflict with their own perspective! The behaviour observed may of course be untypical (with a small sample of time). However, there is also evidence that teachers' reports regarding disruption in lessons may not always be reliable (Kaufman *et al*. 1985). The level of teacher concerns and the nature of their perceptions can lead them unwittingly to 'over-report' incidents of disruptive behaviour and to exaggerate the amount of time necessary for dealing with problems that arise.

Information provided by a school at second-hand about a family also needs verifying, as do possible explanations that a family may give directly about why particular behaviour is occurring. For example, one school might state that a family has moved frequently because of the child's difficulties at school and within the neighbourhood. However, investigation might show that the family had moved house on several occasions because of changes in the employment of the child's parents. Similarly, parents might state that their child's behaviour resulted from medication received. However, direct contact with the medical consultant (with parental permission) might indicate that neither the condition nor the medication were affecting the behaviour presented at school and that the parents had misunderstood the information they had been given.

At all stages of an intervention, information should be carefully considered by the support teacher. Where there is a conflict of opinion, matters should be clarified. Inaccurate information should be challenged, while ensuring that the partnership with the school is maintained (Gray and Noakes 1992a).

4 *Before you start, find out how you can finish*

Support services have finite resources, which will inevitably silt up with demand unless there is a system of case closure. They therefore have a responsibility to make schools aware of the resources actually available and the need for some cases to be closed before others can be taken on. Discussion at the point of initial referral should agree the criteria for success on which a case can be closed. If not, expectations will continue to rise, with the ultimate expectation of the creation of the perfect pupil!

Unless a case is closed through a formal system it will always remain the responsibility of the support service, even when an incident occurs some years later, after involvement has ceased. This prevents a support service from planning effectively even its medium-term work schedules, because numerous cases could reappear at any one time.

5   *Identify factors that will help or hinder change*

Not all factors that are helpful in one case will be the same in another! There is a view, for example, that pupils can be supported more easily at primary school than at secondary. Consistency of approach can be easier to achieve when a child is with one teacher at primary school, whereas, at secondary school, there will be several different teachers with further problems arising during lesson changeover (including opportunities for truancy). However, at primary school there can be personal conflict between a particular teacher and a pupil, and a range of different teachers in a secondary school can be an advantage. Secondary schools also have greater opportunities to re-timetable pupils where particular conflicts occur.

A major factor in achieving a positive outcome with difficult pupils is the flexibility a school has in its approach. This flexibility is about the degree to which the school can adapt to meet the needs of particular pupils. Flexibility is not to be confused with a particular management style. Schools that have informal classroom approaches (which give opportunities for children to move freely around the classroom) may appear to be positive environments in which to achieve behaviour change. However, when a structured behaviour management programme is necessary (requiring restriction in the child's movements in the initial stages), such an informal ethos can present problems. Flexibility is about the school's capacity to adapt its standard practice when needed.

6   *Use questions that will help things move on*

Recent advances in systems approaches (particularly those deriving from family therapy, see, for example, Penn 1982) have emphasised the importance of different kinds of questioning. Questions have a functional outcome (in terms of the behaviour and perceptions of the listener), as well as a formal answer. They can be seen on a continuum between that of 'challenge' and 'confirmation'. If questions contain too much challenge, the 'system' finds ways of rejecting them and simply confirms the *status quo*. Too little challenge, on the other hand, may results in the 'system' accepting the questioner but with little change to practice.

Support teachers need to find an effective balance along this continuum in order to facilitate change. At the point of referral to support services, there is usually a strong belief that the child is the cause of any problems or stress. Schools often attribute difficulties to the child and their home background. In trying to effect change, the support teacher needs to enable both parents and the school to manage the child in a different way and will therefore have to challenge existing beliefs. The support teacher will need to ask the kind of questions that make those within the 'system' reflect and then work towards resolving perceived anomalies. This needs to be done in a way that may result in parents and teachers feeling discomfort at times, but which does not lead to the rejection of the support teacher.

To achieve this there is a need for a mixture of confirmatory and challenging questions. Confirmatory questions such as 'Is he from a one-parent family?' do not move things forward and can simply confirm stereotypes. An acceptable challenging question could be 'He doesn't seem to be a problem in History and English. Why do you think this is?'

Questions that give reasons or interpretations are best avoided. It is usually more productive to ask questions that link people and events together and to test hypotheses by asking 'If' and 'Suppose'. Hypothetical questions about the future, such as 'What do you think will happen if nothing is found that will change the present situation?', can also be valuable, as can questions that encourage new alternatives, such as 'What would have to happen before Johnny would stop behaving in this way at school?'

7 Avoid being the 'knight in shining armour'

It can be a very attractive option for a support teacher to take over all aspects of planning a programme for behaviour management. It can be seen as an opportunity to show knowledge and demonstrate effectiveness. It can also be a short cut, avoiding time spent in discussion. However, unless there is involvement by the school in planning the programme (even though this may involve compromise in structure and design), there will inevitably be problems with uptake and maintenance. It is an easy and attractive option for school systems to reject detailed programmes when they have had no sense of involvement or responsibility in planning.

In practice, schools are in control of day-to-day practicalities and there-fore support services depend on their involvement and should recognise the school's role as internal expert. Tasks should be set for those involved directly, as well as for the support service, when planning and carrying out programmes. Contributions to plans by the school or parents, however small, should be rapidly and positively reinforced. If a programme is to lead successfully to more normal arrangements, then there should be an increase in school and parents' decision-making, allowing the phasing out of the support service.

8 *Stop and think: could your involvement make matters worse?*

The potential number of agencies that can become involved with a child presenting behaviour difficulties is considerable. This is particularly the case when parents have not put up barriers to further agency involvement. Education, social services, health and others in the private sector, such as parent advocates, can become involved in succession or simultaneously.

Unless there is careful joint planning and coordination across agencies, working towards shared goals, the situation can become chaotic. In such circumstances it is not unusual for agencies to work unwittingly against each other, creating what is often described in military contexts as 'friendly fire'.

Before accepting a case the support service should find out which other agencies are involved. This can be done through a formal referral system where the process has a built-in request for information regarding other agency involvement. Where it is felt to be inappropriate to accept a case at a particular stage, clear options and criteria should be given for reconsidering the situation either at the present time or in the future. Clarification should be given to other agencies on what they can legitimately expect from the support service.

Where other agencies are not involved at the time of referral, the basis and mechanism for involving them at a later stage should be clarified (Crombie and Noakes 1992). Preferably, behaviour support services should create structures for providing more coordinated multi-agency networks (Gray and Noakes 1992b).

9 *Ensure change is in everyone's interest*

Unless the school believes strongly that the removal of the child is necessary, then a change in the child's behaviour is always in the school's interest. However, if removal is a clear objective, the situation is more difficult. While other 'low-cost' options exist (e.g. permanent exclusion), incentives for working towards change are likely to be few and there is great dependence on teachers' sense of professionalism.

Effective programmes for pupils with challenging behaviour take time to design and implement. When planning programmes, consideration should be given to ensuring that time demands match the levels of concern and reduce as success is achieved. If there is an increase in concern, support teachers should not shoulder all the additional responsibilities that can arise, but should share these with the school and wherever possible include the child's parents.

It is often useful to start programmes with a high level of structure and formality and to move gradually towards more flexible arrangements as success is achieved. In the case of relapse, there should be a return to a greater degree of structure.

10 *Move from 'special' to 'normal' as quickly as possible*

It is usually very difficult to change the nature of special education resourcing, once this is in place. Thus, when classroom assistant time is allocated, it can be difficult to remove. Once a pupil is placed off-site, reintegration can be difficult to achieve. With finite resources available to meet need, this can be a problem. It is wise, therefore, to ensure that, before any special arrangements are put into operation, people are clear what such resources will be expected to do. How will progress be measured and on what basis or criteria will the resources be changed or removed? To ensure that resources are used cost-effectively, it is also important to establish who is responsible and in charge of the arrangements.

SUMMARY AND CONCLUSIONS

Some of the strategies and ways of thinking outlined above may seem somewhat challenging to teachers and schools. It is easy to believe that solutions for both pupils and teachers should be more simple. Surely schools know the support they require and the only task of support services is to deliver it?

The attraction of such beliefs in an area that is complex and charged with emotion makes the delivery of effective support even more difficult. Beliefs do have to be challenged, but in a supportive way that respects teachers for their ultimate professional responsibility for educating children. Teachers need support, but positive outcomes are necessary too for pupils whose behaviour may be provocative but whose present welfare and future stability cannot be ignored.

Difficult behaviour elicits strong emotions and this increases the chances of conflict between schools and support services. There is a difficult line for support services to tread. Ultimately, support is at its most effective when both teacher and support worker are able to recognise the emotions that are present and are aware of each other's needs and perspectives as well as those of the pupils.

REFERENCES

Coulby, D. and Harper, T. (1985) *Preventing Classroom Disruption: Policy, Practice and Education in Urban Schools*. London: Croom Helm.

Croll, P. and Moses, D. (1985) *One in Five*. London: Routledge & Kegan Paul

Crombie, R. and Noakes, J.S. (1992) 'Developing a service to support children with behaviour difficulties in mainstream school', *Educational and Child Psychology*, 9, 4: 57–67. The British Psychological Society.

Gray, P.J. and Noakes, J.S. (1987) 'Time to stop taking the easy option', *The Times Educational Supplement*, 10 April 1987, p. 21.

Gray, P.J. and Noakes, J.S. (1992a) 'Planning reintegration', in A. Miller and D.A. Lane (eds) *Silent Conspiracies: Scandals and Successes in Work with Vulnerable Children*. Stoke-on-Trent: Trentham Books.

Gray, P.J. and Noakes, J.S. (1992b) School support: towards a multidisciplinary approach. In D.A. Lane and A. Miller (eds) *Child and Adolescent Therapy: A Handbook*. Milton Keynes: Open University Press.

Kaufman, M., Agard, J.A. and Semmel, M.I. (1985) *Mainstreaming: Learners and Their Environment*. Cambridge, Mass.: Brookline Books.

Lane, D.A. (1978) *The Impossible Child*. London: Inner London Education Authority.

Penn, P. (1982) 'Circular questioning', *Family Process*, 21: 267–280.

Pinnell, H. (1993) 'Marching in step'. Report of NAS/UWT annual conference, *Education*, 23 April 1993.

Reynolds, D., Jones, D., St Leger, S. and Murgatroyd, S. (1981) *Bringing Schools Back In*. London: Routledge & Kegan Paul.

Rutter, M., Maughan, B., Mortimore, P. and Ouston, J. (1979) *Fifteen Thousand Hours*. London: Open Books.

Warwickshire County Council (1989) *Special Educational Needs in Warwickshire*. The report of the Members' working party on the implications of the 1981 Education Act. Warwick: Warwickshire County Council.

Willis, P. (1984) 'Youth unemployment: a new social state', *New Society*, 29 March 1984.

Section B

Schools and parents

Chapter 8

Parents and difficult behaviour: always the problem or part of the solution?

Andy Miller

The legislative thrusts of the past decade or so have promoted the position of parents to give them, for example, a greater say in a choice of school, to give them access to their child's attainments in national curriculum assessments, and to allow them to contribute towards an assessment if their child is thought to have special educational needs. Although 'parental involvement' has swept through the educational landscape, seemingly leaving none untouched in its wake, the area of problem behaviour in school has been almost totally neglected and the question of how to work positively and productively with parents in such circumstances has largely remained unanswered, or even, some would suggest, unasked.

Why is this so? Why should relations between teachers and parents be particularly contentious in this area?

> Our evidence suggests that teachers' picture of parents is generally very negative. Many teachers feel that parents are to blame for much misbehaviour in schools. We consider that, while this picture contains an element of truth, it is distorted.
>
> (Elton Report: DES 1989, p. 133)

As this quote aptly illustrates, the topic is highly sensitive and can easily lead to enflamed feelings. This chapter attempts to steer a way through these difficulties by avoiding a rhetorical stance and focusing upon what is known from a research perspective about teachers and parents and the issue of pupil behaviour. For a few people, just raising the issue can be contentious, it can be seen as implying that there may be more to this subject than an open-and-shut case of all parents being always to blame for all unwanted aspects of their children's school behaviour. Although this chapter may break a few eggs in this respect, we hope that the focus upon what has been discovered by means of a fairly dispassionate research approach may at least lead to the mixing bowl, the forum for the exchange of ideas, remaining intact.

TEACHERS' AND PARENTS' IDENTIFICATION OF PROBLEM BEHAVIOUR

A useful starting point is to look at how much common ground there is between teachers and parents in terms of what they find troubling in children's behaviour.

There have been several scientifically conducted surveys that have asked teachers to identify the intensity and frequency of different types of difficult and/or disturbed behaviour among their pupils. These have normally required teachers to complete schedules or checklists specifically devised for this purpose. Some of the studies have also asked parents to complete similar instruments designed to detect problems in the home context. The same striking finding occurs in each study – the *majority* of children identified as problems in one setting are not seen as such in the other!

For example, in the Isle of Wight survey of over 2,000 children – one of the most thorough studies of childhood problems ever carried out – standardised questionnaires completed by teachers and parents both proved extremely effective in being able to screen out children with psychiatric disorders (Rutter *et al.* 1970). However, there was suprisingly little overlap between the two sources, with only one child in every six or seven in the deviant group being identified by both parties.

The lack of a close correspondence between teachers' and parents' perceptions of behaviour problems was also illustrated in a longitudinal study of 343 London children (Tizard *et al.* 1988). At the end of the top infant year, teachers saw 34 per cent of the children as having a mild or a definite behaviour problem and parents identified 22 per cent. However, only 30 per cent of those seen by teachers as a problem at school were also seen as problems at home, and only 34 per cent of those identified by parents were similarly perceived as difficult by teachers.

This is not just a phenomenon confined to British society: similar results have also been obtained from a study conducted in New Zealand (McGee *et al.* 1983). This recurring finding suggests that either some forms of behaviour are context-specific, in that they are more likely to occur either at home or at school but not at both, or that some forms of behaviour have far more salience for teachers and others for parents. For example, Tizard *et al.* (1988) suggest that some types of behaviour, such as a lack of concentration, may be more of a problem in the school setting than at home and that other types, such as fooling around or nervousness and withdrawal, may just be more likely to occur at school.

Straight away, these studies have enormous implications for the initial discussions that parents and teachers may have when a school is concerned about a pupil's behaviour. Parents may not be 'unwilling to accept that there is a problem', it may be that they genuinely are not experiencing the same difficulties in the home setting. Similarly, parents who mention difficulties with their children at home, when these children are models of conformity at school, may not be 'fussing unnecessarily' or particularly 'weak' or 'incompetent' as parents.

THE 'DISINTERESTED' PARENT

'It's the ones who never turn up that you really want to see.' This is a common complaint in many staff rooms, and also the title of an interesting chapter by Bridges (1987) that describes the results of a series of interviews in Cambridgeshire with parents who were regular non-attenders at parents' evenings and social events at schools. Rather than revealing mere indifference and apathy, the interviews identified a range of reasons from practical difficulties such as transport, family ties and shift work, through to a concern about not being as confident as some other parents in discussing educational matters.

But the most recurring theme in the interviews was one of a dread of school, often associated with their own childhood experiences. This was most prevalent among those parents who had minimal or no contact. Dread, fear and anxiety are all emotional states that impair our social interactions and make it more likely that we will hear inaccurately or selectively what is being said to us. It is not hard to imagine such a parent avoiding contacts with school, however welcoming the invitation. If the situation should arise when the school wishes to discuss any matter, but especially behaviour, it is also not hard to imagine this parent's manner, fuelled by adrenalin and defensiveness, coming across as 'aggressive' or 'belligerent' or, at the very least, 'uncooperative'.

As with behaviour that occurs at school but not at home, so too a parental dread of school helps stack the cards against a straightforward collaborative approach towards difficult behaviour being easily achievable.

ATTRIBUTING CAUSES TO PROBLEM BEHAVIOUR

How prevalent is the view among teachers that parents are to blame for their children's difficult behaviour in school?

In the study described in Chapter 3, twenty-four primary school teachers who had each worked successfully with an educational psychologist in relation to a particular pupil who had been causing them great difficulties in their class, were asked about what they saw as the original causes of the child's difficult behaviour. *In all but three of the interviews home factors were cited as being implicated in the original difficult behaviour*, usually in combination with factors concerning the child's character or personality and, to a lesser extent, the effects of the teacher's management style, peers, and school organisation (see Table 8.1).

Table 8.1 Teacher attributions for 'causes' of problem and 'causes' of solution

	Problem	Solution
Home	21	4
Child	23	15
Class teacher	10	21
Peers	9	6
School	6	3
Home/teacher interaction	5	1
Teacher/child interaction	2	4

In particular, the most frequently occurring home factors thought by the teachers to be responsible for the difficult behaviour in school were that:

— parents are separated or divorced, thus leading either to the absence of a natural father, divided loyalties or children's uncertainty about where they will be living   9 cases
— the mother had difficulty managing the child(ren)   9 cases
— the child did not receive enough attention from one or the other parent   5 cases

Factors within their own control were thought by the teachers to be implicated in the origin of the problem in ten cases. The most commonly occurring of these were:

— teacher not selecting work of appropriate interest level   4 cases
— teacher's expectation of unrealistic quantities of work   3 cases
— teachers giving pupils 'negative attention'   2 cases

As well as being asked for their views on the original causes of the problems, the teachers in the study were also later asked why they felt that the pupils' behaviour had improved. Their attributions of who was responsible for the improved behaviour are also shown in Table 8.1.

The teachers attributed the improvement to factors within their control in 21 cases, the most commonly cited mechanisms being:

— teacher's positive attention to the child   13 cases
— teacher selecting work of appropriate level of interest   8 cases
— teacher's expectation of realistic quantities of work   5 cases
— use of tangible rewards/incentives   5 cases
— consistent teacher approach   3 cases

These findings show that many of the teachers in the sample were able to take a self-critical look at their practice and recognise their ability to exert a positive influence on the pupils in question. The interventions involved working with an educational psychologist and parent in most cases, but credit for the improvements was seldom extended to the parent. Despite working jointly with parents and witnessing their input in 18 cases, and despite attesting to and welcoming an increased level of 'support from home' in 16 cases, home factors were cited as making a contribution to the solution in only 4 cases.

A more detailed analysis of these attributional processes is provided elsewhere (Miller 1994a), but these results do suggest that parents may be readily seen by teachers as the cause of pupils' difficult behaviour but that they do not have the ability to effect real solutions, even in partnership with teachers and psychologists. This research suggests that these attributions of blame may become very resistant to modification, even in the face of experiences that would seem to provide clear evidence to the contrary. If we put this information together with the finding that teachers and parents often do not identify the same children as displaying behaviour difficulties, and the dread of school experienced by at least some apparently disinterested parents, then the stage is set for almost inevitable misunderstanding, if not confrontation.

It is this attribution of blame, usually surrounding children with emotional and behavioural difficulties, that, this chapter suggests, singles these children out from those with other forms of special educational need. For children with partial hearing, or Down's syndrome, or for those experiencing bereavement, for example, this level of tension between home and school seems far less likely. And it is highly likely that this seemingly inevitable tension accounts for emotional and behavioural difficulties having been carefully sidestepped by the enthusiastic parental involvement revolution of the past decade or so.

The problem with 'causes' in complex social systems

It seems decidedly sensible to search for the cause of a particular pupil's difficult behaviour, as a first step towards improving it. If the cause can be detected and then removed, we should stand a reasonable chance of decreasing the 'symptom', the difficult behaviour. This is a model of causation that appeals to many spheres of professional endeavour and to our basic human common sense.

However, difficult behaviour in schools is often a different type of phenomenon. We have already seen that behaviour can be context-specific. Research has also shown that the standard of pupil behaviour as well as academic attainment can vary between schools, irrespective of the school's catchment area, and can be partly influenced by factors within a school's control (Rutter et al. 1979; Mortimore et al. 1984).

The problem can be more usefully seen as lying more with our cause-and-effect style of thinking. It may be far more profitable to think in terms of circular causality (Fine and Holt 1983; Dowling and Osborne 1985; Leyden 1991), a concept often employed by therapists attempting to address conflicts within families. Take the example of a primary school-teacher who feels that a mother is not supporting her efforts to manage her son's difficult behaviour, because the mother does not accept that there is a problem to be addressed. The teacher may decide that it is necessary to keep the mother informed of all misdemeanours, so that the classroom behaviour can gradually be more fully appreciated. However, suppose the mother initially interprets this as making an unnecessary fuss over rela-tively minor matters and concludes that the teacher is 'picking on' her son. She may decide that the best way to 'stick up' for him is to argue with the teacher about the seriousness of much of this reported behaviour. The teacher will then receive further confirmation of her view that the mother is refusing to accept the seriousness of the problem and may redouble her efforts to convince her. A 'vicious circle' may then result where each move can be seen to act as the trigger for the next (see Figure 8.1).

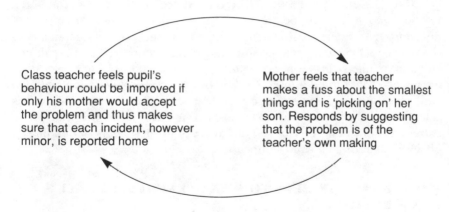

Class teacher feels pupil's behaviour could be improved if only his mother would accept the problem and thus makes sure that each incident, however minor, is reported home

Mother feels that teacher makes a fuss about the smallest things and is 'picking on' her son. Responds by suggesting that the problem is of the teacher's own making

Figure 8.1 A self-perpetuating cycle of attribution between home and school

In order to stop this mutual blaming, it is necessary to abandon the search for one particular cause, however justified one side or the other may feel their position to be (and however much a reasonable and detached observer might be inclined to side with one party or the other). Abandoning attributions of blame is often extremely difficult; it has been the means by which a threatening and confusing complexity has been rendered intelligible, and we do not easily give up these beliefs and return to a position of uncertainty. Of course, dismantling cycles of attribution is made even more difficult because each of these elements may well have become enmeshed within a whole network of 'wheels within wheels'. For example, the teacher may have invited some disapproval from a less tolerant colleague, who believes that more drastic action should be taken by the head teacher because the pupil's behaviour is irredeemable. The class teacher, in response, may become more determined to show that the pupil can improve and try harder to engage the mother's cooperation (see Figure 8.2).

Similarly, we might imagine a situation in which the boy's father feels his wife is being far too sensitive about reports from school and that by responding to each of these she is getting a bad name for herself and in turn causing their son to be further criticised in school (Figure 8.3).

There can easily be any number of circular attributions, rather than just one set, between two people and these will also be linked to many others throughout the social edifices of the school and family systems. Although intimately linked, some of these will be far removed from the original teacher, parent and child, perhaps involving deeply ingrained beliefs and important organisational procedures within the school or family, and may be very resistant to modification for all kinds of reasons.

Although it can sound a trifle trite on first acquaintance, especially to a teacher who feels a desperate need for a solution aimed directly at a difficult pupil, the greatest benefit a skilled external consultant can sometimes bring is to help to stop the spiralling of interconnected and expanding circles of implied causation. *Sometimes internal personnel, the school staff, are unable to perform this task, not because of a lack of skill or goodwill, but because of their position within a wider set of conflicting attributions.* It is sometimes only by slowing down or halting these (and this can prove extremely difficult in some cases) that there is any possibility of building an effective solution to a child's difficulties.

THE INITIAL BARRIERS TO JOINT TEACHER–PARENT CONSULTATION

The research literature and professional casework experience repeatedly indicate that the most difficult part of the work of a consultant attempting to dismantle some of these attributions is in the initial stages of intervention. Consider this quotation from a research study carried out in Newcastle, which attempted to investigate the most effective methods of helping secondary-age pupils exhibiting difficult behaviour in schools:

> Attempts were made to lessen mutual distrust and prejudice and ways sought to increase parental interest in the child's education and progress . . . Occasionally, it was necessary to reassure teachers that parents were concerned and interested . . . There was also the far more difficult operation of helping certain teachers to appreciate their personal impact on parents. This was perhaps the most sensitive area . . . it had to be broached with great diplomacy and caution . . . Sometimes, before

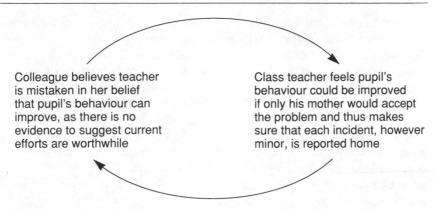

Colleague believes teacher is mistaken in her belief that pupil's behaviour can improve, as there is no evidence to suggest current efforts are worthwhile

Class teacher feels pupil's behaviour could be improved if only his mother would accept the problem and thus makes sure that each incident, however minor, is reported home

Figure 8.2 A self-perpetuating cycle of attribution within school

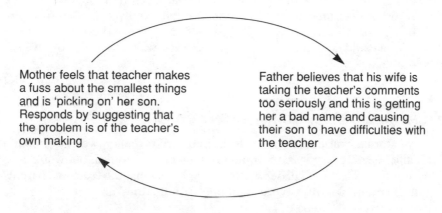

Mother feels that teacher makes a fuss about the smallest things and is 'picking on' her son. Responds by suggesting that the problem is of the teacher's own making

Father believes that his wife is taking the teacher's comments too seriously and this is getting her a bad name and causing their son to have difficulties with the teacher

Figure 8.3 A self-perpetuating cycle of attribution at home

> meeting, parents or teachers proposed angry confrontations with each other . . . Sometimes the teacher thought the school social worker was siding with the parents, while the parents thought the opposite.
>
> (Kolvin *et al.* 1981, p. 194)

A similar point is made by two workers who experimented with offering an advisory service to parents within a London primary school:

> Often a joint meeting with parents and teachers would seem the [next] logical step . . . However, careful and skilful handling is required in bringing the two parties together, as the situation can be so polarized that such an attempt could be perceived by the parent as a potential confrontation. The seemingly humble goal of reopening communication between parents and teachers must not be underestimated . . .
>
> (Dowling and Taylor 1989, p. 26)

In the face of such strong feelings it is perhaps necessary to state again that this chapter is attempting to remain exempt from the procedures of blame, in order better to understand and promote what is known about effective parental involvement leading to mutually acknowledged positive outcomes. But before proceeding, it is worth noting once again that there appears to be a universality about these issues, suggesting that we are perhaps dealing with very deep themes within the Western educational world. Aponte (1976), an American family therapist who was one of the first to attempt this type of work, also identified this tension, and described the additional complications that derived from the position of parents in the light of the professional status that is shared between teachers and an external consultant:

> The teachers . . . do not expect to be treated as clients. The prospect of being interviewed with the child and his parents brings into question the school staff's status in relation to their pupil. And yet the therapists are being called upon to accomplish something neither the family nor the school could do and thus must lead the three-way effort . . . to solve the problem.
>
> (Aponte 1976, p. 304)

A MODEL OF TEACHER–PARENT CONSULTATION

Any external consultant who set forth into such turbulent waters without a reliable means of navigation would not only be very foolish but would also be doing a professional disservice to her or his clients, the teachers, parents and children. So what types of models or theories are there to guide participants in this type of endeavour?

One way of understanding this type of consultation is to think about it as a two-stage process, requiring two different explanatory frameworks (West and Idol 1987; Burden and Miller 1993), as in Figure 8.4. The consultant needs a model (Theory 1) to guide the way he or she works with the teacher and parent relationship, so that barriers are overcome and positive attributions are encouraged, and another set of principles (Theory 2) to inform any joint strategy that may be devised with them to help in the management of the child.

The consultant and the teacher–parent relationship (Theory 1)

Several writers have provided methods and techniques for consultants approaching joint work with parents in respect of difficult pupil behaviour. Some have described attempts to deal directly with the strong feelings that can be aroused in teachers by such behaviour and by unsatisfactory dealings with parents. Both Osborne (1983) and Hanko (1990) provide sensi-

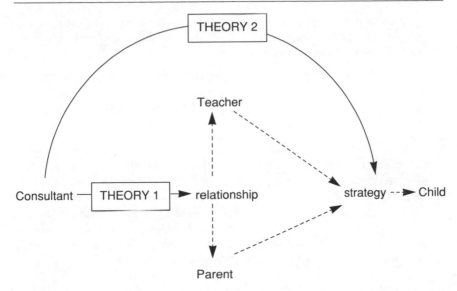

Figure 8.4 The two theoretical frameworks that guide teacher–parent behavioural consultation

tive accounts of groups they have run for teachers, in which it has been possible through discussions of real-life cases to acknowledge and legitimise these feelings and for those present to help each other with possible ways forward. This form of group work, and its equivalent with parents, could be envisaged as a preliminary to that undertaken with both teachers and parents together.

One method by which successful consultants enable teachers and parents to work more effectively together seems to involve helping 'insulate' the teacher from the culture of the school on those occasions when extended cycles of attribution are likely to be a particular problem. In another aspect of the study described in Chapter 3, many of the primary teachers who had achieved considerable success with one of, or the most difficult pupil(s) they had ever taught, had kept the details of what they had been doing from their colleagues on the staff, even though these colleagues often knew how difficult this pupil had been and were also aware of the positive changes in behaviour that had taken place. Instead, the consultation had led to the teacher, parent and psychologist developing a new working relationship, in which it was possible for each party to begin to see the others in a fresh light (Miller 1994b).

Some of their comments illustrate this sense of 'insulation' and hint at why it may on occasions be necessary:

I think a lot of the time when teachers are working with a psychologist they keep it very much to – it's their property almost. It's strange . . . teachers are very possessive of the children in their class and they don't want to share things (Interview 24)

I mean I've come back to teaching after 15 years' break and they've been super, they've been really helpful . . . I can't come in [to the staffroom] and say 'Aren't I good?' . . . It's very big-headed isn't it? . . . (Interview 1)

I was a little unsure and I didn't want to say anything – stick my neck out if you like and say 'Look we're doing this and it could prove wonderful'. I wanted to go very tentatively and then when I could see some sort of hope I turned to the staff and said 'This is what we're doing, will you please bear this in mind' . . . I didn't want to offend Margaret [pupil's previous teacher] in any way by saying 'I shall keep him in the class no matter what'. So it was only very gradually that I explained to her what was happening – that's the deputy head . . . it's very, very delicate (Interview 18)

This type of work would, of course, be far less likely to occur in secondary settings where a pupil is taught by a large number of different staff. The author has been involved in situations where ten or so staff who teach a difficult pupil have taken a cautiously positive approach to a home–school intervention, while two or three colleagues have asserted a more pessimistic view. It is not unknown for this minority to be more influential in terms of the senior management's final decision on how to proceed with the pupil, because it is difficult for more optimistic staff to 'stick their necks out' in case they ultimately find themselves in a position where the pupil's behaviour has changed for the worse and they are then publicly perceived as being unable to manage. Two American studies (Tucker and Dyson 1976; Power and Bartholomew 1985) have employed the methods of family therapy, not only with the parents and siblings of a pupil but also, at the same time but in a modified form, with the formal and informal power alliances and allegiances among the school staff.

Taylor (1982) described another method, which involved an initial family interview in school, attended by two school staff for the first half hour in order to 'voice the complaints of the school' and to obtain an initial response from the parents and pupil. This understandably generated strong feelings in the parents, and these became the focus for much of the rest of that meeting. Strategies were subsequently developed by the educational psychologist with the school staff, in which the parents' perspective was also represented by the psychologist. In terms of the theoretical roots of this form of practice, Taylor suggested:

The would-be consultant . . . owes a debt to many approaches in the field of mental health . . . a psychodynamic understanding of the life cycle; systems theory, learning theory and crisis theory; techniques of brief therapy, family therapy and consultation and, for work in schools, at least a nodding acquaintance with the literature of organizational development. Trying to determine which is the major influence in this or that tactic can lead to the proverbial problem of the centipede.

(Taylor 1982)

It might also be added, in line with the arguments presented earlier, that the most pertinent influences in any specific case may be strongly determined by the particular webs of attribution within which that case is located.

A more forthright approach is provided by Long (1988), who set up meetings between teachers and parents of particular pupils in school and took responsibility for initiating and maintaining an effective communication system in both directions. He considered it important to air and clear up any early differences between home and school as quickly as possible. Then, he outlined the possible alternatives available, such as suspension, special education and home tuition, and the negative consequences that these could have for pupils. At the same time the success rates reported in the literature on home-based reinforcement methods, described below, were presented to the joint meeting. Using this approach, and these methods, Long and two behaviour support teachers in West Norfolk were able to obtain an 82 per cent success or partial success rate with 44 cases, representing the most difficult 1 per cent of the area's secondary school pupils.

The consultant and the joint teacher–parent strategy for child management (Theory 2)

Home-based reinforcement (H-BR) methods have been shown in a number of scientifically controlled experiments and in a succession of carefully detailed case studies to lead to improved pupil behaviour (Atkeson and Forehand 1979; Barth 1979). In a comparative review of a great deal of research into methods for helping disruptive adolescents, Topping (1983) found that training parents in behaviour management and home–school schemes were more cost-effective approaches than using either external resources, such as special schools, or internal ones, such as time-out rooms and special classes. In HB-R, the teacher is basically responsible for specifying classroom rules, for deciding when these have been followed or broken and for communicating this information to the parents. At home, the parents are responsible for consistently dispensing rewards and sanctions to the child, based on the teacher's information. As well as the two major reviews of the American literature above, case studies and research reports have shown this method to be effective in Australia (Leach and

Byrne 1986; Leach and Ralph 1986) and in Britain (Gupta *et al*. 1990; Long 1988).

Similarly, surveys have repeatedly shown that pupils, both at secondary level (Wheldall and Merrett 1988; Caffyn 1989) and primary level (Harrop and Williams 1992), value highly information being sent home to their parents as a reward for good behaviour at school, although the research suggests that teachers are more divided in their judgements on the effectiveness of this (Harrop and Williams 1992).

Topping (1992) has presented a detailed account of how a school can proceed with the practicalities of setting up an H-BR approach. Although the methods are not quite as simple as they might first appear – requiring careful attention to such factors as the selection of rules, the involvement of pupils, the criteria for deciding upon rule adherence, the method for communicating between home and school, the selection of rewards and sanctions, the frequency of their use, the method for ensuring consistency, and so on – their efficacy has been consistently demonstrated, leading Barth in 1979 to exclaim that 'the widespread application of this system need wait no longer'.

And yet it has had to wait. Although effective methods from Theory 2 clearly exist, if the Theory 1 procedures required for getting to the position where these methods may be used are not given equal or more attention by support staff and mainstream teachers, they stand little chance of realisation.

CONCLUSION

The initial stages of this type of work are not easy for any of the major parties involved with the pupil, neither teachers, parents nor consultants. The benefits of persevering in a sensitive and professional manner, however, are revealed in sets of quotes from some of the teachers in the study discussed in Chapter 3. An often dramatic change can be clearly discerned by comparing quotes from the teachers, describing their working relationships with the parents of the children before and after the involvement of an external consultant:

Before involvement	*After strategy*
Darren's mum had been very critical of how he had been handled . . . she's got a hair trigger	Mum came in every single night to check . . . I think she feels the more help she gets the better (Interview 18)
Mum had caused so many problems here. She's a very bristly lady	Mum and I got on quite well . . . I feel she's got some respect for what I'm trying to do for him (Interview 15)

What we lacked before was cooperation from the parents

Any time I meet the parents they're very enthusiastic now (Interview 20)

We did try to get the parents involved. We got very little support from home at that time

The head, after her conversations with the parents, would then come to me and say 'They're really pleased you know' (Interview 22)

The mother had had such negative feelings about any involvement

She said 'You don't know how much you've achieved with him . . .' she's so positive about the improvement (Interview 6)

These quotes substantiate findings from elsewhere in casework experience and the research literature, showing that, even when the process of dealing with initial attributions proves particularly lengthy and fraught, it is sometimes possible afterwards for all concerned to be rewarded with very effective strategies. Challenging pupil behaviour will probably always be a demanding area of work, but as schools continue to develop their working relationships with parents of children with a wide range of special educational needs, it will be worth remembering that, even in the most difficult of cases, the means do exist to make effective parental collaboration a reality.

REFERENCES

Atkeson, B.M. and Forehand, R. (1979) 'Home-based reinforcement programs designed to modify classroom behaviour: a review and methodological evaluation', *Psychological Bulletin*, 86, 6: 1298–1308.

Aponte, H.J. (1976) 'The family–school interview: an eco-structural approach', *Family Process*, 15: 303–311.

Barth, R. (1979) 'Home-based reinforcement of school behaviour: a review and analysis', *Review of Educational Research*, 49, 3: 436–458.

Bridges, D. (1987) ' "It's the ones who never turn up that you really want to see." The "problem" of the non-attending parent', in J. Bastiani (ed.) *Parents and Teachers. 1*. Slough: NFER–Nelson.

Burden, R. and Miller, A. (1993) 'Intervention or prevention? Applying educational psychology to the therapeutic process', in A. Miller and D.A. Lane (eds) *Silent Conspiracies: Scandals and Successes in the Care and Education of Vulnerable Children*. Stoke-on-Trent: Trentham Books.

Caffyn, R.E. (1989) 'Attitudes of British secondary school teachers and pupils to rewards and punishments'. *Educational Research*, 31, 3: 210–220.

Cooper, P. and Upton, G. (1991) 'Controlling the urge to control: An ecosystemic approach to problem behaviour in schools', *Support for Learning*, 6, 1: 22–26.

Department of Education and Science (1989) *Discipline in Schools* (The Elton Report) London: HMSO.

Dowling, E. and Osborne, E. (eds) (1985) *The Family and the School: A Joint*

Systems Approach to Problems with Children. London: Routledge & Kegan Paul.

Dowling, E. and Taylor, D. (1989) 'The clinic goes to school: lessons learned', *Maladjustment and Therapeutic Education*, 7, 1: 24–28.

Fine, M.J. and Holt, P. (1983) 'Intervening with school problems: A family systems perspective', *Psychology in the Schools*, 20, 1: 59–66.

Gupta, R., Stringer, B. and Meakin, A. (1990) 'A study of the effectiveness of home-based reinforcement in a secondary school', *Educational Psychology in Practice*, 5, 4: 197–200.

Hanko, G. (1990) *Special Needs in Ordinary Classrooms: Supporting Teachers* (2nd edition). Oxford: Blackwell.

Harrop, A. and Williams, T. (1992) 'Rewards and punishments in the primary school: pupils' perceptions and teachers' usage', *Educational Psychology in Practice*, 7, 4: 211–215.

Kolvin, I. Garside, R.G., Nicol, A.R., Macmillan, A., Wolstenholme, F. and Leitch, I.M. (1981) *Help Starts Here: The Maladjusted Child in the Ordinary School*. London: Tavistock Publications.

Leach, D.J. and Byrne, M.K. (1986) 'Some "spill-over" effects of a home-based reinforcement programme in a secondary school', *Educational Psychology*, 6, 3: 265–275.

Leach, D.J. and Ralph, A. (1986) 'Home-based reinforcement: a case study', *Behaviour Change*, 3, 1: 58–62.

Leyden, G. (1991) 'Mind the steps! The primary school and children in second families', in G. Lindsay and A. Miller (eds) *Psychological Services for Primary Schools*. Harlow: Longman.

Long, M. (1988) 'Goodbye behaviour units, hello support services', *Educational Psychology in Practice*, 4, 1: 17–23.

McGee, R., Silva, P.A. and Williams, S. (1983) 'Parents' and teachers' perceptions of behaviour problems in seven year old children', *The Exceptional Child*, 30, 2: 151–161.

Miller, A. (1994a) 'The growth of intersubjectivity between teachers and parents in successful behavioural consultations', in S. Gregory and G. Hartley (eds) *Parents, Professionals and Children* (in preparation).

Miller, A. (1994b) 'Staff culture, boundary maintenance and successful "behavioural interventions" in primary schools', *Research Papers in Education* (in press).

Mortimore, P., Sammons, P., Stoll, L., Lewis, D. and Ecob, R. (1984) *School Matters*. Wells: Open Books.

Osborne, E. (1983) 'The teacher's relationship with the pupils' families', in I. Salzberger-Wittenberg, G. Henry and E. Osborne (eds) *The Emotional Experience of Learning and Teaching*. London: Routledge.

Power, T. and Bartholomew, K. (1985) 'Getting uncaught in the middle: a case study in family-school system consultation', *School Psychology Review*, 14, 2: 222–229.

Rutter, M., Maughan, B., Mortimore, P. and Ouston, J. (1979) *Fifteen Thousand Hours*. London: Open Books.

Rutter, M., Tizard, J. and Whitmore, K. (1970) *Education, Health and Behaviour*. London: Longman.

Taylor, D. (1982) 'Family consultation in a school setting', *Journal of Adolescence*, 5: 367–377.

Tizard, B., Blatchford, P., Burke, J., Farquar, C. and Plewis, I. (1988) *Young Children at School in the Inner City*. Hove: Lawrence Erlbaum.

Topping, K.J. (1983) *Educational Systems for Disruptive Adolescents*. London: Croom Helm.

Topping, K.J. (1992) 'School-based behaviour management work with families', *Pastoral Care in Education*, 10, 1: 7–17.

Tucker, B.Z. and Dyson, E. (1976) 'The family and the school: utilizing human resources to promote learning', *Family Process*, 15: 125–141.

West, J.F. and Idol, L. (1987) 'School consultation (Part 1): An interdisciplinary perspective on theory, models, and research', *Journal of Learning Disabilities*, 20, 7: 388–408.

Wheldall, K. and Merrett, F. (1988) 'Discipline: rewarding work', *Teachers' Weekly*, 16 May, pp. 25–27.

Chapter 9

Parents and teachers working together: a case example

Pauline Fell and David Coombs

Children presenting difficult behaviour in school frequently find them-selves in the middle of a situation where, on the face of it, there appears to be considerable mistrust and even antagonism between their parents and their school. A whole range of experiences, beliefs and feelings may contribute to the difficulties. Parents may feel blamed and possibly intimi-dated by school. Schools may see parents as uncooperative.

Consider the parents whose only communications from school are nega-tive reports of their child's behaviour and whose own experiences of school were overwhelmingly negative. How might they feel when faced with another letter requesting their attendance at a meeting to discuss their child's misdemeanours?

Consider the school's frustration at being unable to 'engage' this parent in order to try to deal with the child's difficult behaviour. Their letters have been ignored, meetings arranged which the parent has not attended and the child's behaviour is deteriorating.

This chapter examines a framework which can be used by support teachers, using a detailed case study to help illustrate the strategies involved in working with parents and teachers. A framework for planning intervention is shown in Figure 9.1.

The initial work involves gathering information on all aspects of the case, i.e. a systematic analysis of the factors operating and the building up of effective working relationships with all the involved parties. Individual casework (Lane 1989) involves several important stages, which although distinct are dynamic, i.e. casework is not a linear process but a constant re-evaluation of situations and circumstances. Attitudes may change, circumstances in the home and/or school may change.

The aim of the intervention is to reduce the level of problem behaviour, to effect the development of the skills of all parties and to adopt the role of objective outsider in the dynamic. Perhaps it is as well to be clear that the support teacher should act as facilitator in the process in order that others should share and own any success. If progress is too dependent upon the support teacher, then any level of success will not be maintained when the

INITIAL DEFINITION
↓
INVESTIGATION
↓
ANALYSIS
↓
FORMULATION/PLANNING
↓
INTERVENTION
↓
MONITORING
↓
EVALUATION

Figure 9.1 Framework for planning intervention

support teacher reduces or ceases involvement. It is vital that ownership of the intervention remains with the teachers and the parents who need to continue to interact with each other, and the child, in the future.

CASE STUDY

Stephen Jackson (pseudonym)

Stephen was referred during Year 9 of his school career. He was 14 years old and attending a comprehensive school of approximately 800 pupils, aged between 12 and 16 years.

Stage 1: Initial definition of the problems

These are as listed by the referring school:

1 Truancy from school and lessons.
2 Ignoring staff instructions.
3 Verbal abuse, including foul language to staff and pupils.
4 Temper outbursts in class, often followed by walking out of lessons.
5 Violence to other pupils, e.g. head butting, fighting.
6 Smoking and selling or stealing cigarettes.

On the referral form positive qualities were listed as:

1 Able to hold interesting conversations with adults.
2 Very protective of younger pupils on the playground, often involving himself in fights and inappropriate revenge attacks on others.

3 Likes helping the caretaker or repairing damaged furniture when given such tasks as punishment.

Background information on the referral form stated that Stephen lived with his mother. His parents had divorced when he was 8 years old. Stephen's mother had remarried and there was a brother aged 4 years and a sister aged 3 years at home. The second marriage had broken down shortly after the birth of the baby, and Mrs Smith had care of the three children.

Stage 2: Investigation

This involves gathering as much information as possible about the behaviours and any other possible influencing factors, for example:

1 Observation of the child in a range of school settings.
2 Completion of checklists of behaviour by involved staff.
3 Interviews with:
   (a) Parents.
   (b) Teachers.
   (c) Child.
   (d) Professionals from other agencies, e.g. education social worker, clinical psychologist, psychiatrist, social worker, learning support teacher.

All other agencies involved are informed of the support teacher's involvement, and joint interventions are planned if appropriate.

The first step with Stephen was to arrange an interview with the head of year involved in the school in order to discuss the case in detail.

It was apparent early on that the head of year felt unable to cope with Stephen and was seeking to have him removed from the school. Complaints from staff and parents of other pupils were taking up lots of time, and the head of year felt that all possible methods of intervention had been tried. These were listed as:

1 Long conversations with Stephen.
2 Letters home inviting Mrs Smith (mother) to school.
3 Detentions. Stephen attended on occasion, but walked out when he got bored or disrupted others by talking or being insolent to staff.
4 Stephen had spent considerable amounts of time with the caretaker, cleaning or repairing damage and had always been helpful, polite and hard-working, but had continued to be disruptive in lessons.
5 Stephen had been on school report on four occasions, but over a few weeks had failed to respond and ceased to report.

The head of year was very experienced but felt unable to progress, especially in view of the fact that Mrs Smith, after initially being very anxious and upset when contacted, now did not even bother to acknowledge letters. Despite a previously good relationship, she had telephoned the school and shouted angrily at the secretary, saying she was sick of the school and she had enough problems at home without having to help them to do their job. It was at this point that the referral had been made.

On questioning in detail, it appeared that Stephen was academically able (in middle sets) and was particularly good at Maths and CDT, where staff had few problems except occasional verbal abuse to other pupils when expected to share or wait for use of equipment. Most problems occurred in Science, French and Games, and during breaks and lunchtime. These findings were confirmed by checklists completed by all staff teaching Stephen. Problems at break and lunch usually involved attacks on pupils he thought were bullying smaller, younger pupils. This made him unpopular with his peers.

It was arranged that Stephen would be observed by the support teacher in a range of lessons during the following week and a home visit would be made to Mrs Smith as soon as possible.

Observations were made in Science, Maths and CDT. The results were as follows:

> Stephen had behaved appropriately in Maths and seemed well able to cope with the work. The teacher was firm but good humoured and managed to deflect possible problems with a well-timed comment and use of praise fairly earned. Science was viewed as a problem; the equipment in the lab proved a great temptation for several of the group, who were seen to touch equipment without permission, e.g. gas taps. The lesson started late with the class being noisy and unsettled, the teacher shouting to be heard. She then left the room to collect materials. A boy near Stephen threw paper at him, Stephen retaliated and was seen by the teacher. When challenged by the teacher Stephen was abusive and said 'F . . . this, I'm off' and left, much to the delight of the rest of the group and to the obvious relief of the teacher. The teacher sought out the support teacher and stressed that she was pleased it had happened as 'Stephen is always a problem and the group are unteachable when he is there'.

CDT involved Stephen in making a chess board. He worked alone and ignored other pupils who were trying to attract his attention. He sat at the back and remained on task, even insisting on staying in at break with the teacher to finish off some work and help tidy up.

A pre-arranged home visit was made to Mrs Smith. When the support teacher arrived at the house, Mrs Smith answered the door in tears and said she did not want any more problems and wanted to be left alone, as she was not responsible if Stephen misbehaved at school. Mrs Smith reluctantly agreed to spare a few minutes for the situation to be discussed.

It is extremely important to be aware of the impact such a visit is likely to have on the parent of a pupil who is experiencing difficulties in school. As previously mentioned, a whole range of negative perceptions and experiences may well need to be considered. The problems need to be discussed openly, and also the need for cooperation in order to effect change. The support teacher needs to gain the confidence and trust of the parent(s), remain objective and avoid colluding with any party. The support teacher needs to fulfil the role of counsellor to both teachers and parents individually, but maintain the long-term aim of enabling the school and the parent(s) to negotiate effectively to meet the needs of the child. In effect, the support teacher progresses from being counsellor to mediator and, finally, if the goal is achieved, to the role of outsider (Egan 1986).

Mrs Smith was very anxious and said that she did not want her son excluded from school, as he was 'a good boy and never any trouble at home, he just did not like school because he felt picked on and accused of everything that went wrong'. She was tired of getting letters and being held responsible for Stephen's problems at school. She had had two husbands, who had blamed her for everything and then gone off and left her to cope with three children. Stephen, she felt, was a good boy and she needed him to help her. Mrs Smith knew he could be difficult and she worried as he was out a lot and she didn't know where. He was good with the little ones, but caused problems with the neighbours by threatening children who played with them. Mrs Smith admitted that she felt sorry for Stephen because he and his dad had been close and he had been very upset when he left. He had hated her second husband and was pleased when he left. Mrs Smith said she felt guilty and therefore let Stephen do as he liked to make up for it. In any case when she said 'no' to him he knew she would give in anyway, 'so what was the point?' Stephen liked watching TV, in particular soap operas, and going out. Mrs Smith did not see how she could help, but agreed to try working with Stephen as long as she was told what to do. She said she gave Stephen £2 a week on Fridays for his 'cigarettes', but shared hers with him if he ran out.

An arrangement was made to visit Mrs Smith weekly, as she did not feel able to meet in school with Mrs Brown (head of year). The next meeting was to include Stephen.

Stephen was seen at school, and he was very hostile when sent for by the head of year. Stephen was aware that his mother had been visited. He was seen alone and freely admitted to creating problems in class. He explained that he had been very upset last year when the problems started, but had been picked on for little things so was past caring now. As everyone thought he was badly behaved he had nothing to lose. He said he did not fit in and everyone was on at him. He was aware that he had to attend school and, despite the problems, did not want to change schools. Stephen said that he had a bad temper and lashed out in temper and thought others felt he was bad like his dad, who was always angry and fighting. He said he got fed up with his mum being miserable and that she did not seem to bother what he did any more. Stephen felt that no one could help him and that it was a waste of time, 'Cos they just want to throw me out'. He very reluctantly agreed to consider a programme if he thought it was fair and people would be fair to him. Stephen agreed to meet weekly to discuss the situation with the support teacher and the head of year.

Stage 3: Analysis

This involves consideration of information in an ordered, systematic way: that is, predisposing, precipitating and maintaining factors are identified.

It was felt that Stephen was lacking in self-esteem and lacked the ability to respond appropriately to adults in authority or to children his own age. Adult role models had been aggressive and inconsistent. Stephen's loss of his father, his mother's distress and depression on the loss of the stepfather and family breakdown appeared in his mother's view to have triggered the problems.

Mrs Smith experienced feelings of guilt about her inability to maintain stable relationships, and general feelings of inadequacy had led to her overcompensating and responding passively to any problematic situation. She found it difficult to help Stephen cope with school (Herbert 1988).

As a result of initial problems, teachers had come to view Stephen as deliberately awkward and demanding and had reinforced Stephen's feeling of being socially isolated. Negative behaviour had gained a lot of attention and resulted in Stephen receiving what staff considered to be 'punishment' but which Stephen found rewarding, i.e. helping the caretaker. Stephen had seen inappropriate behaviour as a means to remove himself from stressful situations in class and around school and to do things he was good at and appreciated for.

Stage 4: Formulation and planning

Hypotheses are put forward to explain the situation and formulate a plan of action to try to overcome the difficulties presented. It was felt that any intervention in this case would need a high level of input in all three areas: the child, the parent and the teachers. Any intervention which concentrated on Stephen alone without support for his mother and the school staff would be unlikely to produce long-term results. Needs were identified as follows:

STEPHEN

1   Stephen needed help with developing a more positive self-image and self-concept.
2   Stephen needed to receive social skills training in order to acquire the skills necessary to interact more effectively with other adults and peers.
3   Stephen needed some time to discuss his feelings and progress, other than in a formal meeting with others present. Counselling sessions were to be offered on a regular basis and specific anger-control techniques taught and rehearsed.
4   Stephen needed to take responsibility for his behaviour and have it monitored in a more positive way, with clearly defined guidelines as to acceptable and unacceptable behaviour. Rewards were seen as vital for success, with appropriate sanctions for failure to comply. It was necessary for Stephen to feel fairly treated by staff and to learn to take responsibility for his actions.

MRS SMITH

1   Mrs Smith needed to be taught to be more assertive and to express her views calmly to others.
2   Mrs Smith needed to receive some input, i.e. counselling, in order for her to explore her ideas and thoughts and to increase her confidence and self-esteem.
3   Mrs Smith was to be encouraged to support the school and take some responsibility for her son's behaviour by being involved in the operations of a home/school contract, clarifying expectations and rewards and sanctions for Stephen.

TEACHERS

1   Initial contacts with the school were to be effected via the head of year. A positive progress report system was to be negotiated, which would clarify and simplify staff responses to Stephen. The programme was to involve focusing on positive responses to appropriate behaviour, rather than the previous emphasis on trying to punish the inappropriate behaviour. Consistent responses were emphasised as essential to the running of the programme and were clarified to all staff. Staff were to receive feedback and encouragement via the head of year in order to maintain the programme. Facility for staff comment was to be built in.
2   The head of year was to be consulted and involved in writing the home/school contract to support the intervention.
3   Appropriate interactions with Stephen were to be modelled to both Stephen and his mother at the weekly meetings. It was also felt that there was a need for the head of year to be more assertive in dealings with other staff as, on occasions, she was seen to overreact to implied

criticism and tended to placate rather than advise staff who were experiencing difficulties. Other staff tended to offload problems and expect her to solve all their problems. This was unrealistic.

4 It was felt that the programme in school could be greatly enhanced if staff were aware of the issues and techniques which can be applied for avoiding or dealing with behaviour problems. The staff often encountered difficulties which they attributed to lack of parental support, poor catchment area, etc. It was felt that the Service could negotiate a long-term inset programme in the school, including courses on behaviour management, classroom management, working with parents, playground behaviour, assertiveness, school refusal, etc. This was to be a long-term input, not just concerned with the management of Stephen.

Stage 5: Intervention

1 A contract was written, revised, discussed and negotiated with Mrs Smith, Stephen and Mrs Brown (head of year), clarifying all procedures to be followed and rewards, bonuses and sanctions to be applied. The contract was based around five rules which specified the target behaviours. Stephen was willing to try the contract, although he was not totally committed to it. He doubted anyone else's ability to carry it out. A target was set which would give him access to 30p a day from his mother and to be allowed out in the evening. A bonus of 50p could be earned from home for gaining a set target within a week and the head of year also arranged for Stephen to help the caretaker after school on Friday as a bonus, not a punishment! Reward sessions were also to be provided by the Service for meeting long-term targets.

2 A weekly meeting was held in school, to be attended by Stephen, Mrs Brown, the support teacher, and as soon as possible, Mrs Smith. The purpose of the meeting was to discuss Stephen's positive progress and objectively examine problem areas. It is important for the support teacher to model assertive interactions in order to allow all parties to develop positive negotiating skills.

3 A weekly meeting was arranged with Mrs Smith at home with Stephen. The purpose of this meeting being to 'skill up' Mrs Smith in dealing with the children at home and to help her overcome her anxieties about attending school meetings.

4 A weekly session with Stephen was arranged for anger-control techniques to be discussed and counselling to take place.

5 A Social Skills course at the Service Centre was arranged for a group of 12 pupils from Stephen's year. The group included Stephen. The members of the group all experienced some difficulty with interpersonal relationship skills and the course focused on overcoming these problems (Cartledge and Fellows-Milburn 1986).

6 Mrs Smith and a group of other parents were offered an Assertiveness Training course one evening a week, again based on discussion and role-play. Sessions were concerned with developing strategies for refusing requests, expressing opinions, acknowledging and expressing justified anger, and being assertive with authority figures and family members (Galassi and Galassi 1977). Mrs Smith was very reluctant to attend, as she felt unable to meet the others and thought they would think her stupid as she had not been very bright at school and had only done cleaning work. The support teacher managed to persuade her to attend by offering to collect her and return her home until she felt more confident.

Stage 6: Monitoring

This involves regular contact with all parties to discuss progress and/or adjust the programme.

Stephen's programme ran for 10 weeks. Weekly meetings were held. For the first two weeks Stephen was very keen to try hard and managed to achieve his target every day. In the second week, he even gained his bonus. The weekly sessions in school were interesting for Stephen, who had a chance to access the undivided attention of the support teacher. Mrs Smith became more relaxed and confident. She felt less isolated and appreciated the regular contact with the support teacher. These meetings were used to allow her to express her feelings and anxieties about managing Stephen's behaviour and, with the guidance of the support teacher, to rehearse and discuss alternative strategies for handling Stephen's behaviour in a more appropriate way. These sessions were reinforced by lending her a pamphlet on behaviour management for parents (Wheldall *et al.* 1983).

During the time Stephen's programme ran, most rules broken involved verbal abuse to peers and failure to complete work. Only 10 rule breaks occurred during the three weeks. In the fourth week, an incident occurred at break one day when Stephen had attacked another pupil for hitting someone else. The contract agreed that any reported problems at break or lunchtime would result in Stephen losing his next break or lunch. Stephen ran out of school and missed his weekly meeting. At the meeting the incident was discussed with the head of year, who said she was very disappointed as he had done so well, but that staff were not surprised the system did not work. This was discussed and the support teacher acknowledged that problems often occur when introducing a programme for any type of learning difficulty, academic or social/behavioural, and consequently it might be appropriate to make adjustments to the programme.

The following home visit was difficult, Stephen was embarrassed and Mrs Smith tearful. They both felt that the programme had failed. It was necessary therefore to address their irrational belief that everything must be perfect. This one failure had led them to believe that the situation was irretrievable (Ellis and Harper 1975).

It was agreed that the system should continue and Mrs Smith agreed to attend the next meeting in school with Stephen and the head of year. Stephen was to miss his break and not receive his daily reward. Mrs Smith was worried about being able to stick to this, but Stephen agreed it was fair to stay in and not receive his money, which surprised his mother. Mrs Smith was even more surprised that he actually complied.

Stephen and his mother attended the sessions arranged for them. Weekly meetings continued for the rest of the term. Mrs Brown (head of year) noticed that Stephen was responding to his mother much more positively and incidents were discussed openly. Stephen was admitting when he was responsible, and was also contributing positively to the meeting. Mrs Brown had also been receiving much more positive feedback from staff, Science in particular being noted. As a result of the Social Skills sessions, Stephen was beginning to build relationships with a couple of the other boys involved and spent time with them in school and in the evenings.

Mrs Brown (head of year) adapted the school report system for use with other pupils as she could see that the system in operation with Stephen ensured tighter management. She also put pressure on the staff and the head to arrange INSET on behaviour management with the support service.

Stage 7: Evaluation

The monitoring is continued at intervals during and after the intervention to ensure maintenance of the desired behaviour.

After a few weeks, Stephen earned his way off the programme in targeted stages and accessed the normal school procedures (Gray and Noakes 1993). After 6 months, Stephen was meeting monthly in school with his mother and the head of year. During the summer term it was agreed that Stephen should start Year 10 without the involvement of the service. Criteria were set for reintroduction of the programme if necessary. Mrs Brown (Head of Year) felt able to take over Stephen's case and service involvement ceased at that level. As a result of the progress a project to re-examine the school report system was jointly planned by Mrs Brown and the support teacher. The success of the intervention had really hinged upon the establishment of dialogue between home and school, focusing on the need for positive support of each to the other. Previously school and home had reached a position of distrust and hostility, which had not been helpful to anyone. By encouraging the staff and Stephen's mother to view the problem objectively as a shared concern, Stephen had received the positive reinforcement of appropriate behaviour that was needed for him to achieve success in school.

CONCLUSIONS

We have tried to give an idea of how it is possible to effect behaviour change with a pupil displaying difficulties, by working closely with parents and teachers. The main focus of the work carried out with the parent in the case study was aimed to increase her skill levels when dealing with her children and to provide her with the opportunity to discuss and rehearse strategies for handling situations she found difficult, at the same time as providing the school with alternative strategies for dealing with inappropriate behaviour and encouraging the development of cooperative styles of working with parents whose children are experiencing difficulties.

Obviously, not all cases will need the same level of input, but it is necessary to have a clear framework for approaching cases and to develop a whole range of techniques and strategies if we are to enable pupils, teachers and parents to work together effectively.

The real strength of working as a support teacher is that it is possible to work more closely with parents and families than it is possible for hard-pressed teachers in school. This means that the vital step of forging close working links between home and school can be taken in order that the needs of the child can best be met.

REFERENCES

Cartledge, G. and Fellows-Milburn, J. (1986) *Teaching Social Skills to Children*. Oxford: Pergamon.

Egan, G. (1986) *The Skilled Helper*. Monterey, Calif.: Brooks/Cole.

Ellis, A., and Harper, R.A. (1975) *A New Guide to Rational Living*. Hollywood, Calif.: Wilshire Book Company.

Galassi, N.D. and Galassi, J.P. (1977) *Assert Yourself! How to be Your Own Person*. New York: Human Sciences Press.

Gordon, T. (1970) *Parent Effectiveness Training*. New York: NAL Penguin.

Gray, P. and Noakes, J.S. (1993) 'Reintegration of children with challenging behaviours into the mainstream community', in A. Miller and D.A. Lane (eds) *Silent Conspiracies*. Stoke-on-Trent: Trentham Books.

Harding, J. and Pike, G. (1988) *Parental Involvement in Secondary Schools*. London: ILEA Learning Resources Branch.

Herbert, M. (1988) *Working with Children and their Families*. Leicester: British Psychological Society.

Lane, D. (1989) *The Impossible Child*. Stoke-on-Trent: Trentham Books

Wheldall, K., Wheldall, D., and Winter, S. (1983) *Seven Supertactics for Super Parents*. Windsor: NFER/Nelson.

Section C

Organising support services

Chapter 10

Moving from consumer survey to service evaluation

Phil Watts and Peter Olsen

This chapter will chart the process of setting up a behaviour support team from the first idea, through finding out what type of support schools are wanting, and ending with the results of an evaluation exercise.

STEP 1: SETTING THE SCENE

Sandwell is a densely populated Metropolitan Borough in the West Midlands, occupying much of an area with a heavy industrial-based economy known as the Black Country. As a Local Education Authority, there is a high level of special needs and the pressures and demands on schools are considerable. Within the LEA, a coordinated approach to meeting special educational needs is taken. In contrast to many LEAs where the various support services are often responsible through different line management structures, in Sandwell virtually all the Special Educational Needs (SEN) support staff are part of one multi-professional team – the Child Psychology Service. The various components are shown in Figure 10.1.

Each of the professional teams within the Child Psychology Service (CPS) has a particular contribution to make to the overall service delivery. The teams work together as part of a multidisciplinary team. Between them they offer a range of support to children, schools and parents agreed through a process of negotiation. This support focuses on different aspects of SEN:

Child focus Working directly with children: casework, assessment, teaching, counselling, etc.

Adult focus Working in partnership with teachers, parents and other professionals to help children.

School focus In-Service training and looking at organisation and curriculum in meeting children's needs.

LEA focus Advice to the LEA on policy, practice and provision based on project work, research and evaluation.

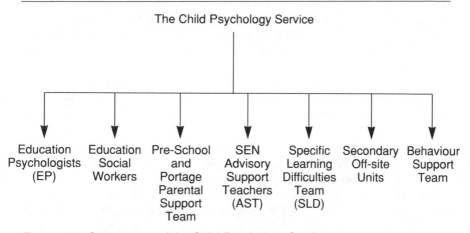

Figure 10.1 Components of the Child Psychology Service

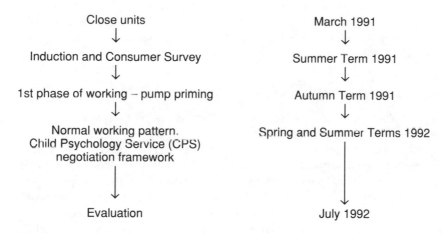

Figure 10.2 Behaviour support team's time line

However, this is rushing ahead. In 1991, the behaviour support team did not yet exist. Instead there were two units for children placed in social services care and who for various reasons could not attend mainstream schools. These were pupils of secondary age who had usually been in several high schools, often having been excluded. As part of a reorganisation of child care facilities, the number of places for these pupils was set to decline as the Social Services Department placed more children in fostering situations. This provided the opportunity to reorganise our own provision by closing the units and using the staff involved to set up a peripatetic behaviour support team. We were concerned about the number of children placed in special education provision and wanted to see if some of these placements could be avoided by early school-focused intervention. This support would be within SEN provision generally available to schools. The time scale for the process of setting up the team is shown in Figure 10.2.

The first stage was information-gathering. One strand was to find out as much as possible about how other LEAs had set up such teams, how they worked, and their effectiveness. Although we had some knowledge within both the Advisory and Support Teacher and Educational Psychology teams, we thought it prudent to pick other people's brains – no sense in re-inventing the wheel! The other important factor was to determine the needs and expectations in Sandwell.

On the one hand we had some stereotyped anticipation that the major behaviour problems were to be found in secondary schools, where the majority of exclusions occurred. However, we were also noting trends in our referrals and working records about an apparently growing number of significant behaviour problems in primary schools, often involving very young children in infant departments. If this were the case, then there would be some significant implications for the organisation and training of the team, as the teachers involved were secondary trained and experienced.

STEP 2: CONSUMER EXPECTATIONS

A programme of visits to behaviour support teams in several other authorities was organised. In reading about other services many similarities were noted, especially in terms of the types of support offered. A feature common to most support teams was that caseloads were driven by logistics rather than by need; hence, most tended to operate in either the primary or the secondary sector only. Typically, one behaviour support teacher would be assigned to a number of schools within a patch and would allocate their time evenly between them. Adopting this system would have limited the Sandwell team to two options: either secondary schools only could be targeted or a greater number of schools including those in the primary sector could be worked in, if schools were accommodated on a rotational basis. Neither of these options, however, address meeting the needs of schools where they are the greatest. Being an integral part of a multi-professional CPS, it was a simple exercise to consult colleagues from other disciplines, who between them were working in every school in Sandwell on a regular basis. Following meetings with EPs and ASTs, at which the issues surrounding logistics and needs were addressed, it was accepted that the team should operate cross-phase in response to requests from schools where the need was greatest. At this stage the mechanism for referral had not been considered in detail, and it was not until a term later that the current system was put into operation.

Having decided to target schools cross-phase, and having identified a number of ways of providing support to schools, it was decided to consult schools regarding their perceived need for the different forms that support could take. A questionnaire was constructed and with an accompanying letter was circulated to all primary and secondary schools in Sandwell. As this was the first official communication that the new team was to have with schools, it was necessary to give a brief background. The letter pointed out that its staff of five teachers had been recruited by the reorganisation of personnel within the CPS as part of the Local Authority's response to the Elton Report. Also, the consultative process would operate in conjunction with other CPS staff, in order that the team could function most effectively in schools and areas of need throughout the borough where additional behaviour support would be most beneficial. It was stated that support during the initial phase following the questionnaire would be allocated using the following criteria:

(a) that schools recognised a need and requested support;
(b) that schools clearly identified the types of support they required;
(c) that the support requested could be met within the resources available.

Schools were advised that following the setting-up phase they would be notified of the procedure for future referral, assessment and negotiation of support. This allowed time for reflection and fine-tuning of the systems initially put into operation.

The questionnaire comprised three distinct parts. The first referred to a menu of different ways of supporting schools, and the other two considered immediate and longer-term requests for support. As was expected, majority of the primary returns had been completed by the head while, in the secondary sector, in the main they had been passed on ity with a management responsibility for discipline.

65 out of 116
11 out of 23

listed twelve items of good practice in other authorities. Respondents were in order to indicate the relevance (most relevant 5, least rele- in ranking order follow- most popular heading

ten of the eleven secondary requested involvement in some

Table 10.1 Twelve items of good practice in supporting schools, placed in ranking order after completion of the first part of the questionnaire

Item	Average score on 1–5 rating
Helping teachers to devise strategies for improving the classroom behaviour of individuals and or groups.	4.1
To liaise with and actively involve parents in managing their children's behaviour.	4.1
Counselling or developing behaviour programmes for individual pupils.	3.9
Assisting in devising strategies for the management of out-of-class behaviour.	3.5
Supporting teachers/pupils in the classroom.	3.3
Assisting in compiling behaviour contracts for individual pupils.	3.2
Involvement in the planning and delivery of school-based in-service training.	3.2
Giving active support in developing whole-school policies on codes on conduct, rewards and sanctions.	3.1
Assisting in the construction of strategies to address the problem of bullying.	3.1
Providing support with induction programmes for probationary teachers.	3.0
Providing training and support for special needs support assistants and class teachers where additional provision has been made.	2.7
Withdrawing a pupil or small group from class for on-site support.	2.7

form. These schools were requested to identify the type(s) of s
required in the following term, using the categories in the menu
names and year group of individual pupils where appropriate.
important so that behaviour support staff could check with
leagues whether or not work was already ongoing with a parti
Finally, areas of work requested to take place later in the sch
as in-service training, were included in a separate section.

STEP 3: TRAINING AND INDUCTION

The results of the consumer survey and our conclusio
ways of working meant that a lot of training and

packed into a fairly short period of time. We felt that it was essential that in setting up a BST as a new venture, we should provide the necessary training and induction that reflected the information we had gathered. There were three major concerns for training:

1 All the teachers in the new team had taught in secondary or special schools, but were not familiar with peripatetic support work.
2 They had a considerable amount of secondary experience, but little in the primary sector.
3 They had extensive practical experience in dealing with pupils with behaviour problems, but little direct practice in advising others how to deal with the problems.

We recognised that delivering a successful support service to teachers in mainstream schools is not merely a question of putting an experienced practitioner in contact with one who is experiencing a problem with a particular pupil. It is far more subtle than this. There are not just the skills of knowing about techniques or approaches but being able to spot which one might be most appropriate for a given situation – depending on the child's needs and the teacher's skills, attitudes and expectations. There are also the skills necessary to be a good seller – persuading someone to try something which maybe they are reluctant to attempt; how to support, encourage and reinforce good practice without being there to do it all yourself. With these issues in mind, together with what seemed like a myriad of others, we organised a one-term period for induction, training and setting up the operating system for the team. The major areas covered were as follows:

A *National patterns of working*

Visits to other authorities to speak to team members of other support teams.

B *Local working and information*

Visits to EBD provision within Sandwell.
Work shadowing of advisory and support teachers in Sandwell.
Attending negotiation meetings as observers.
The role of the Education Welfare Service.
The role of the Educational Social Worker.
The role of the support teacher.

C *Skills, knowledge and techniques*

Observation of classroom behaviour using adapted behaviour checklists in
   both primary and secondary schools.
How to devise a pupil contract.
Strategies in overcoming difficult behaviours.
Counselling/interview techniques.
Delivering a one-day INSET course to ASTs on the Elton Report.
Monitoring techniques.
Behaviour modification techniques.
Use of incentives and sanctions.
Non-verbal communication.
Promoting self-esteem.
Training techniques for use in delivering INSET.
Managing out-of-class behaviour.
Whole-school INSET.

This training programme drew extensively from other colleagues within
CPS and the goodwill of schools in trying out techniques. By the end of the
term, the team felt ready to move onto the first phase of working.

STEP 4: FIRST PHASE OF WORKING

The initial phase of work in schools by the BST began in September 1991.
Though remaining centrally based, in order otherwise to mirror the existing structure of the CPS, each member of the team was assigned to one of
the four area teams. The team leader, also centrally based, was later to
establish his own casework from team members whose caseload would
otherwise have been overstretched.

During the first week of the term, team members were given the
returned questionnaires for schools in their area. By collating the information from these returns and colour coding responses, it was a simple task
to identify schools requesting support immediately for individuals and
those who were expressing their interest for the future. Before schools
were contacted, behaviour support staff first contacted the EP and the AST
of each school that had requested support. Through colleagues' regular
visits to schools, information relating to the ethos of schools and the
implementation of their discipline policies was acquired. In addition, an
insight into some of the referred individuals was gathered.

In building up a caseload there were a number of circumstances which
had altered school needs and influenced the BST response. When schools
were contacted with a view to initiating support, several, especially in the
primary sector, wished to delay any behaviour support intervention, as the
pupils concerned were beginning a new academic year with a different
teacher. In some cases certain children's difficulties paled into insignifi-

cance when in the new situation, while with others the change had only served to delay support. Several had moved schools and some had even moved out of the borough. Where it was found that there was already involvement by an EP, then the case remained with them.

In the completion of the questionnaire, a few requests were totally unrealistic: for example, one school had requested direct support for 16 individuals. In response to these, negotiation with the schools took place to prioritise a manageable caseload in order to offer support to a greater number of schools. The method of obtaining a suitable caseload for the first term of operation on the whole worked well. Although busy, the team did not allow themselves to be overloaded in casework. It was important at that stage that each member of the team had sufficient time with schools to do justice to the learning process which they themselves were going through. For this reason, throughout that stage the team met on three occasions each week to discuss casework, exchange ideas and develop support materials. Supporting each other and sharing experiences proved highly successful in the team-building process and was perhaps the singly most useful activity undertaken during this period.

The CPS uses a system of negotiation visits to schools when current concerns can be discussed, past work reviewed and future work prioritised, agreed and planned. These negotiation visits are conducted by the EP and AST meeting usually with the Headteacher and designated teacher for special needs. The EPs and AST do not just negotiate their own work but also serve as a filter for requests/intervention from the other teams in the service. It was decided that the BST should also work within this framework as this was successful in managing the workloads of other teams. After the initial setting-up phase, the process for BST involvement with schools was as shown in Figure 10.3.

Early in the following term, a booklet was distributed to all primary and secondary schools imparting all relevant information to them about the behaviour support team and outlining this process.

STEP 5: EVALUATION

During the period from September 1991 to June 1992, a total of 80 pupils received some form of individual support from the BST. Of these, 63 per cent were already the subject of a formal referral to the Child Psychology Service, while 37 per cent of cases were taken prior to a formal referral.

In all, the team was involved with individual pupils in 32 primary and 11 secondary schools. There were also some other activities which are not accounted for in these figures. These include supporting individual teachers in the management of whole-class behaviours; supporting newly-qualified teachers who were experiencing problems of establishing their authority and discipline in the classroom; and delivering in-service train-

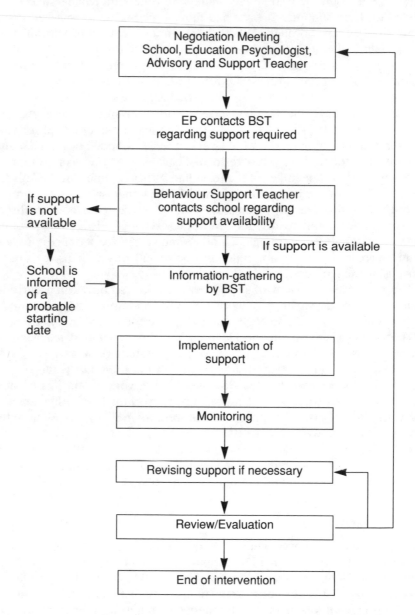

Key: BST = behaviour support teacher
　　　EP　 = educational psychologist

Figure 10.3 Process for behaviour support team involvement with school

Table 10.2 Schools' ranking of team interventions

Intervention	Mean score
Withdrawal of a small group	4.5
In-class support	4.4
Collation of behaviour checklists (Secondary)	4.2
Withdrawal of individual pupil(s)	4.0
Advice on behaviour management	3.9
Progress booklet materials	3.9
Feedback from observations	3.9
Reward systems implemented	3.7

ing. INSET proved to be an ever-increasing facet of the role both for schools and within the LEA. The INSET programme also included training for nursery nurses/classroom assistants (NNEBs), midday supervisors, primary relief supply team, etc.

In order to obtain feedback on the various methods of operation, in June 1992 an evaluation questionnaire was compiled. This was circulated to schools in which involvement had taken place over a period of time. Casework that had only just begun was not evaluated. In total, 60 scripts were issued for completion by the staff concerned. Also, a copy of the questionnaire was included for head teachers to complete should they wish to. A return rate of 58 per cent was recorded.

At the time of issuing the evaluations it was decided that, in order to obtain more openly critical responses, they should be completed anonymously. However, with hindsight, in future evaluation exercises it is intended that this should not be the case, the reason being that if schools are not happy with the support received then it might not be possible to trace the source of the dissatisfaction and therefore the problem could not be addressed.

The first section of the evaluation asked teachers to use a five-point rating scale (5 = most useful; 1 = least useful), to reflect their opinion on a number of aspects of the team's interventions. These are shown in collated form in ranking order with the most useful interventions given first (see Table 10.2).

A further section requested staff broadly to quantify any changes in behaviour both during intervention and after intervention had ceased. The results were interesting, though on reflection not surprising. By reference to the graph (Figure 10.4), it can be seen that in about three-quarters of the cases with individual pupils there had been improvement in behaviour while the intervention was taking place. This figure, however, reduced to 46 per cent after support was withdrawn. It was also noted that the behaviour in 7 per cent of cases actually deteriorated while support was operational and later continued to decline. A possible explanation for this is that, at the time when support took place, the behaviour of these pupils was so extreme that perhaps only full-time support could have been fruitful. It is known from further enquiries that several of these pupils were subsequently excluded or alternative provision was made for them.

Perhaps the most sobering finding from this section was that, although improvement in behaviour can be achieved through interventions, there is a significant number of pupils for whom support needs to be constantly available. Logistically however, this is not practical when staff are carrying full caseloads from schools and it creates problems in withdrawing from these situations. There appear to be no easy answers.

A third section of the evaluation posed an open question, asking staff how they considered improvement could be made to the delivery of the BST. In response, there were many encouraging comments regarding individual staff and what they had achieved. These included not only the influencing of pupil behaviours, but also in helping teachers to feel more confident in their management of behaviour problems. Such comments were very encouraging and added greatly to the team's self-esteem. The main thrust of comments regarding improvements to the support delivered were that:

1 More time be spent with the problem pupil.
2 Full-time support for a defined period would be most beneficial.
3 More work with parents could be undertaken.

Enhanced staffing would obviously help in responding more easily to these suggestions; however, considering present financial constraints, this seems unlikely. Considerable demands regarding a certain number of individuals, if met currently, would be at the expense of denying others any support at all. One aspect of intervention which has figured more prominently as a direct result of the evaluation is the involvement with parents. When new cases are now taken on, if it is thought by the school and support teacher that involvement with parents would be beneficial, that contact with parents is made, usually in the form of a meeting at school, in conjunction with the head teacher and/or the class teacher. This increased contact has brought about a greater consistency in tackling unwanted behaviour at both school and at home. It is often the case that programmes promoted by support staff in school have an element in them in which parents have a part to play in the situation.

In comparing the initial questionnaire with that of the evaluation, a cautionary note should be heeded regarding who is the customer. Basing work on what schools think they would like and what they subsequently find most useful may be two different things. In the initial questionnaire, the item concerning withdrawal of a small group was ranked bottom of the list in terms of relevance of need. It should be noted that primary head

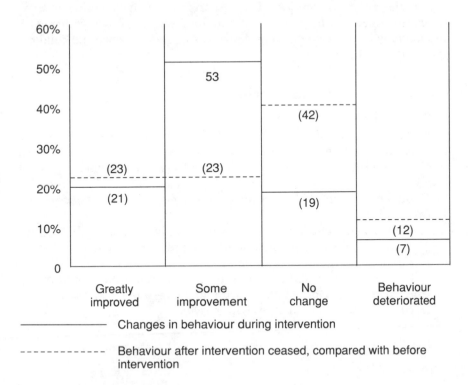

Figure 10.4 Changes in pupil behaviour during and after intervention

teachers accounted for the majority of respondents to this question. In the evaluation, however, returned in the main by class teachers, withdrawal of a small group was ranked at the top as a useful method of operating.

On reflection, these results are not difficult to understand. To date, this form of support has almost exclusively been undertaken in primary schools. Here, the behaviour of one or more individuals can affect the learning potential of the whole class for a complete year. In these circumstances, it is perfectly understandable that by withdrawing a small group on a regular basis the teacher is given the opportunity to teach the class relatively unhindered. Any improvement in the behaviour of an individual or the small group could be regarded as an additional bonus by the class teacher. If nothing else, the evaluation exercise, irrespective of its subjectivity, supported the team's belief that most of what they were doing in schools was on the right track. It also assisted in fine-tuning the delivery to schools and gave the team an indication of how their input was valued. The initial year was not totally without situations which would rather be forgotten, such is the nature of the job. The opportunity of the team to air any difficulties openly with each other and to problem-solve together was undoubtedly a significant factor in consolidating good practice and building upon it for the future.

A summary of general points learned:

1 Training and induction is essential.
2 Collaborative working with EPs and SEN advisory teachers adds to a cohesive approach and effective support.
3 Clear publicity and expectations are necessary in communicating with schools.
4 Good negotiation skills and able to see class teachers' needs and expectations.
5 Flexibility and frequent visits are key parts of supporting behaviour problems – more so than for supporting learning difficulties.
6 Evaluation and feedback must be built into team delivery.
7 It is frequently more difficult to support children with behaviour problems than to support children with learning problems, because of teacher expectations and ethos within schools.

Chapter 11

Induction and training of support staff

Chris Hevey

Teachers appointed to a support service for children with emotional and behavioural difficulties have seldom had direct experience or training in the field, and are more likely to have been appointed through a combination of personal qualities and previous experience in education generally. However, they will be expected to carry out new roles and specialised functions within a range of complex structures, and to resolve problems which have resisted successful interventions from a school's existing strategies. Staff working in behavioural support teams are expected to possess expertise and a knowledge of effective support strategies for mainstream staff and pupils to maintain children in school. However, staff within mainstream schools can often feel frustrated and under personal stress from dealing with challenging behaviour, and they can respond negatively to interventions from an outside agency, possibly because of perceived increases in workload or of accepted wisdoms being challenged.

Advocating changes in the way teachers, schools, families and pupils act and react within the complexity of their social situations can generate conflicts, leading to serious difficulties which the support teacher and the service need to be able to anticipate, understand and resolve.

The increasing and sometimes competing pressures for changes in schools from the Education Reform Act (1988), market economy approaches, Grant Maintained status and LMS have, according to a Panorama TV programme (15 March 1993), contributed to an increase in exclusions from schools of disruptive pupils and truants, to make schools more attractive in the market place. These pressures have added to the stress of working with children presenting challenging behaviour, especially so when schools claim to have less time to devote to children with emotional and behavioural difficulties.

With regard to the above, it is apparent that specific and intensive high-quality training is needed to support staff working in a field where conflict can appear to come from several directions simultaneously.

HOW CAN TRAINING OCCUR?

There have been many ways in which teachers have developed and improved their qualifications and skills. New staff into the profession can still learn by studying the characteristics and techniques employed by established staff, and by gradually adopting these values and styles in their own practices. Bell (1991) refers to this as the apprenticeship model, utilising the concept of anticipatory socialisation whereby new staff assimilate into the profession symbiotically. Unfortunately, as well as learning good habits, they can learn bad ones or work in an organisation lacking direction, clarity or unity. It is haphazard, with no regard to a structured approach to needs' analysis on the part of the individual and institution within agreed objectives.

To avoid such pitfalls some staff choose to attend off-site INSET courses to enhance qualifications, develop existing skills, or acquire new skills with the aim of improving their career choices and the quality of work within their institution. Problems of this approach are that course providers are seen as the experts and teachers can choose whether or not to attend the course and whether or not they intend to use the skills. This also ignores the power of institutional constraints on individual staff's ability to influence changes in the work place (Georgiades and Phillimore 1975).

Just as the use of development plans and funding for INSET have become the responsibility of each institution, so whether a teacher attends a particular course may relate to how this contributes to the development of the institution. With the problems of externally provided courses, a greater emphasis has been placed on school-based and school-focused approaches to professional development. The school-based model advocates the development of training programmes by staff to meet their own needs, though this can become too parochial in ignoring or discounting developments elsewhere and can lead to institutional aims superseding individual teachers' needs. School-focused models build on the expertise of staff within the school, but not exclusively so. External input is utilised and coordinated within the overall needs of the institution, though this assumes sufficient resources are available to meet needs, which may therefore only benefit larger institutions. It also assumes that the institution is able to clearly identify its needs.

Bell (1991) outlines a third model (in addition to apprenticeship and school-based/school-focused models) of professional development, which has emerged out of the defects of the school-based model while retaining its essential school-based nature.

Within an overall policy framework, more systematic and purposeful planning of the professional development of teachers can occur, aided by the provision of resources and time set aside for training. Within this model, a mechanism, which could be an appraisal system, is needed to resolve tensions between individual and institutional needs. Within such a model, teachers are expected to participate in training arrangements and provisions, and to contribute to the training needs of colleagues. Essentially, the professional development of staff is placed at the centre of a coherent set of policies for institutional improvement.

TRAINING FOR THE TRAINERS – WHERE DO YOU START?

The availability of suitable training on a national level for specialist areas in special education may be diminishing (Jones 1993), which probably relates to the move from a dependence on external providers to the model of professional development linking individual and institutional needs.

Staff in a support service need extensive training and supervision in a range of skills and knowledge areas, so that they can offer a professional response to the needs of pupils, their families and schools. They may also be expected to contribute to the professional development of other teachers in schools, though very few will have experience of this when appointed to a support service.

As a means of training, programmes and courses can be developed by support service staff themselves. The process of planning, designing and delivering INSET courses for staff in schools can serve as an excellent vehicle for training support service staff. The remainder of this chapter will outline some of the methods used in a recently established support service to meet the training needs of its staff, and to contribute to the training needs of schools, and their staff.

SCRIPTED COURSES

A support service will need training courses to be planned, organised and delivered by staff to support them in their practice and to create shared views of working practices across a service.

This can be achieved by small groups of staff working together to prepare scripts of INSET courses, covering areas of training identified by staff in the support service and in schools. Such courses could, for example, focus on each of the following areas: introduction to behavioural approaches; managing classroom behaviour; a token economy; contracts in schools; school refusal; rewards and sanctions in schools. On a more personal level, courses on counselling and assertiveness skills can be developed.

There are many advantages in writing course scripts which detail word-for-word what the presenters will say. The script can be typed and stored either on computer disc or as a 'master copy' in a service resource area. The script can also be transferred onto cue cards for staff to refer to when delivering the course, so they stick to the point instead of wandering off into personal homilies or anecdotes. Discussion between participants can follow interesting diversions, but the presenter can retain control and return to the point should the discussion wander. Certainly, for staff delivering INSET for the first time, the cue cards can be useful as 'prompts' should stage fright or nervous anxiety temporarily inhibit the presenter.

Activities, role-plays, use of audiovisual resources and discussion times can be scripted into the course, allowing the course to run within given start and finish times, which can be adhered to. Effective time-management of sessions is obviously important, so that all areas can be covered effectively within given time limits planned in advance.

Schools may repeatedly request a particular course, having heard of it through colleagues, and this can be presented without the need to rewrite it each time. Clearly some parts will need updating and revising (for example, changes in the law regarding non-attendance,) but this need not lead to whole courses needing to be rewritten. Again, demand for places on a course can run at a constant level over a period of time. Having a script allows a range of staff the opportunity to attend and deliver it, improving their own knowledge base and presentation skills. One member of staff is not stuck with repeatedly delivering the same course; expertise is developed and shared across the service, and continues as an element of service delivery even as staff come and go. In the event of illness or sudden absence, other staff can provide cover to enable the course to go ahead, which is essential in circumstances where a school has allocated one of its training days or a series of staff meetings to it, as a part of its own development plan. In this respect, a service is seen as offering a professional response and able to meet its commitments within agreed time-spans. It is not a fickle organisation only able to deliver training dependent upon the commitments, enthusiasm and expertise of staff employed at a particular time. Having 'off-the-shelf' courses available can help schools in their development planning. Precise dates for courses can be agreed in advance without worrying whether particular staff will be available at the time. With a range of staff able to deliver all of the courses, exactly who does it can be agreed within the service nearer the date.

The evaluation and feedback provided by those who attend the course can include specific reference to parts of the script, or the quality of overhead transparencies (OHPs) and thus enable adaptations and changes to be made. It may well be that some of those who attend a scripted course may express a dislike of presenters reading from cards. New staff are more likely to stick to the script, though the cards can be dispensed with, certainly by experienced deliverers who may lead the course through 'prompts' provided by the OHPs.

COURSE DELIVERY

Service staff need to practise delivery skills, including body language, voice projection and contact with those attending the course, before the course is presented outside the service. The actual content of the course as regards its knowledge base, the use of audiovisual aids, the nature of assignments, role-plays and handouts, all need to be assessed.

The course should be presented internally first, possibly at the service centre, to service staff for their constructive feedback. Potential problems can be taken out, so that the course does not go awry in front of an external audience with damaging potential for the reputation of the presenter and the service. Learning curves and concentration spans of those attending the course have to be catered for, with varied activities built in to stimulate interest and learning. Even though the delivery style is a scripted format, it would be difficult to expect anybody to sit still and be read to from cue cards without expressing some form of discomfort.

After finalising details and purposes of the course, a strategy to increase the confidence and effectiveness of staff in delivering INSET needs to be available.

New staff joining a service would attend a course for the first time at the service centre as participants, in order to develop or reinforce their knowledge base. They should then attend the course a second time, again at the centre, taking more note of the delivery styles and structure of the course, how the pace and organisation of the course is maintained and managed by the deliverers, how passive or hostile participants are managed, and how course leaders relate to the audience and to each other and provide links and support for activities. They would note how leaders introduce and conclude the actual course, sessions within the course and activities within the sessions.

The member of staff will then be more familiar with the course and can develop this through again reading the script and background reading, plus discussing issues and problems in supervision meetings.

They will then be in a position to rehearse delivery of the course and to present it to others. They should deliver the course for the first time with a colleague who has previously delivered it and who will take responsibility as course leader. The next time the course is run, the member of staff is likely to be in a position of co-leader, and after two or three deliveries they may become the course leader. Following this sequence a new member of staff can develop into a confident leader of INSET courses, able to deliver INSET courses from the service centre and also to whole-school staff in their schools.

The use of scripted courses implies a blanket approach to all schools and their problems. Although general conclusions and recommendations can be made about the problems faced by teachers and schools, such as in the

Elton Report (DES 1989), account also needs to be taken of a school's specific needs.

It is possible to anticipate demands and needs of particular schools and to adapt scripts to take into account their circumstances. For example, an INSET package on contracting needs to take into account different motivational and situational factors for primary and secondary pupils, and to include examples of contracts used at primary and at secondary-aged levels.

The three-tier model (Galvin *et al*. 1990), focusing on working at whole-school, classroom and individual levels of managing difficult behaviour, is an excellent example of a systematically organised training package which can be adapted to suit individual schools aiming to develop positive and consistent behaviour policies throughout the school.

PROJECT WORK

Schools and teachers are at different stages of development and will require differing levels of input from a service. If staff from schools attend courses at, for example, the Service Centre, this will be convenient and provide necessary support for service staff, but the impact is likely to remain at the level of personal interest and development for individual teachers from outside the service. 'The myth of the hero-innovator and alternative strategies for organisational change' (Georgiades and Phillimore 1975), documents the difficulties of externally based training programmes influencing change in the work place, and provides general points and guidelines to those seeking to influence change in organisations. The importance of initially cultivating a 'host culture' conducive to changes occurring, and working with healthy parts of a system with authority to carry recommendations through, are essential prerequisites to achieving change.

For support service staff this can mean working with groups of staff in a school to bring about organisational changes. Combining training and ongoing work with school staff, focusing on the school as a system, can achieve consistency in the way school staff work as a group (Scherer *et al*. 1990).

To train service staff into operating at a systems level with schools is a long-term process, but can be assisted by building onto the skills and knowledge developed through delivering a training programme into a school. To elucidate how this can be achieved, I shall briefly refer to a specific project, outlining staff, service and school developments.

A newly appointed education social worker (ESW) had no prior training or experience in the field but had previously trained as a teacher without taking it up as a career. On appointment the ESW was provided with reading materials and regular supervision on casework and reading. Subsequently, this supervision moved into planning and structuring a course on non-attendance to meet the needs of staff in the service and schools. The County Solicitor also advised on the legal situation.

By reference to specific examples and models of case work (Lane 1978; Herbert 1985), background reading and the law, a course of four ninety-minute sessions was constructed, focusing on the legal background, possible causes of persistent and poor non-attendance, methods of collecting and recording relevant information, and planning and evaluating an intervention.

Before the course was 'exported', it was presented internally to service staff and to senior ESWs for their views and recommendations. The course was then run on several occasions, reaching approximately 120 teachers and providing training for service staff. One of the course presenters was working in a school which had prioritised non-attendance as an issue for school development, and senior staff from the school attended the course.

The course presenter then agreed to work as the project worker with a committee of staff within the school, comprising pastoral and senior staff.

The objective then, instead of providing a blueprint of new ideas, was to look at and listen to staff's understanding of how the existing system worked, addressing both positive aspects and areas where change or development were needed. To have suggested drastic changes at the start could have placed the project worker in a confrontational and hostile relationship with school staff.

Two groups of pupils considered to have similar attendance patterns were selected: one as a control group, the other as a group into which the project worker made an input within the school. Parents of the second group were visited in the home and came into the school as a group to discuss and develop support strategies.

The school's existing system and strategies for monitoring attendance were looked at within the school and recommendations made by the committee based on their own findings and those of national surveys (Elton Report: DES 1989) regarding action at school level in dealing with non-attendance.

While the INSET course provided a knowledge base and update for school staff, the impetus and influence for change stemmed more from direct work within the school.

STAFF SUPERVISION AND SUPPORT

Although staff may develop their skills and knowledge through producing and delivering INSET in a range of contexts, it is important that ongoing complementary support systems are available. Staff should not be left to 'get on with it' alone or to be 'thrown in at the deep end' for others to study the corpse afterwards.

Personal and professional support strategies are needed on formal and informal levels within a service. Regular team meetings are needed for staff to discuss their anxieties and stresses. It will be necessary for staff to meet to discuss specifically their workload – on cases, projects, INSET and teaching commitments – to prevent overload and ensure reasonable and appropriate distribution of tasks.

The use of staff meetings themselves can be utilised as a training opportunity. By rotating responsibility for organising and chairing meetings, staff can practise group leadership skills such as ensuring that continuity and adherence to the agreed agenda are maintained, interruptions and diversions are dealt with appropriately and all present feel they have had the opportunity to be heard.

Staff also need feedback from senior staff on successes in their work and an opportunity to pass on to colleagues ideas and practices they have found successful, which can be collated into a central resource area for general staff use. This reinforces the concept of a learning organisation by acknowledging a very sound training resource to be the staff themselves.

Bearing in mind that staff can be expected to work on a number of levels with schools, from developing whole-school policies to managing behaviour in the classrooms, then resources and a specific annual budget need to be made available to purchase materials, books, audiovisual and training packages so that staff are in a position to take on self-directed study and work on courses or project developments with other staff. They will also need to be given time to prepare thoroughly and to reflect on the quality of the work.

INDIVIDUAL AND SERVICE DEVELOPMENT

The overlap and interplay between individual and institutional development are well documented (Bollington *et al*. 1990). Service development depends upon staff acquiring and disseminating good practice, which in turn relies on their being trained by those with appropriate skills. A specific system, or interrelated set of sub-systems to review individual and service strengths and weaknesses, is needed to identify training needs (Miller and Watts 1990).

The use of a staff appraisal interview, incorporating a formative approach focusing on career development and training needs (as opposed to summative processes concerned with pay and promotion, redeployment and dismissal procedures), can act as a vehicle for resolving conflicts between individual and service priorities and for identifying and prioritising areas for development. The interview can be structured around three broad but related questions, 'What have I done?', 'How am I doing?' and

'What am I going to do?' and this can help both the management of the service and individual staff within it to identify training needs and formulate training responses.

In addition, the use of personal and professional development checklists (Miller and Watts 1990) can help in initially opening up areas of training need and enabling staff to focus on priority areas for development or to identify areas in which they can offer training.

From the range of systems available, including supervision, appraisal, checklists, team and supervision meetings, themes emerge across a service reflecting training requirements. These can be managed through internally organised training programmes, or through input from an external agency or speaker.

CONCLUDING COMMENTS

The approach outlined in this chapter favours service-based INSET as opposed to the traditional off-site attendance at courses for individuals. In this respect staff within a service can be expected to learn about the work while doing the work. The process of organising and delivering courses needs to be carefully structured within a supportive culture to enable staff to address with confidence the organisation and delivery of INSET.

With small groups of staff working together to prepare scripts, no 'elite' of course writers is needed; groups can disband when the course is completed, and new groups reform when the need for another course is identified. New staff joining a service will work with established colleagues and develop through the training programme previously outlined.

Preparing a number of courses can prove a relatively quick and useful way of training new staff into knowledge areas and delivery skills. For a new service, this approach is particularly useful in enabling staff to provide training for each other and themselves.

Staff in this respect receive and deliver training to each other on a reciprocal basis, as part of an organic rather than a mechanical system. By taking a systematic and structured approach to the training of staff the service is able to deliver a professional response to many of the demands placed upon it.

REFERENCES

Bell, L. (1991) 'Approaches to the professional development of teachers', in L. Bell and C. Day *Managing the Professional Development of Teachers*. Milton Keynes: Open University Press.

Bollington, R., Hopkins, D. and West, M. (1990) *An Introduction to Teacher Appraisal*. London: Cassell Educational.

Department of Education and Science (1989) *Discipline in Schools* (The Elton Report). London: HMSO.

Easen, P, (1989) *Making School-centred INSET Work*. Milton Keynes: Open University in association with Routledge.

Galvin, P., Mercer, S. and Costa, P. (1990) *Building a Better Behaved School*. Harlow: Longman.

Georgiades, N. and Phillimore, L. (1975) 'The myth of the hero-innovator and alternative strategies for organisational change', in C.C. Kiernan and F.P. Woodford (eds) *Behaviour Modification with the Severely Retarded*. Amsterdam: Associated Scientific Publishers. Also reprinted in Easen, P. (1989) *Making School-centred Inset work*. Milton Keynes: Open University Press in association with Routledge.

Herbert, M. (1985) *Behavioural Treatment of Problem Children: A Practice Manual*. London: Academic Press.

Jones, M. (1993), 'Children with special educational needs compounded by severe challenging behaviour', in A. Miller and D. Lane (eds) *Silent Conspiracies*. Stoke-on-Trent: Trentham Books, in association with the Professional Development Foundation.

Lane, D.A. (1978) *The Impossible Child* Vols 1 and 2. London: ILEA.

Miller, A. and Watts, P. (1990) *Planning and Managing Effective Professional Development. A Resource Book for Staff Working with Children who have Special Needs*. Harlow: Longman.

Scherer, M., Gersch, I. and Fry, L. (1990) *Meeting Disruptive Behaviour: Assessment Intervention and Partnership*. Basingstoke: Macmillan Education.

Part II

Methods for improving pupil behaviour: whole-school approaches and specific techniques

Chapter 12

Building better behaved schools: effective support at the whole-school level

Peter Galvin and Peter Costa

This chapter is about how the *Building a Better Behaved School* (BABBS) (Galvin *et al*. 1990) materials were developed and the lessons we have learned from our work in schools in the UK. The chapter will describe the research background to the materials; the contents of BABBS; how the materials were used as the basis of the Positive Behaviour Project in Leeds; the philosophy of this project; the manner in which the project operated in schools; the recommendations to schools which resulted from our work; the evaluation we conducted on our work with schools and the issues raised by this evaluation; and our work generally as a support and change agency working with a whole school to promote better behaviour.

THE RESEARCH BACKGROUND

The early work on BABBS originated from a number of different prestigious, academic sources. The first source was neither prestigious nor academic; simply, it was our dissatisfaction with the service we were able to offer to schools as generic psychologists: too many children with too many problems and too few visits. Even those children for whom we found time often seemed beyond help. Setting up positive behavioural contracts, for example, in schools that espoused and promoted fundamentally punitive approaches to managing behaviour often seemed an impossible task. The feeling that there had to be a better way to help children, teachers and schools is hardly an original one. For us it was the first incentive to develop BABBS.

The second source of inspiration came from the USA. American educators had, for some time, been engaged in working in the area of whole-school behaviour policies, or more accurately, whole-school-district, even whole-state, policies, as a way of managing behaviour (Duke 1986). We were heartened by this work in two quite different ways: first by the notion, inherent in this approach, that well-organised, proactive policy could make a difference to the behaviour of pupils; second, that there seemed to be a number of flaws in this approach that we could improve on.

Briefly, they were that we did not believe that whole-school-district poli-cies could by owned by staff, pupils and parents, nor, we felt, could such broad policies possibly meet the needs of individual schools. Such blanket policies were therefore reduced in their effectiveness. In addition, the policies we saw were essentially negative in their approach to behaviour. Typically, they identified a list of misdemeanours, and alongside these a commensurate list of consequences. 'Rudeness to a teacher' led to a 'report to the Principal', two such offences led to 'parental interview' and so on. We did not and do not believe that managing behaviour can be as simple as drawing up such a list (usually depressingly overlong) whereby misdemea-nour x irrevocably equals consequence y. We had a great deal of concern about such inflexible, packaged approaches to behaviour management.

Our contribution to the whole-school policy debate was, we believe, to suggest that the positive supportive characteristics of a well-conceived behaviour programme for an individual pupil could be reproduced at the whole-school level. The well-established behavioural principles for manag-ing the behaviour of pupils remains the underpinning of most educational psychologists' work. We felt that the principles of changing behaviour at the individual level were a solid basis for a part of the approach we wished to employ in our training with schools at the whole-school policy level.

Our third building block was the massive amount of research which has been conducted at the classroom management level. The work of American educators such as Brophy (1983), Evertson et al. (1984), Doyle (1984), Sanford and Emmer (1988) and many others is typically thorough and comprehensive. Brophy epitomises the confidence of this movement:

> It is clear from research that the key to effective management is preven-tion. Effective managers are distinguished by their success in preventing problems from arising in the first place rather than by special skills in dealing with problems once they occur.
>
> (Brophy 1983)

The classroom management research movement has identified a wide range (almost too wide) of factors that can reasonably be considered as the basis of good classroom management practice. Room layout, classroom routines, managing transitions, maintaining momentum, curriculum issues, managing groups, and getting the year off to a good start are just a few of the key areas of preventing misbehaviour from occurring in the classroom. Although we did not entirely agree with the conclusion that good class-room managers prevent misbehaviour and that very little difference exists between teachers when considering how they respond to misbehaviour, nevertheless, preventive approaches to managing behaviour are clearly important for the teacher trying to take a proactive view of difficult behaviour. If there is a criticism to be made of classroom management research it is that it was rarely set within a whole-school context. It is our view that the efficacy of initiatives at this level is reduced if the environment into which they are introduced is not a sympathetic one. We believe that the impact that teachers make at the classroom level is significantly determined by the organisation and ethos of the school as an institution.

This brings us to the next influence on the development of BABBS. It operates alongside the notion of working at the 'whole-school' level described earlier. In this case the focus originated from work developed in industrial settings. Simply put, it is the notion that organisations have an effect on the groups and individuals who are a part of them (see, for example, Handy 1976). This 'effect' has been given many names –'culture', 'ethos', 'climate' among others. There is an accumulating body of evidence in educational research about the nature of this effect on the lives of children in schools – that is, on their learning and their behaviour (Reynolds and Sullivan 1981; Anderson 1982; Handy 1984). Our view was that if schools have an effect on the behaviour of pupils, whether they plan for it or not, it is better if the nature of this effect is planned rather than accidental. The research told us much about the in-school factors that determined the extent and nature of this effect.

In Britain the work of Michael Rutter and colleagues in *Fifteen Thousand Hours* (1979) was probably the most famous and influential of the early studies which considered what those in-school factors might be. They suggested, for example, that effective schools had common policies on behaviour, they made regular use of rewards, they took trouble to set up a pleasant working environment and thought carefully about what constituted effective classroom management strategies.

HMI reports, such as *Education Observed 5: Good Behaviour and Discipline in Schools* (DES 1987), identified more within-school factors which influenced behaviour. Some of these were: the leadership style of the head teacher; teachers' expectations of the pupils and their work; the opportunities for achievement and success which stem from challenging teaching; the active involvement of the pupils in their own learning and in the wider life of the school; a consensus on essential values and norms consistently applied; an awareness of the school as a social institution which influences groups and not merely individual pupils and teachers.

School Matters by Peter Mortimore *et al.* (1988) added more grist to the mill. This study identified twelve factors which played a large part in determining the effectiveness of a school. Briefly these were: purposeful leadership by the head; the involvement of the deputy head in policy decisions; the involvement of teachers in decisions; consistency among teachers; structured teaching sessions; intellectually challenging teaching; a work-centred environment; a limited subject focus within lessons; maximum communication between teachers and pupils; effective record-keeping; parental involvement; a positive climate. Most of these factors are concerned with academic performance, but given, for example, the link between underachievement and misbehaviour, we felt it not unreasonable to take note of Mortimore's findings.

Finally, there was *Discipline in Schools*, the report of the Committee of Enquiry chaired by Lord Elton (DES 1989). Although this report came out after the greater part of BABBS was written, it was comforting to see our work in agreement with this excellent report. The report made 138 sensible recommendations about how schools could promote good behaviour. Underpinning the vast majority of these recommendations and those contained in the other studies was the central theme that schools can make a difference to behaviour. To take just one quote from the report to illustrate this point, the committee said that they came to the conclusion that:

> While some schools seem preoccupied with bad behaviour, others have concerted policies for raising expectations and improving standards. The schools we saw which had such positive policies seemed to be very successful in creating an orderly and purposeful atmosphere. They had marginalised bad behaviour by promoting good behaviour. The central thrust of our recommendations is towards promoting good behaviour.
>
> (The Elton Report: DES 1989)

We took the findings of these and other reports and studies into account when deciding upon the organisation and content of BABBS.

The final source on which BABBS was formulated extends from this last area. Again it was work conducted in industrial settings that provided the basis for our work. In this case it was the growing body of literature on organisational development (Burden 1981; Fullan 1982; Holly 1986). This literature about *how* organisations can develop and manage change fitted well with what we knew about *what* makes an effective school. This literature was also useful in that it considered the relationship between the organisation, its development and the role of the 'outside facilitator'. The seminal article, 'The myth of the hero-innovator' by Georgiades and Phillimore (1975) was typical of the advice given to those concerned with whole-school organisational development. We believed that we could add to the growing body of knowledge about the process of developing, in this case, good behaviour. We will return to this theme in a moment.

Our main task at this stage was to synthesise these various sources of information into some kind of coherent whole. In summary, the main messages we took from these various sources were:

1 Schools do make a difference.
2 Behaviour can be managed as well or as badly as any other area of school life.
3 To manage behaviour, schools need a philosophy, a policy and a set of practices. (In essence, schools are required to develop a clear ethos, a

recognised set of values about behaviour and to have in place some basic strategies for managing behaviour).

4 The positive approach does work: be clear, acknowledge good behaviour; be fair and consistent with misbehaviour.

THE CONTENTS OF BABBS

With this research background we developed *Building a Better Behaved School* as a package schools could use to promote good behaviour. One key task in developing BABBS was to synthesise these various strands of research and development into a coherent package that teachers would find empowering rather than confusing. We felt we needed to make the research accessible and practical. The task was to empower through clarity. Part of the clarity that emerged was that there was such a thing as good practice in school, which means schools can prevent much misbehaviour and minimise much that they cannot prevent. We believed that this 'good practice' could be made most easily accessible through a three-tier approach to managing behaviour in schools. The three tiers are (a) whole-school, (b) classrooms and (c) individual pupils. The nine units of the pack are based on these three tiers:

Unit 1: *The Effective School* sets the scene for the whole-school approach by arguing that the research evidence suggests that schools can make a difference and that behaviour, like any other area of school life – budget, curriculum, staffing environment, etc. – is there to be managed.

Unit 2: *School Reviews* looks at how a school can review issues around behaviour and so identify areas which need development.

Unit 3: *Positive School Discipline Plans* forms the first level of the three-tier model. It helps schools to develop their practice around four main areas: expectations; reinforcement systems; sanctions systems; organisational factors which affect behaviour.

Unit 4: *Working with Parents* looks at how parents can support and be supported by the school's behaviour policy.

Unit 5: *Curriculum Organisation* examines the relationship between curriculum and behaviour.

Unit 6: *Preventive Classroom Management* begins the second tier of the materials. The next three units of the materials are organised so that the teacher in the classroom is able to consider and implement the lightest possible approaches to classroom management, moving only to more intensive and more restrictive measures if the simple tactics are not successful.

Unit 7: *Rules, Praise, Ignore* (RPI) describes an approach which can be used with a more difficult class, requiring firmer guidelines and a more structured response, positively and negatively, to pupil behaviour.

Unit 8: *Heavyweight Strategies for the Classroom* offers some short-term intensive measures of class control when RPI has not had the desired effect.

Unit 9: *Working with Individual Children* completes the three-tier model by describing an approach to managing the behaviour of the most disruptive minority in the school.

USING BABBS IN SCHOOLS

Until September 1989 the materials that were to constitute BABBS had been used as the basis of centre-based training. When BABBS became commercially available we made suggestions on how the pack might be used, we gave some advice on workshops, but, thus far, we had paid relatively little attention to how schools actually used the materials or how the process of development might actually unfold. The increasing number of requests we received for training days raised our interest in how we could support schools in a more 'hands on' manner over a longer period of time. The literature on organisational development was useful, as we have suggested, in providing a broad foundation for our work, but it was clear that the actual process of supporting schools in developing good behaviour would benefit from closer examination. How can a school set about influencing and bringing under planned control the culture or ethos of the organisation? It is all very well to suggest that effective schools have a consensus on essential values (we might even have guessed this much). The real question is how a school develops this consensus if it does not already possess such a thing. This was one issue that the Positive Behaviour Project, described next, allowed us to explore.

THE POSITIVE BEHAVIOUR PROJECT

The Positive Behaviour Project gave us the opportunity to see how BABBS would stand up to more intensive work in schools, and also to consider the nature of effective support in the context of whole-school work around behaviour. With funding from the LEA we were able to add three important components to BABBS and our early work: (a) the opportunity to work with a smaller number of schools more thoroughly and more closely, (b) to add three teachers to our team to give more credibility and variations to our work and (c) to evaluate our work with schools.

In this context the Positive Behaviour Project was set up in Leeds in September 1989. The multidisciplinary team of teachers and educational psychologists was charged with the tasks of finding out what it was schools needed to do to promote good behaviour, supporting schools in their efforts and evaluating the results of this partnership.

The project team began working in 21 schools: 9 primary, 7 high schools,

4 middle schools and 1 special school (the materials, although organised to be most applicable to the primary school, could, we felt, be used with some adaptations in secondary, middle and special schools; this proved to be the case). We wanted to have as wide a range of schools as possible in the project, so that we might reduce the likelihood (when the project's recommendations were published) of head teachers saying that the report did not apply to their school because there was not a school like theirs in the project. During the second year of the project the number was increased to 33 schools. In the third and fourth years of the project the action research aspect of the project ceased and the project continued to offer support to schools in the LEA. To date this has numbered over 120 schools out of the 340 schools in the LEA.

The philosophy of the Positive Behaviour Project

Before the project began we were conscious of the fact that when inviting schools to be a part of the project we needed to strike a balance between their needs and ours, between what was already decided and what we wanted them to decide. We will return to this issue later in this chapter because we think it is an important one for the support service. We felt that we *did* need to be able to describe clearly to interested schools the philosophy behind the *Positive Behaviour* project and what they might be letting themselves in for. Some of the philosophy or assumptions that underpinned the project we have already touched upon: that behaviour can be managed, that schools can and do make a difference, that we would be working through the three-tier model beginning at the whole-school level. This was not, therefore, a project for those schools interested only in the behaviour of the disruptive minority. The details of this three-tier model developed as the project proceeded. Because the development of the model became increasingly central to the project's work, it is described in more detail in Figure 12.1 (see p. 161).

We wanted to make it clear to prospective schools that positive approaches do work and were not, in some way, a soft option. Another quote from the Elton Report which we used to support this notion, said that 'we are left with the disturbing impression that in some schools a pupil can only get attention in one or other of two ways – by working well or behaving badly' (DES 1989). We told schools that one of our aims was to redress this balance somewhat and make good social behaviour an area worthy of recognition. We argued that it was unreasonable to devote the vast majority of a school's resources – time, staffing, organisation, etc. – to developing 'academic behaviour' while 'social behaviour' was somehow supposed to take care of itself. If, we suggested, schools are concerned with the whole child (which most teachers say they are) and are interested in developing social skills/behaviour (which most teachers say they are) then it is surely reasonable to devote *more* similar (not entirely similar) amounts of time and effort to this area as are given to developing academic skills. We can no longer assume that social behaviour will simply happen or that it is somebody else's job to develop it. We can no more avoid our obligations to manage behaviour than we can to manage the curriculum.

Two final 'assumptions' were presented to schools. First, we felt that behaviour was too important to be left to individual teachers to sort out for themselves. Even though most teachers coped admirably with this task, the way to promote good behaviour was to have a consensus-based message about behaviour from the *school as an institution* rather than from the *teacher as an individual*. Second, we suggested that the school as an *institution* meant staff, pupils and parents all working together to give a message about behaviour. Neither of these two points generated any significant disagreement among school representatives when they were raised at early meetings.

The implementation plan for developing good behaviour

The other aspect of the project that we discussed at the early meetings with schools was the predicted process of development. At its simplest, the process of development in schools over the two-year period consisted of the following:

1 An initial meeting with head teacher and senior management team where the philosophy, the model and the process of development were described. This involved discussion about likely implications for time scales, significant events, the organisation of training days, staffing implications and resources, etc. (As the project developed we were able to identify more clearly for new schools the kind of management responsibilities we anticipated all levels of the organisation would need to assume.)
2 A meeting with all staff to explain the implications of being in the project. (Most schools in the project devoted at least two training days and a considerable number of after-school and lunchtime meetings in two years to developing the three main areas.)
3 A review of the school's strengths and weaknesses in behaviour, based on structured interviews, questionnaires to staff, pupils and sometimes parents, and observations by members of the project team.
4 This review data informed the first training day around whole-school policy. This day drew together the staff's views on expectations, reinforcement systems, sanctions systems and organisational factors which might adversely affect behaviour (Level 1 in Figure 12.1).
5 After the training day the views of the staff were taken by a small working group (usually 6 to 8 people who represented a broad spectrum

of staff) and developed into a draft school policy. This group was chaired by one person, who was the link between the school and the project. This person was vital to the success or otherwise of work done in school. One of our recommendations was that this person should usually be a middle-management person: head of department, head of year, curriculum coordinator, etc.

6 This policy was then circulated to all staff for comments and final amendments.

7 The focus of the second training day was usually classroom management and what the policy means for teachers when applied to the classrooms and also to the corridors and playgrounds of the school (Level 2 in Figure 12.1).

8 Further support was offered to teachers after this day in the form of additional after-school sessions, peer observation, support from senior and middle management, 'surgeries' for particular problems, curriculum materials to support the development of good behaviour–action on bullying, social skills development, self-esteem, etc.

9 The final training day looked at the difficult to manage pupil in the context of the first two tiers (Level 3 in Figure 12.1).

10 At the end of the two-year period the effects of the work done in schools was evaluated. (Some of these final questionnaire results are reported later in this chapter.)

Alongside this central core, the project, in responding to the needs of schools, began developing training courses and training packs on areas such as bullying, race, gender, lunchtimes and parents. All Leeds schools have received copies of these training packs and a pack entitled 'Managing the Difficult to Manage'.

Recommendations to schools interested in promoting good behaviour

At the end of the project's first two years we felt we were in a position, based on the evaluation results (see next section), to make some recommendations to schools on how they might go about promoting good behaviour. At the risk of repetition, some of these recommendations to schools were as follows:

1 Develop approaches for promoting positive behaviour at the three levels of the organisation: whole-school, classroom and around school, individual pupils.

2 Work at the whole-school level means having a philosophy or set of values about behaviour, translating this into a policy and making sure that the policy gets turned into everyday practice.

3 Take developing social behaviour seriously. Use some of the structures that we use for developing 'academic' behaviour. Make behaviour an

issue that permeates the curriculum. In high schools, this would mean through all subject areas, not simply PSE.

4 Develop some evaluation criteria or performance indicators which inform the work done on behaviour.
5 Involve all staff and pupils and, wherever and whenever possible, parents in developing a consensus-based approach to behaviour.
6 Have in mind the behaviour(s) you are looking for.
7 Negotiate and agree these expectations wherever possible and communicate them clearly.
8 Notice and reinforce the acceptable behaviour.
9 Mark the limits of unacceptable behaviour.
10 Find supportive structures for those who find success difficult.
11 Use the lightest possible and the least restrictive structures for managing behaviour.

In the context of the last six items of this list of recommendations, it emerged very strongly that the recommendations we were making on effectively managing pupil behaviour were, in our view, exactly those same basic principles of good management that apply to managing staff. An understanding and an implementation of these principles across the whole school is perhaps one of most important project recommendations.

Evaluation results

At the end of the second year the project reported its findings based on the evaluation it had conducted. There is not room here for all the results. But these are available on request. The evaluation conducted by the project showed some pleasing results. Apart from schools receiving training packs we estimate that over 3,000 teachers out of 6,000 teachers in the LEA have received training in behaviour management. Not all schools felt life had changed for the better for them in the area of behaviour, but overall our results were very encouraging. A random sample of 100 teachers returned the following results:

— 69 per cent felt more confident of their ability to control those factors that influence classroom behaviour.
— 67 per cent felt more supported by school procedures.
— 74 per cent felt that staff were more supportive of each other.
— 66 per cent felt they now used a wider range of strategies.
— 71 per cent had more confidence that schools can make an impact on pupil behaviour.

The head teachers in project schools also responded to questionnaires:

— 90 per cent reported an increase in teacher confidence.
— 89 per cent felt the school had been successful in developing and

reviewing procedures for establishing positive approaches to promoting good behaviour.

— 89 per cent felt they had been successful in developing and reviewing procedures for managing difficult behaviour.
— 90 per cent felt that relationships between staff and pupils had improved.
— 75 per cent felt that relationships between pupils had improved.
— 70 per cent felt that relationships between staff had improved.

What constitutes effective support for schools who wish to promote good behaviour?

During the course of our work before, during and after the Positive Behaviour Project, a wide range of issues emerged about how schools promote good behaviour and, more specifically, the role of the outside support agent in the process.

Advice from head teachers about successful projects

Prior to working in schools we invited all those heads in project schools to a meeting and asked them what they thought would make the project successful or unsuccessful in their schools. The advice is useful for those support services working at the whole-school level. It is reproduced here as it emerged at the meeting. Head teachers said:

AVOID:

×   It being seen as a management-directed initiative.
×   Making some people feel that their contributions are not valuable.
×   Too much paperwork.
×   Having preconceived outcomes.
×   Not enough time for those with credibility and not enough credibility for those with time.
×   Raising hopes unrealistically.
×   Allowing the initiative to die away.
×   Staff feeling that nothing is happening.
×   The feeling that what is being done is based on theory rather than real-life situations.
×   Too many meetings.
×   Information that is sensitive or threatening or that is treated in an insensitive manner.

MAKE SURE:

- ✓ That staff have a sense of ownership.
- ✓ That staff see that there is something in it for them as well as for the whole-school.
- ✓ That you are aware that changes in staff and absences can undermine the work.
- ✓ That parents are involved.
- ✓ That there are clear and agreed objectives (action plan).
- ✓ That the management are prepared to accept constructive criticism.
- ✓ That observation in classrooms is handled sensitively.
- ✓ That the work of the project is integrated into established school practices.
- ✓ That the senior management team is actively involved and supportive of the process.

After a two-year period we asked head teachers about the nature of support offered by the project and the LEA. Certain lessons about behaviour support have been learnt, which should be borne in mind when the nature of future provision is considered. Perhaps the first point of note is that the majority of heads in project schools indicated that, even in a changing climate in LEA provision, they wanted support around behaviour in schools and they wanted it from a multidisciplinary team of workers.

Head teachers were quite clear about which services they valued from the project team. There was almost unanimous agreement that the team should offer consultation with the senior management team, contributions to planning meetings and the organisation of training sessions. Over 90 per cent also wanted the team to provide appropriate training and curriculum materials. Heads also wanted support in the classroom. All the heads expected to need in the future consultation on difficult to manage pupils. Setting up cross-school links and centre-based training were the two aspects of provision least valued.

On the whole, heads have indicated that the project team managed to find the right balance of challenge, theory and directiveness. The fact that 50 per cent of heads felt that some of their staff felt threatened by the project at times suggests that the element of challenge can be quite strong without damage to the relationship existing between a school and a supporting team. Eighty-five per cent of head teachers felt satisfied with the gains made by the school when measured against the time and effort put in. It seems that they valued the research aspect of the project (this is an issue we will raise again at the end of this chapter) and welcomed an approach that encouraged learning through experience.

A successful partnership between the support person/team and the school

If the guidelines in the last section constitute good advice from an inside perspective, it is interesting to compare this with lessons we learned as the project unfolded. Some of our conclusions are perhaps self-evident: for example, we found it easier to promote good behaviour in well-managed schools because policy decisions percolated effectively through the organisation. Nonetheless, if such conclusions serve to reinforce already held opinions, perhaps they are no less valuable for that. We leave the reader to be the judge of their merit:

1 A support agency is only as effective as the person in the school that it interfaces with. The view that the staff will hold about the support person will be determined largely by the view that the members of a school have of their contact person in school. If that person is held in high regard then the likelihood is that so will be the support person. The support person is usually powerless to change this perception, as is the person they make contact with. In this project the group coordinator proved, as we have suggested elsewhere, a vital cog in the change process.
2 Choosing a group with care so that it reflects the inevitable diversity of opinion about behaviour, and then taking some time to build this group into a team is, in our view, time well spent.
3 Beware the grand start that is difficult to maintain. In one school where concern about behaviour was at a very high level, the success of the first training day produced a euphoria we were quite unable to maintain, and expectations were, thereafter, unreasonably high. We learned later to put in some 'high-profile' small events after the first training day that, although not necessarily directly to do with outcomes of the day, served to show staff that something was happening on the behaviour front.
4 Data is interesting and motivating and part of the deal (if you can measure it you can manage it). The review of the needs and strengths of a school is a good way of getting people's interest (staff are always interested in what other colleagues think and perhaps (surprisingly?) even more in the opinions of pupils and parents about what is going on in school). We found less commitment to evaulate the *effects* on any work being done in school. In our view this is an issue which merits further examination.
5 Look at the history of other initiatives in school. There is a lot to be learned about what is likely to succeed or fail in a school by listening to those on the 'inside'. In at least one school we were dissuaded, quite rightly, from making a *grand* beginning which would have alienated most staff.
6 There is a need for a balance between preconceived outcomes (i.e. long-

term goals) and the need for flexibility. One of the recommendations of the heads was to avoid having preconceived outcomes, yet the school must have some long-term goal for behaviour even though this is inevitably and rightly renegotiated as work proceeds.

7 You have licence to make mistakes. There is a tendency in schools to feel that action must be taken and it must be right. Our view is that working on behaviour is a matter of formulating a hypothesis about what action should be taken, putting this into effect, evaluating the action, then keeping the parts that were successful and changing the parts (as there will certainly be) that were not successful. The school's responsibility is not not to make mistakes, rather it is to learn from the mistakes that are made.

8 If the support person wants to prompt schools into action around behaviour they must constantly be looking to reframe the latest educational initiative to their advantage. Local financial management of schools is a case in point. In a situation where, whether we like it or not, schools are in competition with each other, behaviour becomes a marketable commodity. After all, several surveys of parental opinion indicate that what parents look for first in choosing a school is its disciplinary climate. Another example is the National Curriculum, in that one message of the project is: behaviour is an area where we expect so much yet teach so little. Perhaps as the 'academic' curriculum becomes more 'explicit' (through SATs and the like), behaviour should keep pace.

9 The final lesson learned is a message that we have already espoused but, we believe, is worth repeating. Perhaps the greatest service that a support person can give to a school is the rock-steady belief, in times of crisis, that pupil behaviour *can* be managed.

Some final conclusions about the nature of effective support

It is obvious that the nature of the relationship between the outside support agent and the school is a complex one. The support person/team has to strike that fine balance between appearing, on the one hand, almost subservient, thereby giving the impression that they have no professional contribution to make to the school and, on the other hand, appearing so bombastic and self-assured that they do not listen to the schools needs. In the project we felt that the role of the outside facilitator might best be described as that of the *critical friend*.

The critical friend:

1 Lists the problems but helps see the wood for the trees.
2 Breaks down the problems into manageable pieces while seeing the whole picture.

3 Helps the school celebrate success and points out future areas for development.
4 Supplies resources but encourages self-reliance.
5 Provides expert insight but asks naive questions.
6 Empowers by being directive and empowers by following the school's wishes.
7 Can ask sensitive questions to probe hidden agendas but respects privacy.
8 Is uncompromising in own values but respects the values of others.

In practical terms this means that effective support from outside agencies takes into account the issues discussed in the following paragraphs.

An effective support service knows what it can do and what it cannot do – as we have suggested elsewhere; it has a philosophy, a model and a process to offer schools. This also means that the service can provide a clear cost-benefit analysis of any action taken: likely demands on resources, time, etc. It develops with schools clear action plans: the why, what, when, who, where and how of the process of promoting good behaviour.

In the same vein, the service is aware of how it fits alongside other forms of support offered to schools. Given that different support teams have different priorities, it is important, if schools are to gain maximum benefit from support, that support from different sources should interlock but not overlap. Resources are too precious for schools to be using two agencies to develop the same area. The relationship between agencies that offer support to individual pupils and those that work at the whole-school level is a case in point. Sometimes one agency is able to offer a range of services and the problem disappears, although perhaps other difficulties appear.

Effective support helps (perhaps even prompts) a school to evaluate any action taken. The role of evaluation in any school-based initiative is, in our experience, a vexed one. We sometimes felt that schools placed little value on evaluation other than at the initial review stage. They were often more concerned with action than taking time to decide whether their identified targets were the correct ones and whether or not targets were being met. As the project developed we made more use of an action plan format. Schools valued this approach, regarding it as both simple and sensible yet informative in terms of review and change. It would seem to be possible to agglomerate individual action plan results to form an overview of a research project. We recommend that support agencies give careful consideration to how they can put evaluation 'up front', to how they can meet their own needs in evaluating their efficacy without burdening schools with impossible and unnecessary formats for evaluation.

We have already referred to the nature of the partnership between the support person(s) and the school. At its simplest the relationship seems to involve support person(s) meeting school about half-way. This view of effective support meeting schools in the middle ground in a genuine partnership, which empowers the school, raises some interesting issues for those of us who have written training packages for use in schools. Our hope is that the school will be able to adapt the materials to suit their own particular needs. Given that no two schools are quite alike, this would seem to be vital. Our view of the BABBS materials is that, in that they recommend a review of the school's needs and then offer a variety of possible interventions at three levels based on this review, they do allow a breadth and a flexibility that makes this adaptation at least feasible.

Schools do value well-produced training materials and in some ways there seems little point in reinventing the wheel when there is so much that needs developing. We continue to believe that the outside agent, with the benefit of their experience in a variety of schools, has a vital role to play in helping schools to adapt existing materials to their particular needs. Some packages offer only a very narrow focus for development, which gives little indication to schools whether, given a spectrum of possible interventions, this happens to be the correct one. An Assertive Discipline (Canter and Canter 1976) or BATPAC (Wheldall and Merrett 1985) package, for example, takes little or no account of the importance of preventive measures. Such packages contain no mechanism for identifying the lightest possible touch on the helm of good behaviour. Yet it is this touch that encourages the development of self-control, which teachers, in our experience, value so highly. Nor do such packages offer the opportunity of phasing out high levels of support, assuming that they were necessary in the first place. They seem to simply arrive and then they disappear. When, in addition, these packages have to be rigidly applied on pain of excommunication, we begin to hear the sound of a square peg being commercially driven into a round hole.

SUMMARY

Building better behaved schools is not easy, there are so many causes of misbehaviour that it is tempting to see the solutions as equally complex – which of course they are – however, if schools are to feel empowered to promote better behaviour they must see the task as achievable. The relationship between an external support agency and school is equally complex, and here again the challenge would seem to be to keep that relationship clear and simple. Thomas Harris said:

> A winner takes a big problem and separates it into smaller parts
> so that it can be more easily manipulated;
> a loser takes a lot of little problems and rolls them together until they
> are unsolvable.

(Harris 1973)

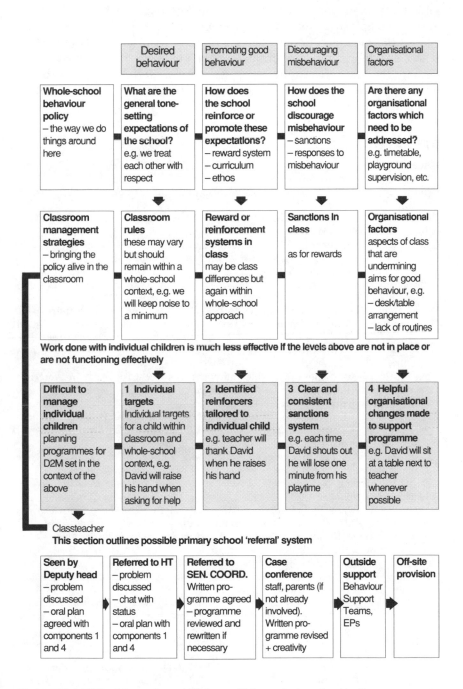

	Desired behaviour	Promoting good behaviour	Discouraging misbehaviour	Organisational factors
Whole-school behaviour policy – the way we do things around here	**What are the general tone-setting expectations of the school?** e.g. we treat each other with respect	**How does the school reinforce or promote these expectations?** – reward system – curriculum – ethos	**How does the school discourage misbehaviour** – sanctions – responses to misbehaviour	**Are there any organisational factors which need to be addressed?** e.g. timetable, playground supervision, etc.
Classroom management strategies – bringing the policy alive in the classroom	**Classroom rules** these may vary but should remain within a whole-school context, e.g. we will keep noise to a minimum	**Reward or reinforcement systems in class** may be class differences but again within whole-school approach	**Sanctions in class** as for rewards	**Organisational factors** aspects of class that are undermining aims for good behaviour, e.g. – desk/table arrangement – lack of routines

Work done with individual children is much less effective if the levels above are not in place or are not functioning effectively

Difficult to manage individual children planning programmes for D2M set in the context of the above	**1 Individual targets** Individual targets for a child within classroom and whole-school context, e.g. David will raise his hand when asking for help	**2 Identified reinforcers tailored to individual child** e.g. teacher will thank David when he raises his hand	**3 Clear and consistent sanctions system** e.g. each time David shouts out he will lose one minute from his playtime	**4 Helpful organisational changes made to support programme** e.g. David will sit at a table next to teacher whenever possible

Classteacher
This section outlines possible primary school 'referral' system

Seen by Deputy head – problem discussed – oral plan agreed with components 1 and 4	**Referred to HT** – problem discussed – chat with status – oral plan with components 1 and 4	**Referred to SEN. COORD.** Written programme agreed – programme reviewed and rewritten if necessary	**Case conference** staff, parents (if not already involved). Written programme revised + creativity	**Outside support** Behaviour Support Teams, EPs	**Off-site provision**

Figure 12.1 Difficult to manage children within a whole-school policy

Ultimately, then, while the task of the outside support person(s) is to take all that complexity, sift through it, look at the possibilities for action, choose the most appropriate one(s), make it accessible and support the school as it moves forward, evaluating and guiding as the process unfolds. Perhaps the best service the support agency can offer is the advice that, in times of difficulty, a school needs to keep it simple. The more difficult the problem the simpler the solution needs to be.

REFERENCES

Anderson, C.S. (1982) 'The search for school climate: a review of the research', *Review of Educational Research*, 52, 3.
Brophy, J.E. (1983) 'Classroom organisation and management', *The Elementary School Journal*, 83, 4.
Burden, R. (1981) 'Systems theory and its relevance to schools', in B. Gillham (ed.) *Problem Behaviour in the Secondary School*, London: Croom Helm.
Canter, L. and Canter, M. (1976) *Assertive Discipline: A Take Charge Approach for Today's Educator*, Santa Monica, Calif.: Canter & Associates.
Department of Education and Science (1987) *Education Observed 5: Good Behaviour and Discipline in Schools*, Report by HM Inspectors. London: HMSO.
Department of Education and Science (1989) *Discipline in Schools*, Report of the Committee of Enquiry chaired by Lord Elton (the Elton Report). London: HMSO.
Doyle, W. (1984) 'How order is achieved in classroom: an interim report', *Journal of Curriculum Studies*, 16, 3.
Duke, D.L. (1986) 'School discipline plans and the quest for order in American schools', in D.P. Tattum (ed.) *Management of Disruptive Pupil Behaviour in Schools*. New York: Wiley.
Evertson, C.M., Emmer, E.E., Clements, B.S., Sandford, J.P. and Worsham, M.E. (1984) *Classroom Management for Elementary Teachers*. Englewood Cliffs, NJ: Prentice-Hall.
Fullan, M. (1982) *The Meaning of Educational Change*. New York: Teachers College Press.
Galvin, P., Mercer, S. and Costa, P. (1990) *Building a Better Behaved School*. Harlow: Longman.
Georgiades, N.J. and Phillimore, L. (1975) 'The myth of the hero-innovator and alternative strategies for organizational change' in C.C. Kiernan and F.R. Woodford (eds) *Behaviour Modification with the Severely Retarded*. New York: Associate Scientific Publishers.
Handy, C. (1976) *Understanding Organizations*, London: Penguin.
Handy, C. (1984) *Taken for Granted? Understanding Schools as Organizations*. London: Schools Council.
Harris, T. (1973) *Winners and Losers*, Jacksonville, Ill.: Argus Communications.
Holly, P. (1986) 'Soaring like turkeys – the impossible dream?' *School Organization*, 6.3.
Mortimore, P., Sammons, P., Stoll, L., Lewis, D. and Ecob, R. (1988) *School Matters: The Junior Years*. Wells: Open Books.
Reynolds, D. and Sullivan, M. (1981) 'The effects of school: a radical faith restated', in Gillham, B. (ed.) *Problem Behaviour in the Secondary School*. London: Croom Helm.

Rutter, M. Maughan, B., Mortimore, P. and Ouston, J. (1979) *Fifteen Thousand Hours: Secondary Schools and their Effects on Children*. London: Open Books.
Sanford, J.P. and Emmer, E.T. (1988) *Understanding Classroom Management: An Observation Guide*. Englewood Cliffs, NJ: Prentice-Hall.
Wheldall, K. and Merrett, F. (1985) *BATPAČ*. Birmingham: Positive Products.

Chapter 13

Promoting peer support among teachers

Barry Chisholm

Over the past decade commentators and schools have recognised the value to teachers of using colleagues as 'critical friends' in helping them to arrive at solutions to classroom-based problems. Hanko (1990: 57) describes one approach, in which groups of teachers meet on a regular basis to discuss particular children whose behaviour in class is a cause for concern. The group is supported by a consultant, who acts as an 'informed facilitator'. Through discussion, the group seeks to support teachers in making informed decisions about what to do next in handling their own classroom difficulties. The process also seeks a high degree of commitment from teachers to following through decisions that they take. Teachers are encouraged to perceive themselves as responsible decision-makers who are entitled to find their own professionally acceptable solutions to the problems they encounter.

Rogers (1990) has also written extensively on the process of peer support for teachers. For Rogers, school-based teacher peer support programmes can fulfil four functions:

1 Enabling teachers to discuss common concerns affecting professional life.
2 Providing opportunities for reflection on practice and problem-solving.
3 Enabling the exchange of ideas on curriculum teaching methods and ways of dealing with student behaviour.
4 Developing approaches to classroom management.

Both Hanko and Rogers emphasise the helpfulness of peer support in generating a climate where issues can be pursued supportively. They acknowledge that peer support reduces feelings of teacher isolation and stress. Both approaches demonstrate the increased level of professionalism developed by participating teachers. However, they differ in three respects. First, Hanko uses consultants as 'informed facilitators' to provide a background context for group discussions, while Rogers simply emphasises the 'basic human relations skills' of facilitation. Second, Rogers's formulation of peer support work encompasses planning specific teacher skill development, as well as generating responses to individual case problems. The Hanko model focuses much more on 'single case' discussions. Third, Rogers's approach looks to developing skills by extending peer support into the classroom via mutual observation. The Hanko approach does not expressly seek to do this.

Teacher peer support has also been incorporated in published materials available for staff development. Chisholm *et al.* (1986) produced a package for secondary teachers focusing on minimising the likelihood of disruptive behaviour in classrooms. The materials were structured to promote a teacher-led progression from peer-supported individual and group work to paired peer-observation in classrooms. It was argued that this would actively and effectively address the issue of developing new classroom skills. The theme of teacher peer support was endorsed by the Elton Report (DES 1989), and in turn this was translated through the Local Education Authority Training Grant Scheme into projects 'to prepare selected teachers to set up and lead school-based peer support groups, the purpose of which is to help improve participating teachers' practical skills in managing pupils' behaviour'. What follows is a description of some of the content, processes and outcomes of a programme of projects within one LEA over a two-year period (1990–92).

THE PROGRAMME

The LEA is organised in three phases – first, middle and upper schools. Over two years, 65 per cent of schools indicated a wish to be part of the programme. Funding allowed 75 schools to take part in the first part of the programme (facilitator training), and 55 schools went on to undertake school-based projects. Those schools which chose not to continue felt they were unable to devote the time necessary to sponsor peer support work. Participating schools selected teachers who became facilitators for school projects. These teachers were then given training, which was led by educational psychologists, who were also available for consultation at each 'step' in the programme.

Facilitator training

Training for the facilitators had the following aims:

1 Ensure that facilitators had a clear understanding of 'peer support' as a concept.
2 Develop an understanding of the facilitator role in school projects.
3 Make available information and materials which would help facilitators promote projects in school.
4 Provide facilitators with techniques of organising groups.

Prior to training, potential facilitators and their head teachers were circulated with materials which elaborated on the peer support concept, e.g. extracts from Elton, the LEATGS funding parameters, and an LEA commentary. Next, they attended a group meeting where they were asked to consider the possible advantages of peer support work and to identify any worries they had about it. Invariably, classroom teachers said they were excited by the prospect of taking control of aspects of their own professional development. Some were not sure that this would be allowed in their schools. Two other points also concerned class teachers. They were worried that sufficient time would not be available to use peer support appropriately, and also about possible links with appraisal. They were sure, however, that peer support approaches would enhance teacher effectiveness. Head teachers were less certain on this last point and wanted reassurance that peer support would benefit the school as a whole as well as individual teachers. Some head teachers expressed anxiety about relinquishing control for implementing staff development to their teachers.

During training, facilitators were asked to identify peer support activities that were already taking place in their schools. Facilitators were also helped to identify the necessary factors that underpin peer support processes in a range of co-worker styles. Facilitators had been identified, because they were teachers who had credibility with their colleagues as good classroom managers. They knew this alone was not sufficient to guarantee successful school projects. They were able to identify additional features of their role similar to other peer support projects (Chisholm *et al.* 1988):

1 Skills in creating the climate in which teachers can take responsibility for their learning.
2 Skills in organising and coordinating practical issues.
3 Skills in utilising appropriate self-disclosure about their own classroom skills.
4 Skills in monitoring and evaluating progress (of individuals and of projects).

The focus of the programme was underpinned by two assumptions: first, that the way teachers interact with pupils and the *manner* in which they convey an expectation of compliance from pupils will influence pupil behaviour; second, that teachers are able to identify and acquire these interactive skills (i.e. good effective classroom managers are not simply 'born' with them). A corollary to this assumption is that teachers will arrive at their own individual ways of putting these skills into operation. During training, therefore, the facilitators were encouraged to identify those aspects of 'climate' which teachers can influence. First, they 'brainstormed' to establish a list of factors felt to influence disruption in classrooms. It was possible to identify those factors which were largely external to school (e.g. limited finance, teacher training, value conflicts, etc.); within school but largely beyond teacher control (size of building, class size, effect of previous lesson, etc.); and those factors – and there were many of these – which were significantly within the influence of the classroom teacher (e.g. classroom rules and routines, teacher expectations, vigilance skills, nipping things in the bud, etc.). Projects were expected to develop around items on this last list. Facilitators also identified resources they felt would be helpful in developing projects in their schools as follows:

> *Preventative Approaches to Disruption* (PAD) (Chisholm *et al.* 1986).
> *Finding Answers to Disruption* (Grunsell 1985).
> *Effective Classroom Management* (Laslett and Smith 1984).
> *Effective Classroom Control* (Robertson 1990).
> *You Know the Fair Rule* (Rogers 1991).
> *Behaviour Can Change* (Westmacott and Cameron 1981).
> *Classroom Management Skills* (Wragg 1981).

Facilitators were also introduced to an active approach to developing skills in which there is the expectation that teachers will arrive at individual solutions to personal development through:

— the implementation of guidelines and principles of management (concepts and content);
— which will be set within the ethos of the school (context parameters);
— and applied in a way with which the individual teacher feels at ease (personal style).

Finally, it was recognised that facilitators would spend some time organising groups of teachers in their own schools to make decisions about how they wished their projects to run, and also as part of the project process itself. Therefore, opportunities were made available for them to practise models of managing meetings to enable group 'business' to be efficiently and fairly dealt with. They were also introduced to a structured problem-solving approach (Problem Zapping – developed by ABRAXAS Management Research) through which individual teachers could gain support from peers in a group setting.

Outcomes

There were no preconceptions about how school projects would develop and, in outcome terms, the programme demonstrated considerable variety and originality. Mismatches between the aims of the programme and project delivery outcomes were rare (only three occurred). In these cases the projects revealed a lack of understanding of the concept of peer support. The vast majority of projects (95 per cent) matched the aims of the programme parameters.

Projects which produced policy

Many projects sought in some way to marry the peer support concept to the development of broader policy in relation to pupil management. A number of projects arrived at *informal policy outcomes*. For example, one school group moved from 'the investigation and sharing of strategies used within the school in the management of pupil behaviour' to providing 'written information which was made available to all staff'. First, the volunteer peer group identified aspects of pupil management in classrooms important to them. Subsequently, these teachers 'tracked' these elements in classrooms with teacher partners. Observations were fed back between the pairs of teachers and then to the larger group. The group has now produced a series of guidelines for the school, on the principles of preventing and managing routine classroom deviance, though there is no intention of endorsing this as full school policy. Some projects became powerful contributors to formal *whole-school developments as unintended outcomes*. In a particularly well-constructed approach, one first school used peer group discussion and paired classroom observation to develop individual teacher practice, and subsequently group practice, around 'Tidy Time' – a time when group management skills are often at a premium! As the group became established, the parameters of successful Tidy Time were explored through structured discussion. Hypotheses evolved and observation schedules were constructed to enable classroom research to be undertaken. Participating teachers were then given structured personal feedback and support for problem-solving by constructive colleagues. It also allowed the evolution of a group view on Tidy Time which could be fed back to the whole-school group – providing a powerful model in the school for developing both school policy and individual practice.

Other projects started with the *intention of producing whole-school policies*. In some small schools the entire school teaching staff have been involved in a process of meeting together to highlight areas of focus, set up peer-based classroom activities to gather information about individual practice and use this for feedback to inform policy documentation. Occasionally, policy-based projects have been limited to discussion/ reflection activities. One upper-school group used published materials (PAD) as the stimulus for support discussions, and also as the basis for generating ideas about a whole-school policy. Proposals from this group were considered by faculties, in order to ensure the school arrived at a consensus-based policy.

In other schools the project proved timely in allowing peer support to be used as a method of *'seeding' policy development*, which was already in progress. In one school a behaviour working party was linked to a project of volunteer staff, who wished to examine their own classroom skills by using peer observation and feedback. By using the two groups, the credibility of the policy development was enhanced; 'paired observation allowed many immediate problems to be addressed and we were able to feed "chalk face" ideas into the Working Party!' Renewed energy and confidence, both at the individual teacher level and within the policy development, was the very positive outcome. Projects like this may best be thought of as 'Trojan Mouse' approaches to introducing peer support work, in that they are relatively small in scale, they address highly critical areas of school and classroom activity, they are not perceived as threatening in any way, yet they achieve significant change within the system, and can provide the foundation for other work.

Projects which enacted policy

A number of projects helped teachers to put school policies into action. One first school identified from their policy the need for a calmer, more controlled beginning and end to the school day. In this project the support group gathered data to highlight areas of their own practice, and the project as a whole was able to feed back into the school guidelines through which policy aspirations might be met. In another school, the facilitator worked alongside other teachers to implement the written behaviour policy at classroom level. This was a clear example of a project with firm parameters at school level, but which attempted to enable teachers to put policy into practice in their own controlled way. Two middle schools used peer support approaches to implement the assertive discipline model within school. In one school, where it was intended to implement assertive discipline as a response to policy, peer support groups were established to find ways of introducing and maintaining the work in school. In the second school, where assertive discipline was already established, the school tried 'to create a climate in which people feel comfortable in asking for support (about assertive discipline)'. Here the support group met regularly to help individual teachers with their own concerns, and provided an organised structure for discussions. Simultaneously, the facilitator encouraged the development of an informal peer support network to meet the day-to-day needs of teachers. The project report again identifies the development of positive staff relationships, which made it easier for staff to discuss practical issues and arrive with some confidence at personal strategies and solutions.

Overall, most school projects included some element of producing or enacting school policy. Perhaps this close structural link between the projects and their schools also helped to defuse the anxieties expressed by some head teachers prior to the inception of the programme. Tying individual peer support in with school policy-based initiatives may be seen as one way of ensuring benefits for the school. Happily, this type of link has not been experienced by participating teachers as negatively affecting their own self-directed development. This group of projects was still organised on a voluntary basis, without selection or coercion.

Possible conflicts in establishing parameters for the projects through competition between 'bottom-up' and 'top-down' approaches did not materialise. A balance between school and individual commitment was maintained. Issues around the confidentiality of information generated by projects were safely negotiated.

Projects with a classroom research focus

Most projects had a direct classroom research component. In some, it was the central feature. In about half of these the focus was on classroom climate – concerned with establishing practices and routines which minimised disruption. For example, in one first school, teachers observed each other's lessons, concentrating on aspects of classroom life such as lesson beginnings, whole-class communication, noise level, etc., and used this information to consider classroom changes. In another school, structured observation by the school facilitator of volunteer teachers allowed the accumulation of a record of achievement of school good behaviour management practice: that is, the facilitator adopted the role of a school-based researcher. As 'a positive attempt to gather good ideas from colleagues about classroom organisation and classroom management in order to promote good pupil behaviour, which can be shared with others', the project was experienced by staff as a reassuring exercise (though without a peer support component it may have been somewhat threatening) and gave an overall picture of child behaviour and child management techniques within the school. In these projects a secondary outcome was the attention paid to specific pupil issues. Some other classroom research-based projects took the latter emphasis as their prime concern. In these, the facilitator sometimes operated as a peer researcher within the classroom. Often the facilitator became a co-problem-solver with the classroom teacher. In at least one school, however, it was clear that ultimately decisions were taken by the class teacher. 'Staff found it very useful having someone else's observations, thoughts and conclusions to use (draw on).'

Projects which use co-teaching

A few projects went beyond participant observation and into the realm of co-teaching. In a middle school, teachers were joined in some of their lessons by an additional teacher, a former member of the school staff. This arrangement impacted far less intrusively on the school organisation than was possible in many projects. The co-teacher helped class teachers in their curriculum delivery. Participating teachers emphasised how this gave them the opportunity to stand back and view their own lessons dispassionately and to reflect on a genuinely shared experience. In a second upper school, autonomous pairs of teachers devised and implemented their own co-teaching programmes. The content for the shared classroom experience was organised together by each pair of teachers beforehand. These two projects moved away somewhat from the overall programme's emphasis on classroom management skills alone, but both offer an interesting perspective on the use of peer support. They also provide important reminders of the interaction between curriculum delivery and group management skills. One teacher commented: 'The mixture of both observation and active participation was, I believe, beneficial to the session. It was interesting to observe for myself a non-art specialist discuss and interpret ideas. As I usually consider the visual complexities I sometimes avoid certain approaches. I feel through discussion with my teaching partner that I may need to concentrate on . . .'

The place of support groups in the projects

In many schools a distinct support group proved to be the central feature of the project. These groups were invariably composed of volunteer teachers, occasionally with an emphasis towards less experienced staff. Groups met in their own time after school, or in directed time, or in a mixture of directed and personal time. A number of facilitators pointed out the organisational difficulties associated with implementing regular group sessions. The control of decision-making by participating teachers about their learning is seen to be a crucial and integral part of the (group) process (Chisholm et al. 1988), but this was sometimes felt to be put at risk by the difficulty of organising the group. Several schools highlighted this dilemma in their evaluation reports.

Most of the groups adopted a general classroom strategies approach to their discussions (i.e. how can I minimise the likelihood of disruption occurring?). They used a range of source materials for their discussions – school-prepared stimulus materials, published staff development approaches, and reflections and insights from their own practice. A smaller number of groups focused on peer-supported case discussions – though in some groups this arose incidentally out of thematic discussions. Some groups got together at the end of school to talk and share ideas round a theme. In others, a framework of pre-prepared activities was provided to stimulate a guided discussion. Other groups were led more formally, adopting a 'managing meetings' approach to ensure a fairness of contributions and outcomes, while at other times using the 'zap' problem-solving approach to allow one member of the group to address a particular issue.

The evidence suggests that groups found value in each of the approaches outlined at the start of this chapter (Chisholm et al. 1988; Hanko 1990; Rogers 1990). No group, however, chose to use an external consultant.

Worries about confidentiality in groups were allayed by the use of a double level of confidentiality within the groups, that is:

— ensuring that discussions were confidential to the group and the room in which they took place;
— ensuring that the content of the discussion became the 'property' of the teacher receiving support at that time.

Groups showed sensitivity to their participants by the way they adopted clear processes, in which feedback was:

— given as soon as possible;
— introduced with positive observations;
— specific;
— used to suggest a range of possibilities;
— 'owned' by the person giving the feedback.

Facilitator training had modelled a process of problem-solving in which the teacher-client used feedback from colleagues as an information base on which to build solutions to problems. In practice, two other variants were also used without participants feeling over-directed by their colleagues. In one version, peer colleagues took over the problem-solving for the client and prepared ready-made answers for teachers to adopt. In the second, the peer group aided the client teacher in arriving at consensus decisions for him/her to implement.

The majority of schools in the programme saw the group meetings as a jumping-off point, and the point of evaluation – within their projects. The progression into other peer-supported activities has proved to be one of the most rewarding aspects for participants, who have always reported back on the positive benefits of classroom research, especially peer observation. Facilitators and participating teachers have without fail made sensitive acknowledgement of the issues to be considered when planning a peer observation:

— defining the parameters of the observation;
— introducing it to the children;
— structuring how observations are to be made/recorded;
— deciding whether the observer joins in with the teaching;
— deciding how feedback should be given to the teacher;
— deciding what the recipient teacher does with the feedback;
— fixing the level of confidentiality of the observation contract.

Classroom research and peer observation have usually developed after a period of work within a larger group. This must, in large part, be a recognition of the facilitator's skill in developing group climate. It is also a reflection of the commitment of group participants to play their part in this process by taking responsibility in:

— giving their time constructively;
— reflecting on and making disclosures about their performance;
— treating the disclosure of others with respect;
— supporting positively in the group;
— being prepared to consider changes in their own classroom performance;
— honouring the contracts made within the group.

CONCLUSION

From the evaluation reports of the project it is clear that the programme of
peer support has been well received by the schools and participating
teachers. Every school-based evaluation indicated a positive view of the
work, typically describing an increased confidence in the use of peer
support and its benefits for teachers. The flexibility and individuality
demonstrated across projects allowed participating schools to accommodate conceptual issues, which it was anticipated might have been
problematic.

Inevitably, there are issues from the programme which require further
exploration and development. For example, the evaluations were school-
based, and school-managed. This meant there were no external measures
of outcomes. Similarly, schools employed few direct measures of actual
changes in teacher practice. Rather, they reported on teacher perceptions
of changes. It is not possible, therefore, to be clear about the extent of
changes in actual classroom practice. It is also uncertain whether teachers,
when problem-solving, focused their attention on developing additional
skills for inclusion in their classroom repertoire *or* on building on existing
strengths that they already possessed.

Similarly, it would have been informative to have received data from
schools about the *precise* nature of the support the teachers gave each
other. At a conceptual level it had been clear that skill development would
best be promoted through the use of a 'critical friend'. This implies a
degree of constructive challenge in the support process – the notion that
peers would be able to 'stretch' their colleague's reflection and classroom
activity. While it is evident that all teachers enjoyed the security and
personal affirmation from time spent working together, we cannot be sure
of the degree to which these relationships tested them in this constructive
sense.

Summary

The aim of the programme had been to establish a peer support approach
directed by teachers themselves within their schools and subsequently self-
evaluated, according to their own criteria. Within this framework the peer

support approach in the LEA has met with considerable approval from teachers for problem-solving, boosting confidence, raising morale and providing a high-quality personal support for managing disruptive classroom behaviour.

REFERENCES

Chisholm, B., Kearney, D., Knight, G., Little, H., Morris, S. and Tweddle, D. (1986) *Preventative Approaches to Disruption*. Basingstoke: Macmillan Education.

Chisholm, B., Kearney, D., Knight, G., Little, H., Morris, S. and Tweddle, D. (1988) 'Developing teaching skills: a preventative approach to disruption', *Pastoral Care*, March.

Department of Education and Science, (1989) *Discipline in Schools* (The Elton Report). London: HMSO.

Grunsell, R. (1985) *Finding Answers to Disruption*. Harlow: Longman.

Hanko, G. (1990) *Special Needs in Ordinary Classrooms*. Oxford: Blackwell Education.

Laslett, R. and Smith, C. (1984) *Effective Classroom Management*. London: Routledge.

Lovejoy, S, (1988) 'How to zap your problems', *Educational Psychology in Practice*, 3, 4: 170–4.

Robertson, J. (1990) *Effective Classroom Control*. London: Hodder and Stoughton.

Rogers, W. (1990) *You Know the Fair Rule*. Harlow: Longman.

Westmacott, E. and Cameron, S. (1981) *Behaviour Can Change*. London: Macmillan.

Wragg, E.C. (1981) *Classroom Management Skills*. Nottingham: Teacher Education Project.

Chapter 14

Resolving conflict in schools

Andrea Higgins and Simon Priest

'I spend up to an hour each working day with pupils helping them to sort out their quarrels – from tittle-tattle about friends to fights and threats of violence. I am here to teach; I have a thousand and one demands on my time. I would like to do more for pupils but I haven't got the expertise for this sort of thing.'

(Secondary school teacher)

'Our arguments are our own. We don't need teachers to help us; it's nothing to do with them.'

(Secondary school pupil)

Conflict between pupils is an integral part of school life and many teachers report a considerable involvement on their part. Evidence of the worst outcomes of unresolved conflicts periodically appears in the newspapers, but what really happens on a day-to-day basis? How much can teachers do to help young people deal with differences between themselves constructively? How should schools organise themselves to facilitate conflict resolution for pupils, parents, staff and governors?

While readers will be aware of the potential for desirable personal growth resulting from the positive handling of life's inevitable conflicts, it is the negative aspects of conflict which tend to figure more prominently in our working experience. Fortunately, the problems in some schools in the USA appear from a British perspective to be excessive: for example, the US National Center for Disease Control Survey of 11,000 high school students in 1987 revealed that 34 per cent of the sample claim to have been threatened with violence in the past year and 23 per cent of the boys admitted to carrying knives. In 1987 the Annual Crime Report for Californian schools noted 14 murders on school premises, of whom seven victims were students. In the same year, 600 guns were seized and there were 25,000 cases of assault, robbery and extortion in junior high schools alone. It is therefore hardly surprising that there is considerable interest in conflict resolution in the US (for a fuller discussion, see Marshall 1987).

The picture is reassuringly different in Great Britain, although research consistently reveals significant groups of children who complain of un-happiness resulting from inter-personal difficulties. In her interviews with top infants, Tizard (1988) notes that two-thirds of them complained about teasing and approximately the same proportion reported fights in the playground, although most of the children said that they did not enjoy fighting and were either provoked or doing so in self-defence. Estimates of the frequency of bullying in schools, which may be regarded as a specific aspect of conflict, vary between 1 in 4 children and 1 in 20 children, depending on how the data is obtained and who is asked (for more discussion here, see Priest 1989).

Following the lead of the US, most approaches to resolving conflict in Britain have involved systems wherein mediators are trained in the follow-ing approaches:

1 To regulate the interaction between the conflicting parties.
2 To help to improve communications between the parties.
3 To help differentiate between conflicting ideas, integrate those which are similar and identify those which are irrelevant.
4 To help people in conflict examine their mutual interests and not try to bargain from inflexible positions (see Fisher and Ury 1981).
5 To encourage mutual problem-solving and the formulation of creative solutions.

In the US, young people, as well as adults, have been trained as mediators in schools, a practice which has been tried on a small scale in Northern Ireland, with promising results. There is growing anecdotal evidence that the most successful student mediators are those youngsters who were themselves actively engaged in negative conflicts. Despite these notable examples the mediation movement is still in its infancy – to the extent that the Elton Committee (DES 1989) was unable to report on any ongoing projects in schools in this country. However, by 1991, Southwark Mediation Centre, a charitable organisation, was advertising nationally for 'a Schools Worker to promote face-to-face mediation between students'. At the time of writing, interest continues to grow and there are now a number of organisations under the umbrella of MEDIATION UK and ENCORE (European Network for Conflict Resolution in Education): further information and training are available from the Education Advisory Programme of Quaker Peace and Service.

This chapter describes two surveys. The first is of a large number of pastoral staff drawn from secondary schools in one Local Education Authority to illuminate their role in conflicts between young people. The responses of these experienced teachers provide insight into the everyday context and perceived causes of conflicts in schools, but, more important, a set of distinct and different strategies emerge which go together to make up 'good practice'. On this basis the authors propose a simple, three-part model to help practitioners reflect upon their efforts to help others.

In a further study, undertaken as a follow-up, a national sample of secondary school students were asked about the sources of their disagreements, how they dealt with them and how they saw the role of teachers. Conflict theory is then considered in some detail and combined with this research to generate practical implications for the prevention and reduction of conflict in schools.

STAFF SURVEY

In 1989 questionnaires were sent to the pastoral deputy head teachers of local secondary schools – 30 in all. The deputy head teachers were asked to distribute copies of the questionnaire to key pastoral staff and, in the event, 103 responses were received from 24 schools. Clearly, it was not possible to calculate the percentage-return, but the authors have no reason to assume that the replies were biased owing to self-selection.

(a) *Frequency* When asked how often they were involved in resolving disputes between pupils, pastoral staff responded as shown in Table 14.1. Resolving conflicts does therefore seem to be an important part of the work of a teacher with a pastoral role – for 80 per cent it was at least a weekly occurrence.

(b) *Source of dispute* When teachers were asked an open-ended question about the source of conflict they tended to offer a list of between 1 and 4 items. The results are shown in Table 14.2.

(c) *Methods of dealing with conflicts* The authors identified a limited number of themes or strategies, which will be described as 'Styles' and discussed later in a three-part model of conflict. In general terms, the overwhelming majority of respondents tend to listen to pupils, either

Table 14.1 Frequency of conflicts

Frequency	Number of responses
Rarely	20
Once a week	37
3 times a week	30
More than once a day	15
More than 3 times a day	1

Table 14.2 Sources of dispute

Source	Percentage of total reasons given
Name-calling	23
Boy/girlfriends	14
Broken friendships	14
Bullying	11
Possessions	9
Queue-jumping	6
Trivia	6
Other (family feuds, tale-telling, games, racism)	17

individually or together, in order to find out more about the source and history of the disagreement. Thereafter, they may draw attention to the views and feelings of others, point out the consequences of various actions or identify alternative ways of behaving/thinking. A very small number of respondents indicated that they would deal with disputes by punishment alone, perhaps due to a misreading of 'conflict' as 'violence'. Some teachers described involving other pupils, either in establishing what had occurred or in the actual resolution of conflict. Parents may be involved in some situations. Finally, teachers varied in their tendency to impose their own solution in contrast to one formulated by the young people themselves.

(d) *Limitations to the role of the pastoral staff* To the authors' surprise, most teachers did not respond that they would adopt different methods if they had more time available, which, taken with the totality of their other comments, suggests that they are not unhappy with the way in which they approach conflicts. However, some teachers did regret that they could not deal with disputes in more depth and had no time for follow-up work. Other respondents mentioned lack of office space and privacy to conduct their work, while others alluded to perceived pressure for 'results' from colleagues, parents or pupils.

A model for looking at conflict intervention

To help practitioners gain greater insight into their own behaviour, the authors propose a three-part model for dealing with conflict between young people:

1 Identify the relevant *issues*.
2 Select the *style*.
3 Implement the specific *tactics*.

1 Some *issues*:

  When practitioners tackle a conflict event it is evident that they must take account of a range of relevant *issues* before acting, for example: Who is involved? Is the time right – is a 'cooling off' period needed? Do we have time now – how long will it take – can it wait? Public or private? Do I need more information? Should I refer on? It is not clear to what extent choice of *style* is affected by perceived *issues*.

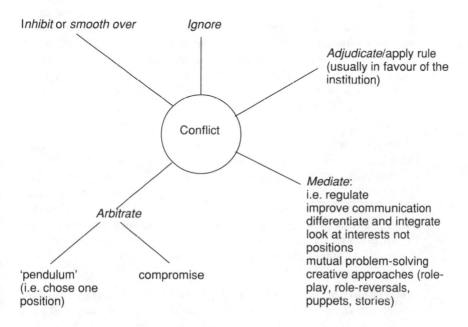

Figure 14.1 Styles of resolving conflict

2 *Styles* of resolving conflict

  From the responses to the survey and the available literature, the authors identified five major styles of resolving conflict (see Figure 14.1). It is important to note that the descriptive terms were chosen by the authors. On the basis of their own personal experiences, and subsequent discussions with teachers, it seems that adults have little initial insight into the styles/strategies which they adopt when dealing with young people in conflict, even though their interventions may be appropriate and successful. It is not suggested here that any particular intervention can be described as being exclusively one particular style and there may be elements of several in sequence.

(a) *Inhibit or smooth over*

(b) *Ignore*

These styles were reported in the survey as sometimes being associated with the use of humour or distracting tactics. There was some suggestion that teachers used these where they perceived the source of conflict to be trivial or unresolvable.

(c) *Adjudicate*

This refers to those situations where the adult makes reference to an external rule, either explicit or implicit (e.g. 'no swearing' or 'no fighting') rather than dealing with the content of the disagreement. Presumably, where conflict has escalated into violence, or grossly anti-social behaviour, adults will necessarily be led towards this more authoritarian style of intervention, with varying degrees of more constructive follow-up work.

(d) *Arbitrate*

Elements of arbitration were frequently mentioned in the survey and, borrowing a concept from industrial relations, could be broadly subdivided into the 'compromise' and the 'pendulum'. In 'compromise', the teacher/negotiator attempts to gain agreement to an outcome midway between the two positions, whereas in 'pendulum' he/she listens to both points of view and then, without modification, selects one of them (i.e. this seems to incorporate the notion of one party in the conflict being 'right' and the other being 'wrong').

(e) *Mediate*

It was of interest to the authors that this term was not used by any of the teachers in the survey, and there was no evidence that any had been exposed to this specific form of training, although many of the respondents described using elements of a mediation process. When it was put to them in the questionnaire, most teachers expressed interest in learning more about mediation and the idea of involving pupils as mediators.

It is suggested here that people do not have ready access to the underlying assumptions which guide their interventions when faced with conflicts. It seems likely that most of us are able to operate more than one style and, as with all social and personal coping skills, it would be dysfunctional if this were not the case. It must be assumed that, to varying extents, an individual adopts a particular style depending on his/her assessment of the background and nature of the conflict. For example, any indication that the conflict is likely to recur would imply that eventually constructive steps must be taken to help the youngsters resolve their disagreement, rather than merely inhibit or ignore it. Since some styles take longer than others to operate, especially mediation, the best use of available time would be an important consideration.

PUPIL SURVEY

In 1990, a follow-up survey asked the young people themselves similar sorts of questions in an attempt to examine their own perspectives on conflicts in school. Teachers who had been attending training seminars linked to the first study presented their tutor groups with the new questionnaire. The 450 responses were grouped in batches of 20 to 30 from schools all over England and Wales and covered years 7 to 11 fairly evenly.

(a) *Frequency* When asked how often they fell out with other pupils, 73 per cent responded with 'rarely' (i.e. less than once a week), while at the other extreme 8 per cent claimed to do so '3 times a week or more'.

(b) *Source of disputes* The responses to an open-ended question were categorised as shown in Table 14.3.

Table 14.3 Responses to an open-ended question on sources of dispute

Source	Percentage of total reasons given
Friendship issues	37.0
Trivia	32.0
Name-calling	7.5
Girl/boyfriends	7.5
Possessions	6.0
Other	10.0

'Friendship issues' included disputes about rumours being spread, not calling for someone, jealousy about who is talking to whom, etc. 'Trivia' refers to indications that quarrels were over relatively unimportant issues, such as 'silly things' or 'nothing in particular'. Conflicts over material resources or school curriculum/organisation were rarely reported.

(c) *Methods of resolving conflicts* Responses to an open-ended question produced the categories shown in Table 14.4. Nearly half the sample reported that they made no attempt to discuss their difficulties, but tended instead to carry on their lives next day as if nothing had happened. Conversely, the other half of the sample did try conciliation. Very rarely were others asked to help.

(d) *The role of teachers* When asked how often they approached teachers for help, 73 per cent of the students reported that they 'never' went to staff and 17 per cent indicated 'rarely'. The personal nature of these disagreements was repeatedly and strongly stated. Finally, when asked what more teachers might do to help, 79 per cent of the students replied that they could think of nothing else.

Table 14.4 Methods of resolving conflicts

Method	Percentage of total reasons given
Ignore the quarrel	45.0
Apologise	39.0
Talk it through	11.0
Involve a third party	2.5
Leave it unresolved	2.5

At first sight there might appear to be a mismatch between the two sets of (admittedly impressionistic) estimates of how often teachers are involved in pupil conflict. It is not clear whether pastoral staff are spending dispro-portionate amounts of their time with a relatively few youngsters. Even if disputes were spread evenly among pupils, the statistical ratio of pupils/teachers is sufficient to account for the pastoral workload. While young people may argue for a private resolution, their behaviour often interrupts the flow of school life to the extent that staff are compelled to intervene. Lastly, spontaneous comments confirmed that, where violence or theft are concerned, adult involvement is seen as legitimate and welcome.

Discussion

Life without conflict is inconceivable. At a cognitive (mental) level we regularly find ourselves with thoughts or attitudes which are contradictory and, as a result, spend mental energy trying to reconcile them. One influential psychologist, Festinger, described these opposing beliefs as causing 'cognitive dissonance' and proposed that people vary in their powers of resolution or tolerance. As with most things in life, moderation would appear to be the key to healthy personal growth: excessive tolerance of cognitive dissonance might entail incomplete learning about life or stereotyped thinking, while the converse might lead to high levels of anxiety or anger.

Argued from this point of view, conflict is an essentially solitary experi-ence concerned with an individual's thoughts and ideas. It may be concep-tualised as an 'internal' process which becomes 'external' when other people are directly involved. This is consistent with the work of rational emotive therapists, such as Beck (1989), who emphasise that events or situations on their own are less important than how we think about them and that this is shaped by powerful internal beliefs or rules (e.g. 'I should always be in control.' 'My colleagues must not make mistakes.' 'My child should be perfect'). They postulate that unrealistic internal rules contrib-ute to a range of emotional difficulties.

In the present discussion, unrealistic rules are more likely to be contra-dictcd by the behaviour of other people, which in turn sets up internal conflict. If this remains unresolved and is of intolerable intensity it may engender feelings of anxiety or anger. In either case the ability of the individual to interact positively with others is diminished. Should the conflict become external, much thoughtful effort will be required to achieve a constructive outcome, whose characteristics are described below (sadly, the salient features of destructive conflict will be familiar to all of us):

CONSTRUCTIVE CONFLICT

characterised by:
— discussion of issues, not people
— willingness to listen and understand

— mutual, creative problem-solving to meet all interests

results in:
— win/win outcomes
— new thinking
— change (personal, institutional or in society)
— contributes to self-knowledge

DESTRUCTIVE CONFLICT

characterised by:
— individuals feeling threatened
— personalities intruding
— emotional outbursts
— conflicts are expected and this leads to self-fulfilling prophecy
— rigid defence of 'position'

results in:
— win/lose outcomes
— unrcsolved problems
— bad feelings

Conflict may usefully be construed as resulting from a perceived psycho-logical threat. It follows that to understand a given situation we need to look beyond the immediate circumstances to take account of the signifi-cance of the events to the antagonists. This is consistent with the assertion that conflict is as likely to arise from a clash of values or beliefs as a disagreement over material resources.

To summarise, both the internal and external aspects of conflict can best be regarded as inevitable and integral parts of life. Although it is often sensible to avoid disagreements, taken to extremes this approach becomes self-defeating. At an individual level, a person who persistently fails to assert his or her point of view, or tries to prevent others from doing so, is courting the risk of unresolved issues and bad feelings. Indeed, apparently irrational anger is sometimes a result of a failure to be sufficiently assertive, and thereby risk conflict, over relatively minor issues, which eventually accumulatc.

At a group level, conformity pressures may inhibit conflicting points of view altogether, resulting in errors of decision-making known as 'group-think': the effects may be catastrophic.

So far, this discussion has been of a general nature and by no means restricted to conflict between students in schools: it is equally relevant to teacher/student or teacher/teacher disagreements. Regardless of age or role, the human qualities best suited to managing conflict successfully are:

(a) to be able to deal effectively with mental contradictions ('cognitive dissonance');
(b) to have practical, detailed and flexible internal rules;
(c) to possess the motivation and inter-personal skills to resolve external conflict when it occurs.

At times mature guidance will be required in the form of listening, supporting, reflecting or occasionally intervening. This is the role into which teachers may find themselves drawn when young people choose not, or are unable, to resolve their conflict privately. At the most basic level, teachers are responsible for an orderly and safe learning environment, but the additional challenge facing them on such occasions is the opportunity to promote 'personal growth' by helping to achieve a constructive outcome.

However, the response of the teachers in the survey indicates that lengthy mediation is usually regarded as impractical or inappropriate. The comments of the young people corroborate this. They indicate that they resolve most disagreements themselves quickly and easily though perhaps not always appropriately or fully. Adult help is sought primarily where violence, bullying or theft are involved. Cullingford (1988) commented on this in his investigation of children's attitudes towards school rules. Universally, the potential for conflict is reduced by the existence of clear, practical and legitimate rules or guidelines, which can be used as an external point of reference either by participants or 'mediators'.

Any analysis of conflict in schools must also take account of the special circumstances of adolescence, the time when young people begin the transition from childhood to adulthood. To understand this progression psychoanalysts talk of a 'second individualisation' (the first having occurred in infancy), while psychotherapists emphasise the change in 'self-image' (from family-bestowed to peer-bestowed), and sociologists talk of the acquisition of new 'roles'. A more pragmatic approach is the idea of developmental tasks which are to be accomplished during adolescence word (Havinghurst 1953):

1 Achieving new and more mature relations with age-mates of both sexes.
2 Achieving a masculine or feminine social role.
3 Accepting one's physique and using the body effectively.

4 Achieving emotional independence of parents and other adults.
5 Achieving assurance of economic independence.
6 Selecting and preparing for an occupation.
7 Preparing for marriage and family life.
8 Developing intellectual skills and concepts necessary for civic competence.
9 Desiring and achieving socially responsible behaviour.
10 Acquiring a set of values and an ethical system as a guide to behaviour.
(Havinghurst 1953)

Although some of these ideas may appear archaic four decades on, the point is well made that young people are faced by a compelling agenda. Perhaps their behaviour can most usefully be understood as pursuing common developmental tasks, while schools may consider their own part in helping or hindering.

IMPLICATIONS FOR SCHOOLS AND COLLEGES

It has been argued previously that unlike some of the behavioural manifestations of conflict (for example, fighting), it is simply not realistic to work towards a total eradication of conflict within an institution. Rich, diverse and sometimes conflicting ideas promote personal, intellectual and organisational growth. It should go without saying, however, that many sources of conflict are unnecessary and avoidable in a thoughtfully run school or college that takes account of the needs of its students and staff. Conversely, organisational or curricular inadequacies, which bring about increased levels of confusion, frustration or under-stimulation, will lead to unresolved or badly resolved conflict.

On the basis of the theoretical backgrounds to conflict and adolescence, these survey data and their professional work with schools, the authors have identified the following practical implications:

1 The senior management team and governors should take responsibility for establishing a culture within which conflict is recognised as an integral part of life. Healthy organisational growth thrives on positively managed conflict. This consideration spans all levels of relationships: from pupil to head teacher and chair of governors.
2 Explicit, proactive approaches to conflicts are essential. These will address how, where and when disagreements involving students, parents, staff and governors will be resolved.
3 Adult confidence and good practice will act as a powerful model for others.
4 An effective pastoral response relies on clear and simple rules aimed at minimising the disruptive effects of student disputes. Usually, lengthy conciliation is neither appropriate nor sought. Equally, staff should be

able to support, listen and intervene when necessary in instances of real difficulty. Organisational planning will need to acknowledge this by making time and space available.

5 Responses to student behaviour should take account of the special circumstances of adolescence and individual levels of maturity.

6 Curriculum leaders should develop cross-curricular themes relating to the needs of others, conflict resolution, individual differences, human rights and citizenship.

7 All staff will benefit from training opportunities in:
(a) theories of conflict and adolescence;
(b) their own role in conflict and management, including the considered use of different intervention styles;
(c) the active encouragement of intellectual differences between students to promote new learning.

If our educational system is going to produce young people who are adequately prepared for adult life and the demands of citizenship, then the issue of conflict must be addressed positively. Ours is a pluralistic, multi-cultural and ever-changing society, within which widely differing perspectives are inevitable. We should seek to equip young adults with personal strategies to deal with differences without them becoming anxious, inhibiting or authoritarian. To achieve this, teachers need time and training opportunities to reflect upon the nature of social interactions in school, and especially in the context of the developmental imperatives of adolescence.

REFERENCES

Antcliffe, J. (1989) 'Some approaches to conflict with adolescents in classrooms', *Maladjustment and Therapeutic Education*, 7, 1.

Beck, A.T. (1989) *Love is Never Enough: How Couples Can Overcome Misunderstandings, Resolve Conflicts and Solve Relationship Problems Through Cognitive Therapy*. Harmondsworth: Penguin.

Cullingford, C. (1988) 'School rules and children's attitudes to discipline', *Educational Research*, 30, 1.

Department of Education and Science (1989) *Discipline in Schools* (The Elton Report). London: HMSO.

ENCORE (European Network for Conflict Resolution in Education) is administered by the Quaker Peace and Service Advisory Programme, Friends House, Euston Road, London NW1 2BJ.

Fisher, R. and Ury, W. (1981) *Getting to Yes*. London: Arrow Books.

Forum for Initiatives in Reparation and Mediation (FIRM). National Office: 19 London End, Beaconsfield, Bucks HP9 2HN (their journal is *Mediation*).

Havinghurst, R.J. (1953) *Human Development and Education*. New York: Longman.

Institute for the Study and Treatment of Delinquency, Kings College London, and Kingston Polytechnic.

Kingston Friends Workshop, Quaker Meeting House, 78 Eden Street, Kingston upon Thames KT1 1DJ.

Kreidler, W.J. (1982) *Creative Conflict Resolution*. Glenview, Ill.: Scott, Foresman.

Marshall, T. (1987) 'Mediation: a new mode of establishing order in schools', *The Howard Journal of Criminal Justice*, 26, 1.

MEDIATION UK, 82a Gloucester Road, Bristol BS7 8BN.

Nicholas, F.M. (1987) *Coping with Conflict: A Resource Book for the Middle School Years*. Wisbech: Learning Development Aids.

Priest, S.J. (1989) 'Some practical approaches to bullying', in E. Roland and E. Munthe (eds) *Bullying: An International Perspective*. London: Fulton, in association with the Professional Development Foundation.

Quaker Peace and Service: Education Advisory Programme (including Friends Book Centre), Friends House, Euston Road, London NW1 2BJ.

Southwark Mediation Centre, 131 Camberwell Road, London SE5 0HF.

Tizard, B.P., Blatchford, P., Burke, J., Farquhar, C. and Plewis, I. (1988) *Young Children at School in the Inner City*. Hove: Lawrence Erlbaum.

Chapter 15

The management of playground and lunchtime behaviour

Andre Imich and Kath Jefferies

Think back to your days at school and the time spent in the playground at breaktime and at lunchtime. What do you remember as the good and not-so-good times?

For most people, this question is likely to evoke strong recollections of playground time which have a distinct balance of positive and negative points. Children spend one-quarter of their school day in the playground, and it therefore represents a considerable proportion of the total time spent in school. However, it is only in recent years that educationists have given much serious consideration to this particular issue. Among the reasons for the growing interest has been the increased clarity over the responsibility for lunchtime supervision, a growing body of research into the psychological impact of children's playground experiences, and the increasing recognition by teachers that playground difficulties can continue into the classroom.

The present chapter presents an overview of the general issues that affect the management of pupil behaviour in the playground. It then outlines one school's strategy to improve pupil behaviour throughout the whole lunchtime period, including the playground. Finally, there is a summary of factors that are likely to be essential in any school-based review of its own lunchtime and playground management structures.

BACKGROUND

A significant issue with regard to lunchtime has always been a need for clarity over the status of lunchtime supervision, and, in particular, the question of whose responsibility is the management of this supervision. The 1968 School Meals Agreement accepted that teaching staff actually had no contractual duty to supervise children at lunchtime. However, primarily through commitment and goodwill, many teachers, particularly at primary school, continued to offer supervision and activities for pupils during the lunchtime.

The introduction of new working conditions for teachers in 1987 reinforced the position that teachers were not required to supervise at lunch-time and, at that time, teachers largely ceased their contribution. However, the 1968 Agreement stated quite clearly that the head teacher is required to retain overall responsibility at lunchtime, and this was main-tained in the new conditions of service. Many head teachers find the task onerous and stressful, particularly in circumstances which were highlighted by Partlington's observation that 'it is now only the presence of the head actually supervising which prevents mayhem or worse' (Partlington 1987: 214). Thus, as head teachers have increasingly carried the weight of lunchtime supervision on their own shoulders, with minimal support from their teaching colleagues, there has been an increased need to determine how best to organise lunchtimes to effect manageable pupil behaviour.

In 1988, Tizard *et al.* investigated the experiences of young children at school in the inner city. They found that playtime and lunchtime were often perceived by young children as either the best or the worst side of school life. The majority of children reported that life in the playground was often verbally and physically aggressive. More recently, studies into bullying have shown that most incidents occur in school playgrounds, where supervision is usually less structured and less adult-intensive than in the classroom.

Elliott (cited in Dorking 1987) investigated the experiences of 4,000 children. She found that more than one-third had been bullied badly or frequently in the playground to the extent that they felt badly upset about it.

In most cases, the victims never told teachers or parents about the incidents, thereby making it increasingly likely that the playground would continue to be a source of anxiety for many pupils. Clearly, educationalists generally regard the playground as a positive opportunity for children to develop a range of important developmental skills, particularly social ones such as the ability to play constructively and cooperatively with others. Additionally, playtime should be enjoyable for children, adding to their enjoyment of the whole-school experience. If, as Elliott's research indicates, a substantial proportion of children find playgrounds a negative experience, then we can hypothesise that these children are at a higher risk of educational failure in terms of classroom performance. There is evidence that for many school non-attenders, it is what goes on outside the classroom that contributes to their non-attendance. For example, Croft and Grygier (1956) noted that truants have few friends and are emotionally and physically isolated – these problems are often highlighted for such children through their playground experiences.

The Elton Report (DES 1989) found that the supervision of pupils at lunchtime was the biggest single behaviour-related problem faced by many schools, even in those schools which were generally regarded as well-ordered. Elton noted that the midday supervisors do not have the same status with children as do teachers, nor are they trained in group management skills.

Elton felt that an important way forward would be to employ some teachers within every school for lunchtime supervision, with appropriate remuneration. These teachers could play the role of leader or midday supervisory teams. With increased autonomy over financial management now in place for schools, this is certainly a real possibility for head teachers to consider. In addition, Elton felt that midday supervisors should be given adequate training in the management of pupil behaviour.

KEY FACTORS IN PLAYGROUND BEHAVIOUR

In order to determine how to improve pupil behaviour in the playground, it is important to identify some of the key factors that are likely to influence behaviour. First, individual differences should be noted. Some children, usually boys, tend to be more physically active and use up considerably more space in the playground. Other children, usually girls, will spend their time chatting to each other or playing word or action games, such as skipping. Perhaps more than any other activity, it is football that epitomises the gender differences. Many men as adults recall football as one of the things they liked most about lunchtime, whereas many women quote football as one of the things they most disliked! What is important in managing lunchtime is to acknowledge that such differences may exist, and to accommodate the needs of all the groups appropriately and fairly.

Racism is a second key factor to consider, although there is little detailed research on the matter. Most of what is known about racism in schools has emerged from the inquiry into the murder of an Asian boy in the playground in a high school in Manchester. This inquiry concluded that this particular violent incident was racially motivated to some degree. The inquiry also carried out some research into other schools and found that racism was occurring constantly. The majority of reported incidents focused on name-calling, which made the individuals concerned feel both angry and upset. The research (Kelly and Cohen 1988) also reported that only a tiny minority of these incidents were being drawn to the attention of teachers. It is important that staff are aware that racism is likely to be occurring in the playground and that a lack of reported incidents should not lead to complacency.

The length of time that children are required to spend in the playground can also be another important factor in determining the levels of difficult behaviour. This is particularly the case at lunchtime, when pupils are often expected to be outside in the playground for well over one hour. This represents a considerable amount of time for young people to find themselves in an unstructured situation. Boredom will inevitably creep in, whether the young person is five or fifteen years of age, and it is not therefore surprising that undesirable behaviour occurs. The provision of lunchtime activities, with suitable materials and supervision, can help to minimise this problem, as can reconsideration of the length of lunchtimes.

The age of pupils needs to be considered. Children entering school for the first time will never have experienced time spent in a confined area with as many as two or three hundred other young people. This can often be a reason for children starting school being overwhelmed by the whole-school experience. There is a particular need for such children to be taught, and shown, by adults how to spend their time in the playground. Similarly, in the teenage years, an expectation that young people will be able to amuse themselves is often misguided.

Weather conditions and temperature are other important variables. Children are often expected to go outside in all extremes of weather conditions. Teachers themselves on playground supervision at playtimes are often unwilling to walk around on very cold and blustery days! For those children who already find the social experience of playgrounds difficult, or who have inadequate clothing, or who are slightly unwell, the playground becomes particularly uninviting under such circumstances. Providing for greater flexibility in arrangements would have great benefits for a large number of children.

The amount of space available in which to play invariably affects the ways in which children will behave. For example, the contentious issues regarding football become even more exaggerated in smaller, more confined spaces. It is often difficult for schools to influence the amount of space that can be provided for playtime activity, but again, with greater consideration, it may be possible to be more flexible through, for example, considering the use of other school areas, such as the school hall, for certain activities.

Finally, the availability of materials, facilities and resources is another key factor. All too often, children are expected to use playgrounds with almost no materials or facilities and are then expected to find ways of amusing themselves. It is again not surprising that this can lead to undesirable behaviour. Increasingly, schools are beginning to consider the availability of materials and facilities and are finding that, where children are gainfully engaged in activity, there are fewer problematic incidents. A range of lunchtime activities can be organised, such as computer clubs, chess clubs, handwriting, homework, and reading, which will be positively welcomed and constructively used by many pupils.

When we consider the range of issues facing those adults who manage pupils in the playground, it is not surprising that midday assistants often find effective management difficult to achieve. This key group of adults, who are always low paid and who usually receive no training, are expected to deal with these key issues. Additionally, they have a wide range of daily tasks to undertake, as was highlighted by the OPTIS materials (1986). These identify a range of tasks that midday assistants undertake such as:

— Control the dinner queue.
— Supervise pupils eating their dinners.
— Collect meal tickets.
— Keep pupils out of classrooms when they should be outside.
— Check that pupils don't hang around places where they shouldn't.
— Control the behaviour of pupils throughout the lunchtime.
— Discipline pupils who break the rules.
— Deal with accidents.
— Keep young children occupied.

In order to improve the behaviour of pupils in the playground, Evans (1990) felt that there were some important prerequisites. Children needed to be given a greater say in devising the rules of the playground. By talking about playground behaviour in the classroom, children can begin to see the importance of this issue, and are more likely to implement changes in behaviour if they have been involved in deciding what the changes need to be. The ultimate aim is to give children more responsibility for their own behaviour in the playground.

Evans also pointed out that many positive benefits accrue from consideration of the physical structure of the playground itself. He noted that there were fewer behaviour problems in playgrounds which were structured to provide children with a range of play opportunities.

Rules, or codes of conduct, for the playground, when devised by pupils, will tend to be simple yet considerate. In one primary school Blatchford found the following playground rules:

1 We will always be kind and considerate to everybody in the playground.
2 We will look after the playground and make sure it is always a nice place to be in.
3 We will share the playground space so that other games, besides football, can be played.
4 Even if we are doing something exciting and important, we will stop and listen to any instruction an adult may give us.

(Blatchford 1989)

A WHOLE-SCHOOL APPROACH

The first step in dealing with problems related to lunchtime is to acknowledge their existence and to recognise that they are problems in *educational* terms. This is what the head teacher of a large junior school did in seeking support to deal with this particular issue (Jefferies and Imich 1987). The head teacher was finding that an increasing amount of time was being spent in having to deal with a succession of unruly pupils referred to him by the midday staff; he felt that the situation could be managed more effectively.

It is important to note that this school did not suffer a greater amount of pupil misbehaviour than did neighbouring schools. As the Elton Report recorded, lunchtime supervision arrangements were 'a source of difficulty even in the best ordered schools' (DES 1989: 122). In this instance, the head teacher was merely acknowledging the existence of these difficulties and was actively seeking solutions.

Through discussion with the school's educational psychologist, a number of possible ways forward were explored. At that time, the school had access to a behaviour support teacher, whose role was to support school initiatives in the field of behaviour. It was agreed that it would be a reasonable, and desirable, extension of the support teacher's role to investigate what was happening in this hitherto 'grey' area of the school day.

In order to gain a clearer picture of existing practice and problems, the behaviour support teacher undertook an observation schedule over a three-week period. This included shadowing the midday supervisors, discussing issues with them, finding out the views of pupils, observing the pupils' play, and examining the logistics of feeding three hundred and sixty pupils in little more than an hour in the school hall. This observation period generated the following findings:

1 Midday supervisors spent a large proportion of their time in verbal conflict with pupils. Pupils would automatically question instructions from midday supervisors and noisy exchanges were common.

2 The majority of the pupils behaved reasonably, but received little or no positive acknowledgement.

3 Many pupils tended to be rather familiar or dismissive towards midday supervisors. One pupil remarked that 'they've got no right to tell us off – they're not teachers, they're only dinner-ladies'.

4 The perceived effectiveness of individual midday supervisors varied among the pupils. Some were identified by pupils as 'naggers' or as being unfair, while others were thought to be 'soft'. Some pupils complained that midday supervisors did not take notice of, or respond to, problems that were reported.

5 Midday supervisors reported that insolence, rudeness and being sworn at were the most unacceptable behaviours that they faced. They were more tolerant of fighting, which was fairly rare, and dealt with these incidents competently.

6 Poor communication between midday and teaching staff could lead to resentment over pupils sometimes being allowed into classrooms,

which was against the rules, and midday supervisors felt that some teachers were unreasonable in not providing activities for wet lunchtimes.

7 Wet lunchtimes were universally disliked and posed extra problems of supervision – the seven midday supervisors were not able physically to cover the inside and outside classrooms.

8 The high level of pupil movement in and out of the main school building caused the most frequent problems of supervision, especially in determining who had legitimate access to particular areas.

9 There was a tendency to rush pupils through the dinner system, with queues forming in several places to service the main queue. Observation showed an example of one child having to wait fifteen minutes to collect his dinner. While waiting in line, unruly pushing and noisy behaviour was common.

10 Pupils complained of boredom in the playground. They would have liked to take toys or games out, but this was either not allowed or other pupils interfered with their games. It was interesting to note that midday supervisors were well aware that pupils misbehaved because they had little else to do, but felt that they as a group were powerless to effect change.

11 Boys presented most supervision problems. They broke the rules more, were told off more and were more often cheeky to midday supervisors.

One conclusion from the period of observation was that the apparent low status and low self-esteem of the midday supervisors needed to be regarded as a key issue of supervision at lunchtime. Pupils treated the midday supervisors differently from the rest of the school staff and they were obviously considered to be 'fair game' for 'winding up' by difficult pupils. This difficulty was compounded by a lack of effective rewards or sanctions through which midday supervisors could establish their authority. A key aim of change was seen as increasing their status in the eyes of pupils if they were to be taken seriously.

The second key issue identified was pupil boredom, which contributed strongly to poor behaviour. If pupils were given access to legitimate activities, they were less likely to misbehave and supervision would be more successful.

Once the observation findings had been clarified, meetings were held between the head teacher, the midday supervisors, and the behaviour support teacher to discuss the implications and jointly to seek possible solutions. As a measure of their commitment to work positively towards change, it is important to note that the time used for these meetings was out of working hours for the midday supervisors, i.e. they were not being paid for their attendance.

Initially, there had been concerns by the head teacher and the support teacher that the midday supervisors could have felt undermined by this project, but once they had been fully involved in consultation meetings, they were eager to cooperate. They too were unhappy about the current organisation and management of lunchtimes.

Through continued discussion, four broad aims for an alternative system for the management of lunchtime behaviour were outlined:

1 To establish a consistent approach among midday assistants when dealing with pupils and to improve their management skills.
2 To improve the behaviour of pupils towards the midday staff.
3 To improve the status of midday supervisors in the eyes of the pupils.
4 To identify organisational practices which could be improved.

A significant change in the organisation of the school dining system was proposed. A more structured system for the seating arrangements would be introduced. In future, pupils would be required to fill each table as directed by the midday supervisor.

Only when *all* the pupils at each table had finished eating could they all raise their hands and seek permission to leave. The midday supervisor would allow them to go if the table and floor areas were free of litter. This would avoid the common problem of messy floors and argument about who should clear it up. Permission to leave would not be given if the area was not clean. The midday supervisor could award a 'team point' to willing volunteers!

The issue about low status was seen as a priority for change, and a range of proposals were formulated. A simple but extremely effective step of giving each midday supervisor a name badge and encouraging pupils to address them properly was introduced; this helped to establish their identity.

Strategies and principles for the management of pupil behaviour were discussed. These included the need for good behaviour to be observed and commented upon, and the expectation that pupils would address all midday staff by title and surname. Midday supervisors were encouraged to deal only with what they had actually seen, rather than listening to tale-telling, and to deal equally with all those involved in an incident. In addition, a new system, which included a range of sanctions, for dealing with misdemeanours in the playground was made available. This was aimed at increasing authority and effectiveness and consisted of three distinct stages.

Stage One – Time Out: For minor offences the pupil was seated in a designated area, away from other pupils, for five to ten minutes without communicating with others. When the time was up, the pupil was given permission to leave by the midday supervisor who had placed him there.

Stage Two – A Yellow Card: This was reserved for serious offences, examples of which were agreed by the midday supervisors in advance to ensure consistent application. The midday supervisor would give the offender a card detailing the offence, which the pupil must hold until the same midday supervisor's signature is obtained for five subsequent days of good behaviour. When the five signatures had been obtained, the pupil would present the card to the head teacher, who would sign the pupil off. Each day the head teacher was to be informed of the names of pupils given cards. A pupil could be given a card by any midday supervisor and carry more than one at a time.

Stage Three – The Red Card: This would be the automatic consequence of receiving three yellow cards within a defined period of time (e.g. one school term). A period of time at home during lunchtime would follow, after the head teacher had informed parents.

These proposals, along with a variety of minor suggestions, were open for discussion at a subsequent meeting with the midday staff. It was made clear by the head teacher that the midday supervisors should approve any change, i.e. nothing would be introduced without their agreement.

The midday supervisors were able to express their views and concerns, thus enabling the meetings to contain a strong training element. The importance of behaving consistently and positively, how to deal with difficult situations, how *they* could deal with unacceptable behaviour, the importance of avoiding confrontation and argument, etc., were addressed. This was the first opportunity that midday supervisors had ever had for these vital issues to be discussed in an open, positive way. This initial meeting proved to be very productive; most proposals were accepted, some were amended and a few were rejected. Agreement was reached and all were eager to set the ideas into motion.

As a result of this meeting, the head teacher produced a detailed record of agreed practice, which would serve to maintain consistency and act as a comprehensive job description for future midday staff. In addition, it was agreed that the head teacher would hold regular meetings with midday supervisors on a half-termly basis. These meetings would of course be voluntary, since resources to pay for the training of midday supervisors were unavailable at that time.

The first step involved in implementing the new system involved a detailed letter being sent to all parents, focusing on the school's desire to encourage politeness and good behaviour at lunchtime. The system was then introduced to the pupils by the head teacher during a lengthy assembly, where pupils were able to ask questions until it was clearly understood. It was made plain that receipt of a yellow card was to be regarded as a serious matter. Lunchtime behaviour was then referred to occasionally at future assemblies to ensure that it remained a high priority, and pupils were provided with feedback.

The new system was carefully and regularly evaluated. At the first review, six weeks later, undertaken by the behaviour support teacher, it was noted that the pupils had adapted to the system very quickly. The midday supervisors found it easy to operate and were keen to make it work. All parties were still full of enthusiasm, partly bolstered by unexpected publicity from the local media, which undoubtedly contributed to improved self-esteem for the midday staff.

The head teacher was extremely pleased – lunchtimes were generally happier for both pupils and midday supervisors and there had been almost total cooperation from parents. Very few yellow cards had been given out and the few that had been issued were taken very seriously by pupils. Regular meetings were planned for the future and the head teacher remarked that 'for the first time, I feel that the middays are part of the school'.

Further evaluation was undertaken by the behaviour support teacher a year later. In follow-up discussions with the midday supervisors, it was evident that they were more confident in their management of pupils. They still found a few pupils difficult to manage, in that their poor behaviour had not reduced significantly, but what had changed was the willingness of midday supervisors to accept this as their responsibility and not that of the head teacher. They met regularly with the head teacher, even though they were still unpaid for this. They appreciated the consultation process and felt much more a part of the school. Newly appointed midday supervisors were pleased to have clear guidelines and settled in to their roles and responsibilities quickly and easily. The midday supervisors did not wish to change the system – it is significant that they felt they had the power to do this!

The head teacher was satisfied that the system was working well, and placed great value on the cooperation of the lunch staff and their regular meetings, commenting that perhaps the consultation process had more to do with bringing about change than did the system itself. The head teacher had, after all, helped to give the midday supervisors self-respect through the introduction of a genuine consultation process.

This was essentially a management-focused activity. On the whole, schools are often more concerned with the problems of control than the underlying causes of poor behaviour. During this project, and in subsequent replication in other schools, several ideas for improving the playground experience have been put forward but not taken up, usually on the grounds of lack of both human and material resources. Some schools have attempted to tackle the 'boredom factor', but this was generally regarded as of secondary importance to the control of pupil behaviour.

More recently, however, a more positive trend seems to be emerging. Some schools are beginning to look at their playgrounds with new eyes, introducing games and apparatus, providing seating areas and generally making playground areas more interesting places. Examples of this can be seen in the work of Learning Through Landscapes, a national organisation that provides advice to schools on how to optimise the physical environment of the playground. Schools which have pursued these developments report striking improvements in pupil behaviour.

THE WAYS FORWARD

It is evident that playground behaviour and the management of lunchtime are areas of concern for many schools, and several factors have been put forward to account for this. However, change and improvement are possible, as has been illustrated in the outline of a project in one large primary school. Subsequent work with other schools has produced encouraging evidence of change, and suggest that success needs to be built on the following factors.

By having a job description, midday assistants are given a clearly defined role. They, and those for whom they have responsibility, have an explicit set of guidelines that form the backbone of their duties. The quality of the induction process for new midday assistants is also greatly enhanced. In addition, full constructive support from the head teacher is paramount in effecting any positive change.

Lunchtime supervision is the ultimate responsibility of the head teacher and he or she needs to be seen by all those involved, particularly midday assistants and children, in leading change. The head teacher plays an important role in the information dissemination of new structures and procedures, and in the provision of meaningful feedback.

One of the most important facets of change is the 'humanisation' of midday assistants. All too often, midday assistants can be perceived, not just by the pupils but also by other members of staff, as peripheral to the school, and this attitude is reflected in their low status, poor remuneration, and lack of clarity over precisely what they do. By recognising that lunchtime is a key part of the school day, we can then recognise the importance of the role played by midday assistants and support them accordingly.

In considering issues about improving lunchtime, it is not sufficient to introduce change that effects only one element, i.e. the time spent in the playground. Strategies need to be considered that take account of all areas of pupil activity during the lunch period, including the arrangements for eating food (i.e. queuing systems, seating arrangements, how tables can be vacated), pupils being allowed in and out of school during the lunch period, dealing with minor cuts and bruises, toilet arrangements, and the facilities and supervision available during wet lunchtimes.

The training of midday assistants is another key aspect. The existence of a clear job description forms a useful starting point. However, as already discussed, midday assistants have a broad range of duties for which they have no training or qualifications, and which teachers themselves often find taxing. Input on basic behaviour management techniques, such as avoiding confrontation and noticing and praising good behaviour, as well as a basic foundation in first aid, would form important starting points. The opportunity to meet regularly with each other and with the head teacher can form a useful forum for shared problem-solving, as well as demonstrating a willingness to involve midday assistants.

The positive involvement and cooperation of teaching staff is important. Through their interest, teachers can demonstrate to pupils that the lunchtime period is indeed an integral and valuable part of the whole school day. Teachers can also play a crucial role in providing feedback about how their pupils behave at lunchtime, and in reinforcing good behaviour. They can also be helpful in making available some facilities and resources.

Finally, further evidence of effective change can be seen in the following feedback to the support teacher from a senior midday assistant of another school, two months after new systems for the management of pupil behaviour at lunchtime had been introduced: 'To date, my job in particular and that of all the midday assistants has been made a lot easier when dealing with incidents occurring during the lunchtime period. The new system was explained in detail by our head teacher to all of the pupils and all of the teaching staff. This enabled us to carry out the new system with ease.'

REFERENCES

Blatchford, P. (1989) *Playtime in the Primary School: Problems and Improvements.* Windsor: NFER–Nelson.

Croft, I.J. and Grygier, T.G. (1956) 'Social relationships of truants and juvenile delinquents', *Human Relations*, 9: 434–466.

Department of Education and Science (1987) *School Teachers' Pay and Conditions of Service.* London: HMSO.

Department of Education and Science (1989). *Discipline in Schools* (The Elton Report). London: HMSO.

Dorking, L. (1987) 'Bullying scares the child', *The Teacher*, 5 October 1987.

Evans, J. (1990) 'Teacher–child interaction during yard duty: the Australian experience', *Education 3–13*, 18, 2 June.

Imich, A.J. and Jefferies, K. (1989) 'Management of lunchtime behaviour', *Support for Learning*, 4, 1: 46–52.

Jefferies, K. and Imich, A.J. (1987) 'Showing the yellow card', *Times Educational Supplement*, 6 November 1987.

Kelly, E. and Cohen, T. (1988) *Racism in Schools: New Research Evidence*. Stoke-on-Trent: Trentham Books.

Learning Through Landscapes. *Making the Best of your School Grounds*. Video, available from Learning Through Landscapes, Technology House, Victoria Road, Winchester, Hants.

OPTIS (1986) *The OPTIS Lunchtime Supervision Pack*. Oxford: Oxfordshire Programme for Training, Instruction and Supervision.

Partlington, J. (1987) 'Heads you lose at lunchtime', *Education*, 11 September 1987.

Pink, H. and Brownlee, L. (1988) 'Playground politics: pairing off', *Times Educational Supplement*, 12 February 1988.

Tizard, B., Blatchford, P., Burke, J., Farquhar, C. and Plewis, I. (1988) *Young Children at School in the Inner City*. London: Lawrence Erlbaum.

Chapter 16

The role of non-teaching assistants in school responses to difficult behaviour

Carol Stewart-Evans

This chapter reviews some of the literature relating to the use of ancillary staff, and outlines a survey of such staff working with children with behaviour difficulties in one local authority. It describes the work they do, the problems they identified, and suggests some possible solutions.

Although ancillaries have been employed both in mainstream and special schools for many years, their numbers have increased considerably since the implementation of the 1981 Education Act. Many LEAs are appointing increasing numbers of ancillaries, particularly in the primary sector, to help teachers support children with special educational needs in mainstream schools (Goacher *et al*. 1988). In many authorities, pupils with difficult behaviour are maintained in mainstream schools only by virtue of being allocated additional help in the form of non-teaching personnel, often through the procedures of the 1981 Education Act. Such personnel may be known by a variety of titles, including welfare assistants, ancillaries, auxiliaries, nursery nurses, and teacher aides.

ROLE OF NON-TEACHING ASSISTANTS IN SCHOOLS

There has been very little research until recently into the role of ancillaries. Prior to the 1981 Act, they were commonly regarded as general helpers who would take on non-professional duties relating to care or supervision (Kolvin *et al*. 1981), thereby freeing the teacher from such tasks. Hegarty *et al*. (1981) described four roles taken on by ancillaries:

— 'care' – related both to physical care and promoting independence; particularly important when working with a child with physical disabilities.
— 'educational' – freed the teacher from routine activities or involved carrying out direct instruction under supervision from the teacher.
— 'para-professional' – involved helping with such activities as physiotherapy and speech therapy exercises.
— 'general' – a less defined role, but included acting as a mother figure, friend or confidante!

Hodgson *et al.* (1984) identified similar roles taken by the ancillary while more recent research (Clayton 1993) showed that ancillaries supporting children with special needs in mainstream primary schools 'spent most of their time on nine core activities most of which were educational in nature and to a lesser extent to do with behavioural management'. Only four of the 100 assistants in his survey spent all their time with the 'named' child, half worked with other special needs children or undertook general duties and 92 per cent said they also worked with normal children.

The current role of ancillaries in mainstream schools seems to be quite extensive. Although still involved in care and supervision duties, they now appear to have a more important role to play in educational activities.

SURVEY IN ONE LOCAL AUTHORITY

Other than the survey outlined in this chapter, there seems to be no British research specifically into the role of ancillaries in mainstream schools who work with children with behavioural problems, and their numbers are unknown. This survey (Stewart-Evans 1991) examined the use of ancillaries appointed in mainstream primary schools to support children whose statement of special educational needs related to behaviour difficulties. A detailed postal questionnaire was circulated to 73 ancillaries identified as working with children with behaviour difficulties in one LEA, which contained both inner-city and rural localities. The questionnaire covered conditions of employment, approaches to working in the school, activities undertaken, training and support, and issues related to job satisfaction. The overall response rate was 49 per cent. Children being supported had behaviour difficulties or a combination of behaviour difficulties and (specific) learning difficulties, with the majority (82 per cent) being boys. Some of the main problem areas arising for the ancillaries are identified below, and possible solutions are suggested.

PROBLEMS IDENTIFIED

The nature of the work

The majority of the assistants in the study said that the major difficulty with their named child was behavioural, with many descriptions of difficult behaviour falling into the category of those which cause harm to the child, to other children, to adults or to the environment. Other behaviours described caused no actual harm, but would obviously interfere with the child's learning. Verbatim descriptions indicated that assistants were having to cope with behaviours that could cause much anxiety, concern and stress. One of the many examples reported was: 'Climbing around the classroom or on the school roof and outbuildings, hiding behind or under the furniture, irritating other children by pulling faces, making silly noises, hitting, throwing things (including furniture). Eye contact and physical contact like touching hands or an arm round the shoulder, etc., used to be impossible . . . very hostile in both action and language.' The question arising is how well prepared assistants are to cope with such demanding behaviour, since only 24 per cent reported that they were currently working on either a behavioural programme or using recommended behavioural strategies and few had received any training.

Most children were integrated into the classroom for the majority of the time, with 73 per cent being withdrawn for small group work. Only 15 per cent of assistants worked solely with the child to whom they were allocated, with 67 per cent working in some way with small groups of children with special needs, and 18 per cent working generally in the classroom but focusing on the child when necessary.

Most assistants were engaged in both general educational activities and more specific educational activities. The most frequent duties reported by assistants were talking to their child, talking to other children, encouraging their child, helping their child with lessons, watching their child, preventing disruption by their child, preventing disruption by other children, listening to their child read and playing with their child.

Although the majority of assistants discussed their child with the teacher on a fairly regular basis, there were differences in practice with regard to record keeping. Under half reported that record keeping was a frequent activity, while over half said it was an infrequent activity. Stone (1990) emphasises the importance of keeping detailed records on children with both learning and behaviour difficulties in order to monitor behaviour and plan efficient strategies. The assistant is in a key position to observe and record such information and could have an important role in the communication system in the school relating to the needs of the child and in monitoring the effectiveness of the non-teaching provision.

A great number of assistants reported that additional difficulties with the child related to learning difficulties, although only 36 per cent of assistants said they were frequently involved in individual learning programmes. As the literature relating to learning difficulties suggests that children benefit from regular periods of intensive practice in specific skills, assistants could be trained to implement such programmes, such as direct instruction, and to monitor progress.

To summarise the work of assistants working with children with behaviour difficulties: they are most frequently involved in general support, educational activities and behaviour management with their child. They are also involved in activities with other children, although less frequently. 'Care' and 'para-professional' activities traditionally associated with ancillaries are rarely undertaken.

Job description, roles, and interpersonal factors

Clayton (1993) noted that many LEAs still do not issue their welfare assistants with job descriptions. In the current study, more than one-third of the ancillaries reported that they had not been given a clear job description, and almost two-thirds of assistants said they had not been given any advice or guidelines when they started working with the child. It should be a matter of concern that so many assistants had not been clearly briefed about their job, particularly since many have few qualifications, little previous experience of this type of work and little or no training. Advice on management strategies for children with behaviour difficulties should be an important aspect of the initial briefing.

Although 88 per cent were aware that the child they supported had a statement of special educational needs, 59 per cent had never seen it. Since the statement includes detailed information on the child's needs and the special educational provision required, usually detailing approaches and facilities, it would be valuable to communicate such information to the person appointed to support and work closely with the child.

In response to questions on the way the assistants worked in the school, it was apparent that, in some cases, classroom roles and responsibilities had not been clearly defined or agreed, and this was a source of confusion and discontent. Where roles had been clearly agreed and planning shared there was a greater degree of satisfaction. While 64 per cent of assistants were very satisfied with the way they worked with the class teacher, of those who expressed some dissatisfaction the most frequently mentioned problem was some aspect of their relationship. Changes required were more consultation, involvement, support and structured planning. Strategies on managing difficult behaviour need to be clearly worked out and agreed if they are to be effective. Tension and irritation can grow between staff if areas of responsibility are not clearly agreed, so it is important for the adults to negotiate and clearly understand their roles.

Poor communication and lack of support and training

Most of the ancillaries were not very satisfied with their degree of consultation and involvement in discussions about their child. The greatest degree of satisfaction came from their involvement in discussions with the class teacher (58 per cent), the head teacher (39 per cent) and other school staff (30 per cent). The greatest source of dissatisfaction was their lack of involvement in discussions with people from outside school, such as parents, the educational psychologist and other professionals. It may be that such meetings take place when ancillaries are not in school. However, since they work so closely with the child it would seem sensible to involve them in discussions, both to keep them fully informed and so that they can report on the child and share ideas. There is no guarantee that relevant information will be transmitted to the ancillary.

The highest degree of satisfaction with the amount of support and advice was within the school from the class teacher and head teacher. The greatest degree of dissatisfaction was with the amount of support offered by the educational psychologist and other school staff. The most frequently mentioned sources of support *required* by assistants was from the educational psychologist, from other assistants in the form of support groups, and from courses for assistants.

Although 88 per cent of assistants had identified behaviour difficulties as the major difficulty with the child, only 24 per cent said they were currently working on either a behaviour programme or using recommended strategies. This suggests many are coping as best they can, without the benefit of approaches that can be effective in improving behaviour, and there is the danger that difficult behaviour may at best be contained rather than improved by the support available.

Only one assistant had received advice on behaviour, strategies from a special needs coordinator. The school coordinator for special needs should be a key person in helping all staff to make the most of opportunities for children's learning. However, Lewis (1991) reports that only two-thirds of schools visited in a HMI (1989) survey had special needs coordinators and only a small percentage of these had qualifications in teaching children with special needs.

The training available to ancillaries was very limited and two-thirds had received no training from any source. Of the third who had received training, over half had been involved in in-service training at school. This lack of training available for ancillaries has been commonly noted, and Goacher *et al.* (1988) reported that only 28 per cent of LEAs said they provided training for ancillaries to help implement the 1981 Education Act. The majority of assistants wanted more training to be available, with 76 per cent saying they were not satisfied with the amount received.

Most of the ancillaries felt they would have benefited from an induction course to allow them to prepare for working with a child with behaviour problems and consider strategies to use. One ancillary commented: 'I had never worked with badly behaved children before and had no idea how to deal or cope with his tantrums, etc. I have just had to learn as I went along.' In relation to current training requirements, behaviour management was the area that most assistants wanted to know more about, with 94 per cent rating it highly. Particular areas of learning difficulty (82 per cent) and general problems of slow learners (79 per cent) were also rated highly. Many also wanted to know about their role in the school and what other ancillaries do.

'Professionalism'

Conditions of service

Several studies have pointed to the fact that poor conditions of service can be a source of dissatisfaction, and Clayton (1989) suggested that as long as pay, conditions of employment and career prospects remain so low, it is unlikely that LEAs will be able to recruit better qualified personnel. Most ancillaries are employed on a part-time basis. In the present survey 61 per cent were employed for less than twenty hours a week. The majority had been employed on a temporary basis, with only 33 per cent having permanent contracts. The lack of job security has been commonly noted, with temporary contacts being associated with this type of work. Although the majority of assistants (76 per cent) saw their job as a long-term career, two-thirds mentioned job security as a major concern.

Qualifications and experience

Currently, apart from the Nursery Nurses Examination Board (NNEB) training, there are no generally recognised pre-service courses available for ancillaries, whether working in a general capacity or with children with special educational needs. Furthermore, it was only in 1980 that the training was revised to include developmental deviations, physical handicap, learning difficulties and social and emotional difficulties.

In addition, LEA recruitment policies vary and recruitment procedures can vary even within the same authority. Hegarty *et al.* (1981) found that only one LEA appointed qualified staff, two preferred to employ trained staff and one relied more on employing staff with experience of bringing up their own children. While some schools make their own appointments, others have an assistant supplied by the LEA.

Ancillaries surveyed were not well-qualified. Only 27 per cent mentioned that they had any relevant qualifications, which were either an NNEB qualification, a teaching certificate or a college certificate. This confirms the picture of assistants described in other studies. Clayton (1990) found that half of the assistants in his study held no school or further education qualifications and one-third did not have qualifications of any kind. We must question the value of the educational support offered by those with few academic qualifications themselves.

Just over half of the assistants reported that they had had previous experience of working as an ancillary before working with their present child, although they had not necessarily encountered behaviour problems. Many mentioned other experience they felt was relevant to the job. There was a wide variety of voluntary work with children: in schools, youth work, play schemes, toddler groups, scouts, cubs and playgroups. Previous paid work with children, other than as an ancillary, included work in the community, day nurseries, special schools and libraries. Clayton (1990) also found that, although ancillaries had varied and substantial experience of children of different ages and in a variety of settings, their exposure to special needs was limited.

Status

While three-quarters of the ancillaries saw their job as a long-term career, despite conditions of employment and lack of training, nearly half felt that they were not treated as a professional in their job. This has to be a matter of concern from the point of view of job satisfaction. The reasons given were primarily related to the attitudes of other staff and to their treatment in school. Some assistants did not feel valued and felt left out of the communication system. This issue has been raised by other authors, and Balshaw (1991) emphasised the importance of teamwork, recommending that assistants should be included as part of the school team and regarded as partners in team development. Some assistants mentioned that they would like day release so that they could gain further qualifications and others wished their experience were acknowledged by the provision of a recognised career structure

THE WAY FORWARD

Many of the problems outlined above have suggested their own solutions. Assistants supporting children with behaviour difficulties are enabling them to be integrated into mainstream classrooms. However, it seems they are not used to maximum advantage in every school.

Responsibilities of the LEA

One of the conclusions that must be drawn from the present study is that if LEAs are to recruit and keep suitable applicants for ancillary posts supporting children with behaviour difficulties, a number of changes have to be made.

Policies and procedures

Currently, although the LEA is responsible for financing assistants working with children with statements of special educational needs, it is frequently left to the school to make new appointments. If the LEA wishes to recruit applicants with relevant qualifications, appointments would need to be monitored. Many of the ancillaries in the present study were offered the post following previous work in the school, either on a voluntary or paid basis. This previous experience was not always relevant to working with behaviour difficulties. Often contracts were temporary and even those with permanent contracts could be moved from school to school, which caused resentment in some ancillaries because their original appointment had been made by a particular school. Some LEAs are now improving this situation by creating a central pool of qualified ancillaries who are offered permanent contracts and training.

Many ancillaries are concerned about their low status. This could be greatly enhanced by the issuing of permanent contracts, the provision of a recognised career structure so that previous experience is valued, the development of support networks, and changing attitudes in schools. Some ancillaries feel isolated in their work and would like a support network of groups of ancillaries who can meet, discuss problems and consider approaches.

Support, training and monitoring

The LEA should have a responsibility to ensure that special educational provision is effectively monitored and evaluated. If LEAs wish to continue with the recruitment of unqualified staff, training needs need to be identified and adequate support and training provided. An investment in training would make the issuing of more permanent contracts cost-effective.

Since so many ancillaries are working with groups of children on tasks of an educational nature, support and training should take this into account. Suitable arrangements for training ought to ensure that ancillaries are not financially penalised, since some are expected to train in their own time. Some training would be best provided via a centralised course, where ancillaries can meet together. However, other areas may best be addressed within the school. Some LEAs are now developing induction courses for ancillaries: Balshaw (1991) describes one in Cambridgeshire and Clayton *et al.* (1990) describe the Wiltshire approach. The two most documented LEA courses for ancillaries are OPTIS 'Working Together' (Oxfordshire) and SAINTS (Wiltshire). The benefits of training have been recognised: for example, Farrell and Sugden (1984) found that ancillaries benefited from a behavioural skills training course, and Balshaw emphasised the value of such courses in increasing the ancillaries' confidence, increasing skills, meeting other assistants for mutual support and identifying further needs. Most of the ancillaries in the present study said they would have benefited from an induction course.

Although centralised training for ancillaries may be most suitable for induction courses, there is a good case for a flexible system of training and support in school. Many ancillaries support the same child for a number of years and training needs to be flexible enough to cope with the changing demands on the ancillary over this period.

Support service staff need to ensure that ancillaries are adequately supported, and included in discussions. Support teachers could offer in-service training and ongoing support. For example, ancillaries could be instructed in the use of such techniques as precision teaching and direct instruction to work with small groups of children with learning difficulties. Record keeping and monitoring would be essential aspects of such learning programmes. The educational psychologist or behavioural support teacher could provide both training and ongoing support in behaviour management techniques. For all children with special needs the educational psychologist has a responsibility to review the suitability of the provision.

Responsibilities of the school

Whole-school approaches

Although many ancillaries were happy with the way they worked in school, the study suggests that there are several areas that may need addressing. In some schools both organisational and attitudinal change to special educational needs may be necessary. The Elton Report (DES 1989) clearly referred to the responsibility of all staff to share in the development of school processes and procedures in order to influence children's behaviour so that effective learning and teaching can take place.

Responsibility for special needs should rest with the school, and the development of whole-school policies on special needs, which should include policy on behaviour, could greatly facilitate the clarification of aims, ethos and provision for special needs. Without effective approaches and policies there is the danger that individuals will feel they are working in isolation. Implicit in the notion of whole-school approaches is the communication system. When ancillaries are not asked to attend staff meetings, relevant discussions and in-service training, they are likely to feel under-valued.

Policy and procedures

Ancillaries need to be fully aware of the child's difficulties and to have a clear job description and guidelines. They should be clear about their role and responsibilities within the classroom and there ought to be a system of regular monitoring and review. Staff appraisal should include the ancillary as a member of the school team.

Training, support and monitoring

It is important that ancillaries receive adequate ongoing support for their work from school staff. Obviously, the class teacher will be the main source of support, although there is an important role for a special needs coordinator in providing support and advice on suitable programmes. In addition, if relationships with the class teacher are difficult, it is important that the ancillary has someone else in school to turn to. If the special needs coordinator has a clear responsibility in this area, communication could be improved. The role of the special needs coordinator could be clarified in the development of the school policy on special needs.

Within the classroom, it is essential that roles are clear and management strategies agreed. Although many ancillaries were happy with their role, some were clearly not, making it unlikely that support was being used to its best advantage. Several authors have drawn attention to the fact that, in order to make best use of staffing and resources following the 1981 Act, it is becoming increasingly necessary to pay attention to effective management in the classroom. Thomas (1987) suggests that, for integration to be truly effective, the focus of attention needs to move away from helping *individual* children and towards ways of *managing* resources, time and personnel within the mainstream classroom in such a way that it is possible to offer individual help.

A system of room management is described by Thomas in various papers and books, the latest of which provides a useful overview (Thomas 1992). Room management (RM) is a possible system of classroom organisation, which could maximise the potential of resources and personnel and make communication and clarification of roles clearer. Three specific roles are identified which can be taken on by the adults: an 'individual helper', an 'activity manager', and a 'mover'. During a focal 'activity period' the adults are allocated their roles – each having specific tasks allocated. The individual helper(s) works with successive children for set periods, giving specific and detailed teaching. The activity manager(s) deals with the rest of the class, while the mover(s) aims to maintain the flow of activity in the class by dealing with minor distractions which may arise. The system is adaptable and roles may be changed by agreement through advance planning. An experiment by Thomas (1985) showed significant increases in on-task behaviour after using this system of room management in a classroom with parents, an ancillary and a teacher. The system was of greatest benefit to those children who initially had the lowest on-task behaviour.

Stone (1990) suggests: 'More adults do not necessarily produce more effective management strategies. It is the effective deployment of adults that will help children overcome their behaviour problems, rather than the number of adults available in the classroom'. Room management offers a clear and consistent approach, which would be particularly valuable in dealing with children with behavioural problems. Time needs to be made available in order that teachers and ancillaries can effectively plan and evaluate together.

With the increasing numbers of children with special needs being integrated into mainstream classes with ancillary support, it is necessary to consider both the training needs of ancillaries and the training needs of teachers to manage adult helpers in the classroom. It should not be assumed that all teachers are able to manage personnel resources efficiently. Goodman (1990) points to the lack of teacher training for the productive utilisation of ancillaries in the mainstream classroom. This makes it unlikely that teachers, without the benefit of training or experience, will be able to use this support to maximum effect.

Some of the training needs of ancillaries would best be met within the school, since an 'outside' system of training cannot address many issues arising in a school. Whole-school approaches to special educational needs will emphasise the importance of the ancillaries' role in the team. There is a good case for training ancillaries and teachers together in some areas. A survey by Frith and Lindsey (1982) showed that 97 per cent of respondents thought that teachers and para-professionals should be trained together. Many teachers will have limited experience of children with special needs and many benefit from training in learning programmes and behaviour management. Room management techniques would best be taught to ancillaries and teachers together, since both would be implementing them.

The literature shows clear evidence that behavioural methods of classroom management are effective in bringing certain problem behaviours under control (Merrett and Wheldall 1984, 1987): therefore, we would anticipate the value of teaching such approaches to ancillaries dealing with children with behavioural problems. Behavioural approaches can be taught effectively to teachers (see Merrett and Wheldall 1984; Presland 1974; Clayton 1985; Harrop 1974) and to ancillaries (Farrell and Sugden 1984; Kolvin et al. 1981). The preceding discussion has emphasised the importance of relationships both in the classroom and in the school as a whole. Perhaps consideration should be given to joint ancillary/teacher training in the form of whole-school courses in behavioural management, since both groups have to deal with difficult and disruptive behaviour wherever it occurs in the school.

REFERENCES

Balshaw, M. (1991) 'Classroom assistants: staff development issues', in G. Upton, *Staff Training and Special Educational Needs*. London: David Fulton.

Clayton, T. (1985) 'The workshop approach to training behavioural skills', *Educational and Child Psychology*, 2, 1: 69–83.

Clayton, T. (1989) 'The role and management of welfare assistants', in T. Bowers (ed.) *Managing Special Needs*. Oxford: Oxford University Press.

Clayton, T. (1990) 'Welfare assistants: are they equipped for their role?', *Support for Learning*, 5, 4: 193–198.

Clayton, T., Moore, S., Parker, R. and Powley, V. (1990) 'Induction courses for special welfare assistants', *Educational Psychology in Practice*, 6, 2: 71–75.

Clayton, T. (1993) 'Welfare assistants in the classroom – problems and solutions', *Educational Psychology in Practice*, 8, 4: 191–197

Department of Education and Science (1989) *Discipline in Schools: Report of the Committee of Enquiry* (The Elton Report). London: HMSO.

Farrell, P.T. and Sugden, M. (1984) 'An evaluation of an EDY course in behavioural techniques for classroom assistants in a school for severe learning difficulties', *Educational Psychology*, 4, 3: 185–198.

Frith, G.H. and Lindsey, J.D. (1982) 'Certification, training, and other programming variables affecting special education and the paraprofessional concept', *Journal of Special Education*, 16, 2: 229–236.

Goacher, B., Evans, J., Welton, J. and Wedell, K. (1988) *Policy and Provision for Special Educational Needs: Implementing the 1981 Education Act*. London: Cassell Educational.

Goodman, G. (1990) 'Utilising the paraprofessional in the mainstream', *Support for Learning*, 5, 4: 199–204.

Harrop, A. (1974) 'A behavioural workshop for the management of classroom problems', *British Journal of In-Service Education*, 1, 1: 47–50.

Hegarty, S., Pocklington, K. and Lucas, D. (1981) *Educating Pupils with Special Needs in the Ordinary School*. Windsor: NFER–Nelson.

HM Inspectorate (1989) *A Survey of Pupils with Special Educational Needs in Ordinary Schools*. London: Department of Education and Science.

Hodgson, A., Clunies-Ross, L. and Hegarty, S. (1984) *Learning Together: Teaching Pupils with Special Educational Needs in the Ordinary School*. Windsor: NFER–Nelson.

Kolvin, I., Garside, R., Nicol, A., Macmillan, A., Wolstenholme, F. and Leitch, I. (1981) *Help Starts Here: The Maladjusted Child in the Ordinary School*. London: Tavistock Publications.

Lewis, A. (1991) *Primary Special Needs and the National Curriculum*. London: Routledge.

Merrett, F. and Wheldall, K. (1984) 'Training teachers to use the behavioural approach to classroom management: a review', *Educational Psychology*, 4, 3: 213–231.

Merrett, F. and Wheldall, K. (1987) 'British teachers and the behavioural approach to teaching', in K. Wheldall *The Behaviourist in the Classroom*. London: Allen and Unwin.

Presland, J.L. (1974) 'Modifying behaviour now', *Special Education: Forward Trends*, 1, 3: 467–472.

Stewart-Evans, C. (1991) 'The use of non-teaching assistants appointed to support children with behaviour difficulties in mainstream primary schools in one local education authority'. Unpublished dissertation, University of Nottingham, Child Development Research Unit.

Stone, L. (1990) *Managing Difficult Children in School*. Oxford: Blackwell.

Thomas, G. (1985) 'Room management in mainstream education', *Educational Research*, 27, 3: 186–193.

Thomas, G. (1987) 'Extra people in the primary classroom', *Educational Research*, 29, 3: 173–181.

Thomas, G. (1992) *Effective Classroom Teamwork: Support or Intrusion*. London: Routledge.

Chapter 17

Activity analysis as a means of clarifying teachers' expectations of pupils

Michael Pitchford

There are few jobs which rival teaching for the complexity of day-to-day organisation which has to be mastered. Children have to be taught, work marked, registers checked, dinner money collected, materials handed out and returned, wet breaks survived, disputes resolved and parents placated and, it goes without saying, the requirements of the National Curriculum fulfilled. In the face of such relentless *busy-ness* the day can feel like a treadmill. Just as wearying is the knowledge that something is going wrong at certain times of the day, that certain activities routinely cause trouble, and yet it is somehow impossible to put your finger on what the problem is. And anyway, Wednesday's swimming trip is now over so forget it until next week because now you've got to think how to make sure this afternoon's lessons run smoothly.

How to analyse and manage behaviour in the classroom has been a topic which has been woefully neglected in the past, although there are increasing signs of this changing. A technology which has proved very useful is one which has come to be known as 'Rules, Praise, Ignoring' after the title of an extremely influential article by Madsen *et al.* (1968). These techniques have been more fully described elsewhere (see Medland and Vitale 1984; Pitchford and Mann 1991) and there are now commercially available packages which are underpinned by this technology (e.g. Canter and Canter 1992). However, the essentials of RPI are easily summarised. The teacher selects 3–5 rules (preferably positive 'Thou shalt', rather than negative 'Thou shalt not' ones), which are then explained to the class. Once this has been accomplished the teacher aims to 'catch the children being good' and praise them for following the rules. Infractions of the rules are discouraged with a hierarchy of mild sanctions, starting with ignoring and proceeding through verbal reprimands and warnings to separation from the class. The research evidence on these sorts of approaches is unequivocal – they work, often spectacularly well (e.g. Frankland *et al.* 1985).

Obviously, part of the trick of making RPI work is to ensure that you've got the right rules and this is where activity analysis comes in. Basically, there are two ways of arriving at the set of rules which is to be used. The first is to use what might be called a blanket approach. List a rule for each of the following areas:

Academic work
Peer and adult relations
Classroom routines
Safety

Using this sort of approach we can come up with a set of rules that would look something like this:

Work hard and quietly   (Academic work)
Be polite and friendly   (Peer and adult relations)
Put up your hand   (Classroom routines)
Don't run in the classroom   (Safety)

Providing the teacher backed up these rules with praise and other rewards for following the rules and mild sanctions for breaking the rules, then he or she could expect the behaviour of the class to improve. This being the case, why bother with activity analysis?

The weakness of deriving rules in the way described above is that it doesn't illuminate why problems are occurring in the first place. Activity analysis, by contrast, does illuminate problems in ways which help the teacher to locate precisely where problems start and even to *predict* when things are going to go wrong.

So how is it done? Every lesson or activity in which children and teachers take part in class follows a cycle from beginning to end. For example, the children listen to the teacher while she explains what they are to do: work on the task given to them by the teacher, correct mistakes, and then clear away ready for the next part of the school day. The first step in activity analysis is simply to list this activity cycle as follows:

Teacher presentation
Independent work
Work check
Clear away

Of course, as teachers we know that nothing in life is so simple and the complicating feature here is the kids and their uncanny habit of sabotaging our apparently well-laid plans. This then determines the next step in activity analysis, which is to determine what the perfect child would do during each of the activities listed above. For example, our perfect student would look at the teacher throughout the course of the teacher presentation, listen carefully to what was said and only interrupt by raising a hand and waiting quietly until called on. Consequently, a completed activity analysis would look something like the one shown in Table 17.1.

Many readers will probably think this is an excessively traditional and

Table 17.1 Activity analysis of teacher-led lesson

Activity	Students' behaviour
Teacher presentation	Students look at teacher. Students look at relevant displays, models, demonstrations, etc., when directed to by the teacher. Students ask or answer questions by raising their hands and waiting quietly to be called on by the teacher. Students accept their own and other students' mistakes when these occur during questioning by the teacher.
Independent work	Students start on the assigned task quickly and quietly. Students allow their friends to work without interruption. Students seek help by raising their hand and remaining in their seat. Students work at a rate sufficient to enable them to complete the assigned work. Students who finish early read a library book.
Work check	Students stay in their seats to have their work checked. Students accept their own and others' mistakes. Students correct mistakes.
Clear away	Students complete the clear up chores assigned to them quickly, carefully and quietly. Students do not pester for chores. Students walk around the classroom without interfering with others' work, hitting or teasing one another. Students check the floor under and around their tables and throw away litter and put away any equipment they find. Students sit in their seats and wait for the next activity.

simplistic sort of a lesson, implying as it does 'chalk and talk' and whole-class teaching. Leaving aside the fact that such lessons can be highly efficient and even enjoyable, the startling fact about even such a simple sort of lesson is the high number of complex requirements and expectations (frequently unspoken) we are placing on our students. If we look at the student behaviour column we will see that there are 17 behaviours the youngsters must get right if our lesson is to run smoothly. And this is without any differentiation, group work or multiple groups following multiple activities.

However, the main point which needs to be emphasised here is a practical one. In completing your activity analysis, never neglect the obvious! The more thorough your list of activities and student behaviours the more powerful your eventual analysis will be. In completing this list of things which you would like the perfect student to do, you should consider not only *what* they should do but also *how* they should do it. Supposing your activity analysis reveals that you want your students to line up quickly to collect some games equipment. How do you want them to line up, like a bunch of wild animals or in an orderly line with no pushing and shoving? Presumably the latter, although we all know the former is an ever present risk with youngsters. It is in answering these sort of questions that a picture will start to emerge for you of the weaknesses and strengths of the classes you take. I shall return to this point in the final activity analysis in this chapter, where a seemingly trivial, 'obvious' but previously unstated assumption about how children should behave held the key to solving what had seemed a complex problem without resort to behavioural overkill.

Having obtained a list of activities and the student behaviours which match these activities, you are now ready to analyse what is going wrong or, if you're being (awful word) proactive, what will go wrong. To do this, simply go through your list and put a check against any activity which is new to the students, or complicated, or hazardous or has a history of problems. This is done in Table 17.2.

Having completed the analysis, we can see that the problems that occur in this class are due to students teasing one another about mistakes, which in turn leads to youngsters becoming upset if they make mistakes. Exacerbating the problem further, the teacher often finds himself swamped by children leaving their places to seek help when they could have stayed in their seat with raised hand. Finally, the teacher is finding himself becoming irritable at transition times because well-meaning children are pestering him for jobs. Unwittingly, he has been assigning responsibilities to those who shouted loudest, in order to get some peace.

In this example the problems that are encountered are not hazardous, nor are they new to the class, but they do have a history of problems and for younger children they might well be considered as complicated.

The next step is simplicity itself: all that is required is to turn the

Table 17.2 Activity analysis: status of students' behaviour

Activity	Students' behaviour	Status
Teacher presentation	Students look at teacher. Students look at relevant displays, models, demonstrations, etc., when directed to by the teacher. Students ask or answer questions by raising their hands and waiting quietly to be called on by the teacher. Students accept their own and other students' mistakes when these occur during questioning by the teacher.	X
Independent work	Students start on the assigned task quickly and quietly. Students allow their friends to work without interruption. Students seek help by raising their hand and remaining in their seat. Students work at a rate sufficient to enable them to complete the assigned work. Students who finish early read a library book.	X
Work check	Students stay in their seats to have their work checked. Students accept their own and others' mistakes. Students correct mistakes.	
Clear away	Students complete the clear-up chores assigned to them quickly, carefully and quietly. Students do not pester for chores. Students walk around the classroom without interfering with others' work, hitting or teasing one another. Students check the floor under and around their tables and throw away litter and put away any equipment they find. Students sit in their seats and wait for the next activity.	X

Key: X = New *or* complicated *or* hazardous *or* has a history of problems.

behaviours that we have put a cross against into rules to teach the class and reward the children for following them. This is illustrated in Table 17.3.

In Table 17.3 certain parts of the rule are placed in brackets as they represent parts of the rule which would be explained to the children but which would not be displayed simply for the sake of brevity. Additionally, this example shows how one rule 'Raise your hand and wait quietly' can often be used to solve multiple problems. Unlike the technique discussed in the early part of this chapter (that is, the blanket coverage of all areas by selecting rules concerning academic work, peer and adult relations, classroom routines and safety), activity analysis has enabled a precise understanding of what is going wrong and a corresponding increase in the teacher's technical ability to identify and solve problems.

Having identified the problem area in this way, the teacher's next task is to teach the students the required rules, emphasise why they are important, post the rules somewhere conspicuous so that they can serve as reminders to the class, and then start to use praise to students who follow the rules and mild sanctions for those who do not.

Sometimes activity analysis takes shape as you introduce something new to a class and can be used as a means of refining your technique as you go along. Some years ago I was trying to introduce peer-tutored paired reading to a class of top infants. Since this was going to be something new for the class and to some extent complicated, it seemed appropriate to frame some rules in order to try to shape the children's performance. I had already decided that the children should read in unison aloud, so, on the first day, I introduced this to the class. I demonstrated what I wanted and introduced the rule 'Read together'. Much to my delight the classroom was soon echoing to the sound of peer-tutored paired reading to the accompaniment of a running commentary of praise from myself and the class teacher, 'It's great to see you all *reading together* . . . Kiranjit and Joanne, I really like the way you're *reading together*, etc., etc.'

However, it soon became apparent that we were running into teething problems. True, the children showed every sign of enjoying the activity and the time on task looked high, but it was also obvious that, although children were reading aloud from the same page, they were not necessarily reading the same part of the page, some were at the bottom of the page while others were still at the top of the page of the book they were reading. After some thought, we decided to alter the rule slightly so that it read, 'Read together carefully'. The rule was discussed and demonstrated to the class and then backed up with praise and soon, in the teacher's judgement and my own, that particular problem had been overcome. Next, though, we became concerned about the noise level which, while it bore testimony to the children's enthusiasm, was too high for comfort. Once again the rule was reworded slightly to read as follows: 'Read together carefully and quietly'. By the end of the third lesson we were happy that by a combi-

Table 17.3 Activity analysis with rules

Students' behaviour	Rule
Students accept their own and other students' mistakes when these occur during questioning by the teacher.	Accept your own and others' mistakes.
Students do not pester for chores.	Raise your hand and wait quietly (if you want a chore).
Students seek help by raising their hand and remaining in their seat.	Raise your hand and wait quietly (in your seat if you need help).

nation of observation, analysis and the use of rules and praise we had the programme working satisfactorily and no other changes were required.

Activity analysis is invaluable in clarifying where the problem actually lies as opposed to where everyone supposes it lies. In an experience which is common to many educational psychologists, I was once told that a year group of Year Twos who came from a disadvantaged area but who for all that looked entirely normal to me, were the worst children that anybody had ever seen. Theories as to why this should be, social, psychological, criminological, and for all I know astrological, abounded. After some fairly persistent questioning it became clear that problems started at lunchtime, the children were getting into trouble, sometimes fighting, and this was spilling over into the afternoons. Now we were making progress, not only were the children to blame, the dinner supervisors were at fault too! However, over the course of a few dinnertimes I was lucky enough to get to know the dinner supervisors sufficiently to undertake the activity analysis shown in Table 17.4.

This activity analysis was revealing to everyone for a number of reasons. Firstly it demonstrated that the dinner supervisors were having to manage probably the most complicated part of the day. For the dinnertime to go smoothly there were no fewer than 31 behaviours, many of them requiring quite difficult discriminations (e.g. 'after I've eaten my dinner do I need my coat? If not, I must remember to come back at one o'clock to get it from the dining block and take it back to the cloakroom in the main school building'), which had to be managed by the supervisors and accomplished by the children. Quite clearly too, the layout of the school, with a separate dining block with access requiring a walk across the playground, was a complicating (in fact crucial) element here.

Having completed this analysis with the supervisors, I asked them to vote on which area was the most problematic and which should receive our attention first. They were unanimous: the problems started with the walk

Table 17.4 Activity analysis of infants' dinnertime

Activity	Students' behaviour
Preparing to leave classroom	Walk to cloakroom. Collect coat. Return to classroom. Line up and wait to be counted so dinner registers can be completed.
Go to dining hall	Walk (no running) with lunchtime supervisor across the playground to the building containing the dining room. Carry lunchboxes sensibly, without hitting one another with them. Stop and line up sensibly outside building.
Queuing for dinner	Go into building without pushing. Hang up coats. Line up outside dining hall without pushing. Holds hands out so that they can be checked by the supervisors. If necessary, wash hands and return to line. Go and collect food tray and cutlery. Go to counter to be served. Tell kitchen staff what food is wanted.
Eat food	Sit where told to by staff. Ask for help cutting food if required. Eat food.
Leave dining room	Take trays and cultery to table by hatch so they can be cleared away. Walk out of dining room. Collect coats if necessary because of weather. Leave coats until 1.00 in cloakroom attached to dining room if weather permits.
Play outside	Play nicely (no teasing or fighting). Stay off the grass unless weather dry and adult available to supervise. Avoid nets, walls, railings, steps. Go to toilets no more than two times.
Return to class	Fetch coats and lunchboxes when told to. Walk to get coats and lunchboxes. Collect lunchboxes quickly and line up ready to return to class.

across the playground to the dining block. If that could be sorted out all the other problems would be nipped in the bud. They were, of course, quite right.

This is what was happening. As far as the average infant is concerned the playground has one main function, it is the place where you escape the irksome confines of the classroom and *run*. So, as soon as the supervisor and the class set off from the main school building for the dinning block many of the children would start to trot. This inevitably would lead to jostling, banging, the occasional trip or retaliatory clout with a lunchbox, to the accompaniment of anguished shouts and pleas from the dinner supervisors. But worse was to come. The playground sloped down towards the dinning block, so the children would inevitably pick up speed as they went along. By this time the dinner supervisor faced the same predicament as the driver of a runaway horse and cart, to try and stop the runaway now and risk a spill as the faster children at the back slammed into the children who'd stopped at the front, or hang on in the hope that they'd begin to tire later on? A lot now depended on whether or not there was a queue of children waiting at the dining block door and the temper of the children leading the pack across the playground. If there was a queue and the leaders of the pack were feeling game, they would go for the infant equivalent of a multiple pile-up, shunting those ahead of them in the waiting queue in a highly pleasing way.

Of course, this was all hugely enjoyable for the children (well, at least for those who didn't get hurt, who would spend at least some of the remaining time trying to get their own back), but it annoyed and worried the supervisors, who responded by shouting. This shouting was generally ineffective and only confirmed the view of some of the children that supervisors were there to be goaded. Thus was the pattern set for the rest of the dinnertime.

With the insights gained by this analysis, the supervisors were ready to fight back. By some small adjustments it was possible to make sure that the children did not set off across the playground until the supervisor was at or near the front of the line. Before the children had even left the classroom they had been given a pep talk about the importance of being grown-up and walking sensibly across the playground. Class teachers and supervisors stressed how pleased they would be if the children could manage this. Next, the children were walked across the playground, with the supervisors taking pains to praise the children for the sensible way in which they were walking across the playground. Because the supervisor was not vainly trying to keep up with children far more nimble than herself, she could take an interest in the children and talk to them on the walk across the playground as well as praise them for walking. By the time the line had got to the dinning block everybody was far more likely to be feeling favourably disposed to each other, the scene had been set for quite a different sort of dinnertime. And yet none of this would have been possible without the insight which comes from activity analysis, stressing as it does the contribution to success or failure made by the complexity of the tasks we often ask children to perform with little or no preparation.

To conclude, activity analysis consists of the following steps:

1 Determine the activity cycle for a particular lesson or part of the school day.
2 List all of the student behaviours that are required for the activities to run smoothly.
3 Place a cross against any student behaviour that is new, complicated, has a history of problems or is potentially hazardous.
4 Frame rules, train students and provide consequences as required, dependent on the results of the activity analysis and ongoing observation of the students.

REFERENCES

Canter, L. and Canter, M. (1992) *Assertive Discipline. Positive Behavior Management for today's Classroom*. Santa Monica, Calif.: Lee Canter and Associates.

Frankland, S., Pitchford, Y.M. and Pitchford, M. (1985) 'The use of video recording to provide repeated monitoring of the successful use of "rules, praise, ignoring" with a class of 14 to 15 year olds in a comprehensive school', *Behavioural Approaches with Children*, 9, 3: 67–78.

Madsen, C.H., Becker, W.C. and Thomas, D.R. (1968) 'Rules, praise and ignoring: elements of elementary classroom control', *Journal of Applied Behavior Analysis*, 1: 139–150.

Medland, M. and Vitale, M. (1984) *Management of Classrooms*. CBS College Publishing, New York: Holt, Rinehart and Winston.

Pitchford, M. and Mann, R. (1991) 'Teacher strategies for improving children's classroom behaviour', in G. Lindsay and A. Miller (eds) *Psychological Services for Primary Schools*. London: Longman.

Chapter 18

Helping children to become more self-directing in their behaviour

Dave Traxson

In this chapter I shall attempt to outline a general model for the self-management of behaviour derived from practical approaches that have been tried. I shall then look at a real example of a self-directing approach, and from that specific example try to illustrate the potential variety and versatility of the approach by providing menus of components and possible designs. My intention is to motivate teachers to use their knowledge of an individual young person and their creativity to facilitate the young person to produce a personalised programme that leads to significant positive change in certain behaviours.

Early in my work with children who were experiencing a range of academic and behavioural problems I became interested in how many young people seemed to communicate to me that they had little control over their own behaviour. A useful therapeutic metaphor emerged over time, which was that they saw themselves as a string-puppet on the stage of life, with strings which led from their body to their youth culture, to their close friends, to their parents, to their teachers, to the TV, to religious and political beliefs or leaders. These strings brought about the movement of their body by a complex interaction of the influence of those factors acting on the individual at any particular time. What was apparent was that there was often no clear connection between the body of their puppet and their own control centre, their brain. Thus, the dance or movements they exhibited were often seen as a result of external influences or pressures only. How many times have we all despaired at phrases like, 'they made me do it', 'I did it for a laugh because I saw it on TV', or 'it wasn't me!' when clearly and inescapably it was?

I started to see that we have a role helping the puppet to become also the puppeteer and 'pull its own strings', encouraging it to take more responsibility for the choice that it has made and for opening up a new range of choices for the future. I began from the assumption that a young person (or indeed anyone) has the perfect right to stay the same or to change, and that they need to become aware of the consequences of any choices that they make. The skill lies in illuminating the nature of their difficulties (using

their own language), in their problem-solving what the options or consequences are, and in motivating them to be in the 'driver's seat' for more of
the time.

I believe that the work done on self-management during the last twenty
years offers to us as educationalists many useful strategies that have not
been as systematically applied as they might have been to the classroom
situation. One of the most obvious and useful strategies is that of giving
young people the responsibility for recording and monitoring the behaviours that they have concerns about and which they openly accept are
important for them to change. So often we as adults fall into one of the
major traps in any counselling process, which is that we become judgmen-
tal and try to take charge of this behaviour by imposing an externally
controlling set of conditions. This satisfies our need for doing something,
but immobilises the young person, further increasing their helplessness and
producing dependency on others for solutions. Surely the purpose of any
intervention is to achieve lasting change by helping the young person to
choose a new way of behaving that brings about more acceptable outcomes
for all parties.

> The goal of any behaviour management system is to help children to
> manage their own behaviour in a socially acceptable way. Mature
> individuals can process information, make decisions, take action, and
> then evaluate their behaviour. Unfortunately, these skills are rarely
> taught in schools. Children are expected to acquire self-management of
> their behaviour independently. When children learn the necessity for
> regulating their behaviour in an acceptable manner, and experience the
> rewards for doing this, they are well on their way towards becoming
> responsible persons.
>
> (Haring *et al.* 1978)

THE EFFECTS OF SELF-ESTEEM

In my view, the pivotal issue in order to increase the chance of a young
person making a more acceptable choice is their self-esteem. If the dispar-
ity between how they view themselves (self-image) and how they would
like to be (ideal-self) is too great then their self-esteem is lowered along
with their motivation to change. We all daily carry out a 'thumbs up or
thumbs down test' on ourselves, which is that we look in the metaphorical
mirror and check out how we are going to do in particular aspects of the
day ahead or the whole day. If we give ourselves more of a thumbs up than
a thumbs down then invariably that aspect is more successful. We, therefore, have to ensure that as adults we foster and develop a more positive
self-image in the children in our care, without challenging their essential
individuality or goodness. We must focus, therefore, on behaviours which

need changing as opposed to the topical view of the child being 'a nasty piece of work', which is more likely to generate a self-fulfilling prophecy. In short:

> The more children like themselves
>> The more they like to behave themselves
>>> (Spencer Johnson, MD 1983)

RECENT RESEARCH

In a recent review 'The use of behavioural self-management in primary school settings' (Panagopoulou-Stamatelatou 1990), the author showed that there is a consensus emerging that the more of the skills that are included in a programme from the Self-Management Cycle (see Figure 18.1), the more likely there is to be a successful outcome. She is also optimistic that these skills can be taught to children who have not fully developed them.

That supports what I have found in practice and is what I have now defined as the self-directing behavioural sequence (see Figure 18.4 on p. 238), which is far more complex than the simple self-monitoring programmes (i.e. self-observation and self-recording) with which I started some years ago.

The self-management cycle (Figure 18.1)

This cyle is a useful summary of the stages in which a young person can be involved when a key person or counsellor is trying to support them to develop more self-control. Its success depends on whether the young person has the social maturity and self-awareness to start the process. All disciplinary methods need to be matched to their stage of social development, and we should be aiming to move them in the direction of more personal responsibility when they are ready.

Several theorists in this area, such as Piaget and Kohlberg, have suggested a natural progression: from responding only to the external control of an adult at ages from 2–7 years, to a stage reached at secondary school age where children, if they have been educated appropriately, will develop the skill of being able to self-direct their behaviour. Rigid application of external control, as some people currently advocate, is likely therefore to impede an individual's ability to achieve self-direction.

If a young person has a realistic view of their own strengths and difficulties and possesses the ability to comment honestly on their own performance, then they have, in my view, the entry requirements for benefiting from the processes outlined in the cycle. These processes are largely self-explanatory.

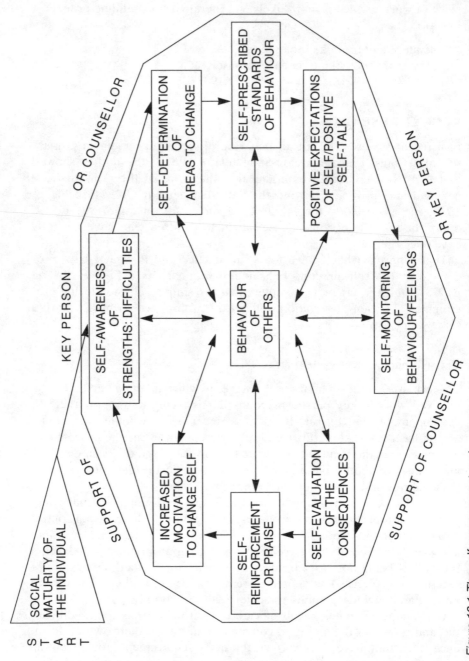

Figure 18.1 The self-management cycle

Increasing the involvement of the young person in stages such as determining areas to change and setting their own standards for behaviours automatically gets us away from any absolute standard where the unrealistic goal of perfection is expected. Rather, a more healthy relative standard of improvement is accepted. Progress has to be seen as difficult behaviours are happening less often, less intensely and with more improvement being gradually achieved. This allows us all to celebrate significant, even if small, steps forward. These small steps, in turn, I know do have a dramatic effect on the levels of internal motivation. It is this upsurge of motivation from within and increased self-confidence that turns the cycle ever forwards in small healthy steps. We can facilitate this intrinsic motivation by ensuring that tasks are chosen at the right level, and that we give high-quality positive feedback that gives them specific pointers to what has been pleasing and what might be the next area for them to tackle.

The planning conversation

The quality of the conversation we have with a young person at a planning stage will dramatically affect how successful the resulting programme is. Our questions should be phrased in a way that elicits the most useful kind of response. Clever questions, which leave the person they are aimed at struggling for an answer, are of no use in motivating a person to change. A simple but thought-provoking question, which provides a lot of useful information to work on, is what we should be aiming at.

If we are clear about our purposes for the conversation, then this will be reflected in the questions we ask. Our purposes should include our intentions:

— to indicate that we are optimistic about the future for the young person.
— to demonstrate that we believe that the problem is not an integral part of their make-up, i.e. we care for them and so try to externalise or separate them from the problem and give them more control over it. This automatically allows movement, as we are not asking them to alter as a person but just for them to change some of the things that they do.
— to explore and map the extent, nature and characteristics of the problem, using, wherever possible, the person's own labels, descriptions and explanations. This will help to personalise the approach, and the child's ownership of it.
— to understand the difficulties from the young person's perspective, because their ownership of the problem is vital to their seeing that it needs solving. Often the problem is ours as adults, because it affects us more than the child.
— to discuss how they would like the situation to change and the actions that they can see themselves taking in order to get there.

Some questions which I find useful in this regard are listed below, but there is no intention to suggest a particular order, as questions will need tailoring to each individual case.

Useful questions for the planning conversation

— Describe how you see the difficulties and successes that you are having at the moment? What would I see if I watched it on a video recording?
— Which people are affected most by these behaviours (positive/negative) and in what order would you put them in terms of the effects?
— What do other people think about you? If I was to ring all the important people in your life on my 'Magic Telephone', what would they say about you? (Cue with strengths and difficulties, if necessary, and prompt with people's names.)
— What good news has there been recently in any area of your life? (Remember we are looking for any rays of sunshine that can be capitalised upon as outcomes of any of the questions.)
— How would you like things to change in the next six months? What things can you see yourself doing differently?
— What will be the easiest things for you to change? What will be the hardest? (Put them in order.)
— Which people will be most affected by these changes? (Cue – where do you come in? – if necessary). Who will notice and be pleased the most? Who the next most? (and so on).
— Who or what you will be doing this for? (Put in order of importance.) Who will be pleasantly surprised if things improve?
— How will you feel when you get to this stage? (Check out feelings at all stages – legitimise the use of the real emotions.)
— How are you going to make a start? Which behaviours are you prepared to record and how will you record them?
— How will you reward yourself when progress is achieved?
— How would you like to record these changes? (Use menu of options, given later, as a prompt if necessary.)
— Whom do you want to talk this over with on a regular basis, where and how long for?
— What other people would you like to be told about any improvement as the problem goes away from you (i.e. becomes externalised)?
— How should these people be told/involved?
— What would 'better' feel and look like? (Imagine you are a fly on the wall watching your own life in the future.)
— How will you know when you have got there (i.e. to an improved situation)?
— How will you keep the progress going?

In a nutshell, these questions put the young people themselves in a position of paramount importance in exploring, understanding, commenting on and changing their own behaviour. For this reason it is important for the young person to use 'I . . .' statements when talking, for example: I think I could make it different by . . .; I know that I can achieve . . .; I will feel very happy if I . . .; and I will deserve . . . if I . . . This focuses their mind on what they honestly can do and gives a greater indication of a commitment to change.

Discussion of an example of a self-directing programme (Figure 18.2)

Paula's behaviours were clearly a manifestation of stresses building up from outside and inside school, with name-calling being the last straw. So this approach allowed her to regain control in the short term and discuss the underlying problems as the relationship developed.

Work completed was selected as behaviour 1, as this was an area in which Paula was usually successful (see Figure 18.2). Behaviours 2 and 3 were the key targets for improvement, as two weeks previously Paula's behaviour had been of grave concern to the pastoral team when she reacted very aggressively to other students calling her names, on some occasions throwing chairs at the people concerned and also throwing punches at other students and any staff who tried to restrain her. Eventually, when removed from the situation, she usually broke down in tears, explaining that she was unable to control herself. Serious incidents of name-calling were being dealt with in line with the school's policy on bullying, but there was an agreed need for Paula to resist smaller provocations, hence the asterisks, which were self-reinforcement for ignoring minor irritations or teasing.

Clearly, break had had a negative influence on Paula on this day, as soon afterwards she had to use the red card. She was out of the room for thirteen minutes, which was an improvement on the time taken when she used to totally lose control, then often half an hour was lost with the member of staff having to sort out the problem. This way everyone continued working, as did Paula when she had regained her composure and returned to class.

The codes at the top of each column allow some privacy if the book were to be found by another student. The red card was felt to be necessary to allow Paula to ask permission to leave the class if she felt a severe loss of control coming on. In order to prevent abuse and to monitor the use of the card, the teacher entered when she left and re-entered the room, initialling it on each occasion. Effectively, this is a request to 'leave the field of play' to have 'a cooling off period'. This helps young persons to increase their control over the adrenalin rush released by the fight-or-flight response.

Other rating methods appropriate to programmes similar to the one

This chart was produced by Paula, a fourteen-year-old girl in a West Midlands comprehensive school, who wanted to control her outbursts of aggressive behaviour and get more work done in class. This example shows one day's record in the second week of the programme. Paula's record book also contained a red card, for use when loss of temper threatened, and a letter to staff from the form tutor and Paula, regarding endorsement of Paula's self-ratings.

Period	Behaviour 1 (work completed) WC	Behaviour 2 (controlled temper) CT	Behaviour 3 (behaviour acceptable) BA	Teacher comments TC
1 (English)	4	✓	3	Worker calmly all lesson. A.H.
2	4	✓	4	Excellent contributions to discussions. F.L.
Break	–	**✓	3	–
3 (History)	3	* RC used (Red Card)	1	Came back in better mood after incident with J.R. C.A.
4 (Maths)	3	**✓	4	Dealt with name-calling very well and worked well. S.T.
Lunch	–	**✓	3	Agree with rating. R.P. (Lunchtime supervisor)
5 (Science)	3	✓	2	Took a while to settle but enjoyed practical and wrote up well. A.R.
6 (Science)	4	*✓	3	

(1–5 rating) (✓ if controlled) (1–5 rating) (1–5 rating)

Paula (10H)	Time T.L. left	Time T.B. back	Initials + date
has permission to leave the classroom to find me in order to avoid a loss of temper. Signed: *Mrs Hand* (Form tutor)	11.22	11.35	C.A. 2.2.93
	2.17	2.31	P.T. 16.3.93
Red card (Front)	Red card (Back)		

Red card = in folder in front of book, to use when student is clear that a loss of temper will occur unless they leave the situation to calm down (i.e. fight-or-flight reaction is judged to be imminent).

Key to symbols used in chart

♩ = controlled temper – no major outburst
* = Resisted being provoked by others
1 = Very poor
2 = Below average
3 = Average for group
4 = Above average
5 = Excellent

Other instructions to staff (on inside cover of book) to endorse Paula's self-ratings:

Please only use positive comments, and be specific about the behaviours you are pleased with, as this gives the most effective feedback to her.

If you do not agree with her rating and/or cannot think of anything positive then leave the space blank.

I will be discussing Paula's ratings with her on Wednesday at 9.05 am and Friday at 3.15 pm.

Thank you for your cooperation.
Signed: *H. Hand*–Form tutor
Paula – student

Figure 18.2 An example of a self-directing programme

described are ticks at the simplest level, colour coding, or just a written description of what the child did. The comments by the teacher might be requested by the child at the start of the programme, but after a period, say a month, it might be advisable to phase out the comments so that the young person has an increasing responsibility for his/her own behaviour.

For younger pupils, it might be more appropriate to focus on an agreed definition of acceptable behaviour and for the child to use a simple method such as writing yes/no or ticks/crosses to describe whether the behaviour was acceptable or not. Endorsing comments by the teacher can be backed up by the head teacher giving stickers or drawing a smiley face at the end of the day. Parental backup can be obtained by sending the sheets home for the parents to add their comments.

Name ....Date ....

Job/Tasks to be done	Time to be taken	Whether achieved	Teacher comments
Quite detailed and clear descriptions are given of what the child is expected to do, so as to reduce uncertainty.	Achievable target times should be set.	A tick could indicate that it has been done.	These should highlight the rules that the child has followed to reach the target.

Figure 18.3 Example of a task sheet

Task sheets or job sheets for lessons

Moving to a more general example, some children benefit from having clearer information about what it is that they are expected to do lesson by lesson, and how long they are being given to do it. Each lesson might have three or four targets, but it is usually best to write down just one target at a time. (An example of a task sheet is given in Figure 18.3.)

Again the teacher has some information to fill in, as does the child, and as more work is completed the child's self-esteem and competence will increase. This method can quite radically alter what is being produced by a child and is something that they realise is used in real-life jobs.

So there needs to be a maximum involvement in the young person selecting every aspect of the programme. I shall later attempt to list as a series of menus all the possible approaches and methods of which I have made use since I began encouraging the use of the self-directing approach.

The purposes of the self-directing approach

1 Self-directing is one strategy which can be used easily in the classroom, which helps make students less dependent on external adult control and moves them towards self-regulated social behaviour.
2 It enhances the young person's view of what they are doing, how this affects other people, and what they are able to change.
3 It releases important time, which the teacher spends on controlling behaviour, for other functions such as facilitating the learning of the children in the class.
4 It helps to achieve a primary goal of education, which is to turn out self-motivated, self-aware and self-controlled young people.
5 It encourages young people to set realistic and achievable goals for their behaviour and to be clear about what would constitute progress.
6 It brings about a generally more effective way of achieving the maintenance and generalisation of a skill to new situations.
7 It provides clear, useful feedback to young people regarding the success that they have achieved in changing their behaviour, thus enhancing their self-esteem.
8 It enhances the motivation of young people who have recognised that there is a problem that needs addressing.
9 It establishes a process for reviewing progress, which is totally child-centred and should make use of the language they use to describe the changes in their behaviour.
10 As the approach develops, aspects of it can be selectively faded out, in a negotiated order so as to put increasing responsibility on the young person, via his/her own internal dialogue.
11 It should encourage a developmental progression to a constructive state of self-discipline.
12 It should become a positive cycle of growth rather than a vicious circle of self-perpetuating and increasingly complex problems.
13 It reduces the need for a power relationship over children, thus increasing their personal efficacy. It is a paradox that, as adults, if we over-use or abuse power we automatically lose our influence and the respect/trust of the young person.

Ways of increasing the success of a self-directing behavioural programme

1 Only *positive information* should be recorded, in order to avoid demotivating the child and, more importantly, to put the responsibility for describing any problems onto the child's shoulders. The key person should facilitate this by encouraging the child to describe what happened honestly, e.g. by pointing at the blank space on the form.

2 The *locus of control* is within the child, and adults have to believe this and convey this message clearly in all conversations e.g. 'It's you that has achieved this, well done!' or 'Who made the decision to have a "wobbler"?' Encouraging 'I . . .' statements also help to achieve this.

3 We need to acknowledge the *'fight-or-flight reaction'* as a normal part of human behaviour. Some people, for a variety of reasons, have a lower threshold to this biological reflex. When the adrenalin rush has occurred and a child is involved with a member of staff, the best professional approach is to allow the child to 'cool off' in a safe place without further confrontation, which would only end with an increased risk of aggression. Once the kidneys have flushed out the adrenalin, in 10–20 minutes, this is the right time to talk it through. This action creates a 'both win' situation out of a potentially major confrontation.

4 *Self-directing needs to be distinguished from other, punishment programmes*, such as report cards. By all staff accepting this distinction the chances of the students shifting their ground are enhanced.

5 The primary aim is *honest and open communication* between the young person and their confidant. An honest appreciation of the effects of their behaviour and what could be done to change it will be far more motivating in the end than any hammer hanging over a child's head.

6 *Being average is OK*, we must not expect an absolute improvement or we will be disappointed. A child behaving within the normal range of acceptable behaviour *must* be seen as a success.

7 *Flexibility of the programme* and adapting it to meet changing needs is essential, so the regular meetings between the child and key person should be a way of negotiating changes and revisions of targets. This freshening up of the programme is a way of avoiding the 'two-week wonder' phenomenon that one gets with a lot of behavioural interventions.

8 *The role of the key person/counsellor* is fundamental to the success of the approach. The young person should select a person they trust and who they feel will give them the attention they need. Imposing someone just because they have 'the pips on the shoulder' and because 'it should be their job' is one way to guarantee failure. School secretaries and lunchtime supervisors, if selected, might be delighted to be involved in such an important process.

9 *Maximising the involvement of the child* or ownership of the approach are not buzz phrases in this approach: THEY ARE THE APPROACH. Consent and agreement are vital, at all stages.

10 *Awareness or recognition of a problem* needs to be accepted as the essential prerequisite of change in behaviour.

Thus: Attitudes, beliefs and inner thoughts change behaviour, *not* vice versa.

11 *Talking about feelings* is a fundamental part of open communication. The four basic emotions can be summarised as:

> Glad – Joy/Satisfaction
> Sad – Down/Depressed/Tears
> Mad – Angry/Frustrated/Agression
> Bad – Frightened/Self-doubt/Poor self-esteem

Emotions are the legitimate domain of any helping relationship. Also, a balanced dialogue on head or heart statements is necessary, as it is often the heart that pumps the warming sense of motivation through our bodies. We want it to be more than an intellectual exercise.

12 *Let's take a risk* and do it the child's way, because individuals are the best judges of what is possible for them to tackle as well as what is the most appropriate way to do things at a particular point.

A menu of components of a self-directing programme

SWOT analysis of agreed changes in behaviour. (Strengths, weaknesses, opportunities and threats, i.e. what will stop it from happening?).

Rehearsal either orally or physically and the use of cognitive preconditioning (mental rehearsal of successful outcomes).

Encouraging positive self-talk/ego-strengthening via relaxation.

'*Secret messages*' written invisibly on the hand to act as a prompt, e.g. TAME = think about my excitement.

Behaviours to focus on – increase success by using at least one that can already be achieved along with ones that need to be achieved.

Developing self-observation skills.

Methods of recording – written, oral description in interview or on tape

Adult/teacher positive feedback to endorse child's view of behaviours. If there is a disagreement the child is given a choice to change his rating.

Key person – Who does the child want to be involved?
          – When/How often to meet?

Where would be a good place to discuss it?

To whom else should feedback go? – tutor, head teacher, parent or teaching staff, as children find this rewarding.

Self-reinforcement – when resisted reacting to a provocation.
– when achieved progress.

Criteria for behaviour – what is acceptable/average?
– what would constitute a relative improvement?

Choosing approaches for rating/recording behaviours

Yes/No	— did it fit self-definition of acceptable or not?
Marks out of 10 or 5	— a very versatile method, which children can apply very accurately.
Colour coding	e.g. traffic lights: Red: unacceptable – stop it! Amber: halfway there. Green: going well.
Everyday measuring devices (drawings of)	— thermometers: the hotter it is the more unacceptable the behaviour. — barometers: fair to stormy. — speedometers: too slow, to good speed for the conditions, to too fast.
Codes	— letters/numbers/simple pictures/shading that represent the range of responses.
Graphs	— for feelings, behaviours. Plotted lesson by lesson or at regular time-intervals.
Tallies	— either by using a stroke or mark for each occurrence or by using a hand-held counter. Counters could also be moved from one pile or pocket to another. For use with specific behaviours that need reducing.
Guesstimates	— frequency of unacceptable and acceptable behaviours (teacher acts as moderator).
Leave it blank	— if behaviour was very unacceptable, as this puts the onus on the child to explain to the key person what happened.

Child's descriptive labels, e.g.
> — 'Grump' rating.
> 'Bluey' count.
> 'Paddy' score.
> 'Smile' count.
> 'Bolsh' rating.

Use numbers to help define the degree of the behaviour.

A menu of formats that can be used

Daily sheet	— child designs layout
Exercise book	— with explanation to staff in front cover. Child takes responsibility for drawing it up.
Booklet	— using computer graphics based on child's design. (NOT mass-produced as it would lose personalised effect.)
Diary	— feelings, e.g. anger, happiness. — behaviours, e.g. lesson by lesson. — reactions to problem situations.
Calendar	— with coding or rating for each day.
Computer	— store information on own disk with password.
Discussion only	— using possibly a counselling framework, e.g. Exploration – Understanding – Action. (Egan 1990)
Tape recorder/dictaphone	— lesson-by-lesson observations, ratings and comments on progress.
Video analysis	— intermittent use of video recorder, which the child then comments on.
Self-mediated essays	— free writing on a regular basis about how they are dealing with their difficulties.
Good News Book	— child comments on areas that are successful and positive achievements.
Comparison to self-generated model example of work:	— e.g. for handwriting, maths layouts, science write-ups, etc.

Slips of paper	— child records information then stores it (e.g. 'blueys': blue pieces of paper to record rather than say unacceptable thoughts; 'red rags to a bull': red pieces of paper to record provoking incidents and how child responded).
Board game layouts	— e.g. a car racing circuit with the child moving on a square for each good lesson.
Popular pictures	— e.g. an aeroplane or a zoo. The picture is broken down into numbered sections which can be coloured in, in the correct order for each acceptable lesson or for each piece of work done to an acceptable standard.
Yellow and red cards	— these could be included in a programme where the young person needs to be helped to handle their temper. The yellow card could be a warning to a teacher that he can feel things building up, and the red card could signal that he needs to leave 'the field of play' to 'cool off', thus allowing any fight-or-flight reaction to dissipate before things are talked through. A teacher might just write the time on the back to show when the card was used and also when the child returned to the classroom.

Parallel teacher and child assessments
— here both parties record the rating for the target behaviours for the session and then discuss the ratings in order to reach a consensus.

Parallel peer and child assessments
— a bit more risky, but here the two students reach a consensus before the target child passes on the information.

PULLING IT ALL TOGETHER

The self-directing behavioural sequence (Figure 18.4) is intended to be a useful descriptive, metaphorical summary of the stages and processes involved in developing a programme for a young person. If the young person gets stuck or misdirected on the journey, then a problem-solving approach needs to be adopted to shed new light and to 'brainstorm' a range of solutions to the current situation.

The key strands in the approach are using all our supportive skills to

Stages using direction-finding metaphor   **Stages from
                                                    self-management model**

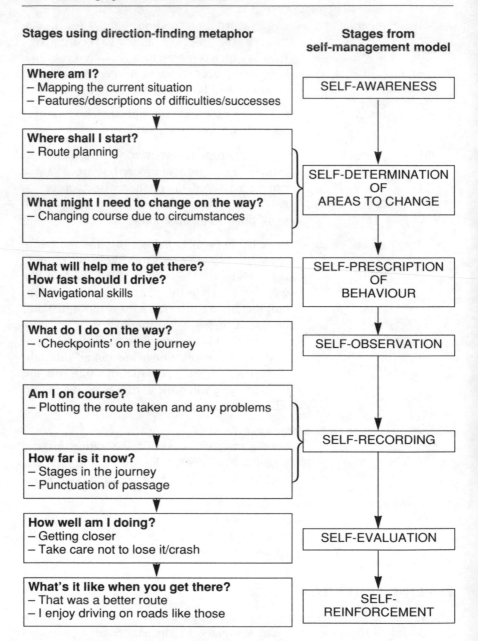

Figure 18.4 The self-directing behavioural sequence

enhance young people's internalised control of their behaviour and, by our conversations with them, to encourage them to think that the problem behaviours can be separated from them, i.e. externalised. So 'grumps' can be locked in this cupboard for much of the time, and 'paddies' can be increasingly left outside the school gates. The distancing between the person's self-control and the problem behaviours illustrates clearly what progress is being achieved, and gives plenty of scope for effective feedback on changes in a positive direction.

To conclude, I hope that by using the model reflexively I have been able to encourage an increased professional awareness of what options are available for use with young people and, by following through the self-management cycle, have increased the motivation to experiment with, elaborate on and share these self-directing strategies. The flexibility and possibilities offered are exciting, and I finish by asking you to try out this model with some lower-level problems initially, to gain confidence, and then to widen it to a whole gamut of problems, but in an individualised, child-focused and carefully negotiated way.

REFERENCES

Claxton, G. (1989) *Being a Teacher*. London: Cassell.
Dyer, W. (1978) *Pulling Your Own Strings*. London: Arrow Books.
Egan, G. (1990) *The Skilled Helper*. Pacific Grove, Calif.: Brooks/Cole.
Frederickson, N. (1991) *Social Competence* (Developing Self-Discipline series). University College, London.
Gordon, T. (1991) *Discipline that Works – Promoting Self-discipline in Children*. New York: Times Books.
Gross, A. and Wojnilower, D. (1984) 'Self-directed behaviour change in children: Is it self-directed?' *Behaviour Therapy*, 15: 501–514
Haring, G., Lovitt, T., Eaton M. and Hansen, C. (1978) *The Fourth R – Research in the Classroom*. Columbus, Ohio: Charles E. Merrill.
Johnson, S. (1983) *The One Minute Father*. New York: William Morrow.
Kanfer, S.H. and Spates, C.R. (1977) 'Self-monitoring, self-evaluation and self-reinforcement in children's learning: a test of the multi-stage self-regulation model', *Behaviour Therapy*, 8: 9–16.
McNamara, E. (1992) 'Motivational interviewing – the gateway to pupil self-management', *Pastoral Care*, 10: 22–28.
Maher, C. and Zins, J. (1987) *Psychoeducational Interventions in the Schools*. New York: Pergamon Press.
Maines, B. and Robinson, G. (1988) *The Bag of Tricks*. Portishead, Bristol: Lame Duck Publishing.
O'Leary, K. and O'Leary, S. (1972) 'Classroom Management'. New York: Pergamon Press
Panagopoulou-Stamatelatou, A. (1990) 'The use of behavioural self-management in primary school settings: a review', *Educational Psychology*, 10: 207–224.
Piaget, J. (1950) *The Psychology of Intelligence*. New York: Harcourt.
White, M. (1988) 'The externalising of the problems and the re-authoring of lives and relationships', Adelaide: Dulwich Centre Newsletter.

White, M. and Epston, D. (1989) *Literate Means to Therapeutic Ends*. Adelaide: Dulwich Centre Publications.

Wong, N.Y. (1988) 'Effects of self-monitoring and reinforcement on problem-solving performance', *Educational Psychology*, 8: 153–160.

Wragg, J. (1989) *Talk Sense to Yourself*. London: Longman

Wright, A. (1991) *Motivation* (Developing Self-Discipline series). University College, London.

Chapter 19

Balancing school and individual approaches

Penny Holland and Phil Hamerton

This chapter has been written by two members of the Nottinghamshire Elton project team, a psychologist and a teacher. It is based on our experiences, before and during the project, as individuals and as members of the team. We owe much to all who have been involved in the Nottinghamshire Elton project, particularly the schools upon which this work is based. Our experiences have shown us that there are opportunities in some schools to improve the support offered to pupils who, otherwise, may be excluded.

The title of this chapter suggests that there may be some tension between meeting the needs of individual pupils, those whom teachers regard as the 'most difficult to teach' because of their behaviour, and the needs of the whole-school community. We shall argue that the tension can be resolved by careful balancing of resources *within a whole-school approach*. By a 'whole-school approach' we mean an approach to matters to do with behaviour and discipline that maximises involvement and consistency and minimises confusion and isolation. Such an approach is essentially preventive, rather than reactive, forming part of the normal, planned provision of the school. We recognise that there is also a need for reactive procedures, but we believe that these are not the essential approach that the school should adopt and upon which they should rely.

We shall describe a process by which schools may begin to develop such a whole-school approach and we shall discuss the potential for change within many schools. We shall not prescribe policies or plans, recommend structures or approaches; it is essential for each school to go down that road anew.

Observations of school classrooms have confirmed for us that pupils' difficult behaviour is, to a large extent, a product of time and context. This should come as no surprise and supports many earlier writers (e.g. Mortimore *et al.* 1984; Rutter *et al.* 1979; Hargreaves 1972), whose works are well summarised in the Elton Report (DES, 1989). The difficulties are usually experienced by teachers as preventing the smooth-running of the classroom, hence the term 'difficult to teach' (Hanko 1989) as a descriptive label when one is required.

THE BACKGROUND

The report of the Elton Committee (DES 1989) was not altogether welcomed by teachers. This report argued strongly that teachers and the schools in which they work can dramatically affect the behaviour of their young people. The report made recommendations regarding the responsibilities of parents, the police, broadcasters, local and national government, as well as teachers and pupils in schools. Ninety-eight of the one hundred and thirty-eight recommendations relate directly to what happens in schools and classrooms. The report did not, however, suggest simplistic solutions, nor did it conclude that schools were about to be submerged under the welter of large-scale disruption that some earlier surveys and press coverage had suggested.

One recommendation, quickly acted upon, was that funds be made available to support local authority initiatives between 1990 and 1993. The aim of such initiatives was 'to support schools in working with their most difficult pupils by improving the coordination and delivery of a range of support services and improving the provision generally made within schools for them'. Nottinghamshire was one of the authorities that bid successfully for funding.

Initially focusing on six comprehensive schools in the city of Nottingham, the objectives of the Nottinghamshire Elton project were to:

— improve the provision generally made within schools for the most difficult pupils, including intervention at pre-exclusion stages and support for reintegration;
— support schools in managing their most difficult pupils and in developing effective approaches and policies that highlight both staff and pupil needs;
— make more effective use of existing mechanisms for managing difficult pupils and improve the coordination and delivery of a range of support from Support Services;
— to enlist positive cooperation and mutual understanding between schools and parents to form an effective response to the needs of pupils with difficult behaviour.

City secondary schools were invited to submit bids to the local authority for inclusion in the project. Successful schools were to receive support from a team of three seconded teachers and a seconded educational psychologist.

As the team was being appointed, one of its first duties was to mount a county-wide in-service event which was open to all secondary schools. The aim of this event was to enable schools to begin or continue to develop policies for meeting the needs of young people who exhibit emotional or behavioural difficulties. Thus, in what follows, references to schools are not necessarily to the six in which we worked most intensively: a total of forty-two secondary schools across the county had some direct project support and all have contributed to the development of our ideas.

DEFINING THE PROBLEM

What we did

In order to help schools identify their development objectives, and in negotiation with them, we agreed to examine aspects of their existing practice.

We agreed to:

1 collect, analyse and try to interpret data on exclusions; identify some pupils who were considered to be at risk of exclusion, and to shadow them for some time to explore the provision made for them; and conduct retrospective case-studies on a small number of permanently excluded pupils, examining their educational histories and identifying successful interventions, etc.;
2 look at existing policy documents and interview teachers about existing support provision for the difficult to teach;
3 undertake classroom observations;
4 interview external support agencies and examine their links with schools;
5 produce an attitude survey for all six schools.

In consultation with the local Area Education Office, it was agreed that we should be supplied with details of all excluded pupils transferring into project schools and of the exclusions of pupils from all Nottingham city's secondary schools. This was to enable us to monitor changes in our project schools' rates of exclusions and thereby evaluate the success of the project. We would also be able to see whether some schools were being asked to admit large numbers of excluded pupils and if any of these schools were being particularly successful in the reintegration of these pupils.

What we found

1 *Patterns of exclusions*

Our data indicated that the schools had clear expectations about the number of times different types of exclusions should be used. Typically, this pattern was that, for any individual pupil, there should be no more than three fixed-term exclusions, one indefinite exclusion and, finally, a permanent. This pattern, which we knew from other data was not universally applied within the county's schools, also hid the extensive use of unofficial sending home of pupils. Use of exclusions was not consistent according only to the actual offence but was influenced by a number of factors, such as who else was involved; the verbal abuse of a caretaker, for example, might result in a reprimand from a member of staff, while the verbal abuse of a member of the school's senior management team would usually result in a fixed-term exclusion. Indeed, one head teacher said that defiance of him by a pupil was 'intolerable' and 'indicated a complete disregard for the authority of the school and could therefore *only* be met by exclusion'.

It also became clear to us that schools operate a 'totting-up' system in regard to punishments, so that, for example, repeated trivial offences can lead to extreme sanctions being applied. This does not reflect the recommended approach that punishment should reflect the gravity of the offence.

> the system of punishments should be designed to signal the degree of disapproval involved. This should mean for example that the most severe punishments, such as exclusion from school, should be reserved for the most serious offences such as violent behaviour.
>
> (DES 1989)

In addition there seemed to be misunderstanding of the 'five days in aggregate' as the trigger for the parental right of appeal. The legal limit to exclusion, during any term, before the parents have a right to appeal to governors, is five days in total. We found that many schools believed that five days' fixed-term exclusion in any term was the legal maximum. Subsequent exclusion, they thought, had to be indefinite or permanent. As a result, very few schools used fixed-term exclusions as part of a systematic holding strategy with a pupil.

2 *Schools' policies for behaviour, communication, rewards and sanctions*

In many schools we found complex documents describing their policies; some schools had no written policies on aspects of the above. The policies we found had often been drawn up several years ago, and they were usually not well known by the staff of the school. Furthermore, some of them were extremely complex and unworkable. Evidence from classroom and other observations, as well as interviews with staff, confirms this view. This evidence also shows that the use of these policies varied between teachers and, in some schools, was seldom seen.

It became clear to us that distinctions between pastoral support structures and disciplinary functions were often muddled. For example, form tutors often repeated punishments given by other teachers or were expected to oversee those given by the subject teachers. Others simply saw their role as collecting information about concerns and marking the register. This finding echoes earlier work (Johnson *et al.* 1980). Form tutors were identified as key people within pastoral systems who are frequently given extensive duties to be undertaken in unrealistic amounts of time. Senior pastoral staff, such as heads of upper or lower school, heads of house and heads of year, who often have important responsibilities for ensuring the effective work of their form tutors, typically are only given one or two hours each week to do this and, in reality, might spend half this checking registers with the education welfare officer. Many subject teachers bypass the channels of communication laid down in the school policies by taking matters such as persistent lateness directly to senior pastoral staff. This carries the danger of marginalising and disempowering the form tutors, overloading the senior staff and escalating the potential consequences. This is most obvious in cases of verbal abuse of a teacher by a pupil, which was often reported to a member of the senior management team who was expected to take responsibility for resolving the difficulty. Apart from the risk that in a moment of anger the pupil will now verbally abuse the senior member of staff, or at least refuse to apologise, the range of low-key options for resolution appears to decrease. By circumventing the tutor and, possibly, the head of pastoral care, opportunities to support the pupil and de-escalate the conflict are frequently missed.

3 *Classroom observation*

Our observations of pupils who were identified by their teachers as causing the most concern showed that teachers are not always accurate in identifying the pupils who are the most difficult to teach. Identified pupils frequently behaved better than teachers had predicted, while other pupils were sometimes observed to be more disruptive. Observation was aimed at pupils, but there is, clearly, an interaction between their behaviour and that of the teacher. Amid much good practice by teachers, some were observed not to adhere to the school's stated procedures and practices. For example, in some schools there were classes where: little praise was observed; minor misdemeanours were allowed to go unchallenged; and rules were not consistently applied. On occasion, pupils were observed to go all day without doing any work of their own and some pupils attended all lessons but were not observed to have any direct interaction with a teacher.

Where classroom support was made available for pupils it often seemed to be unplanned and it did not necessarily seem to be available in lessons where teachers and pupils experienced the greatest difficulties: for example, where classes were largest or where there was a history of disruptive incidents. Some lessons did not seem to be well prepared. In other lessons there was little evidence, in the face of a clear need, of differentiation in task, level or method. Teachers sometimes had inadequate equipment and occasionally left classes to get equipment that had been left behind.

4 *Outside support agencies*

In addition to working with the schools, we worked with the county's Special Needs Support Service, the Education Welfare Service and the Educational Psychology Service. Our work indicates that there is frequently a mismatch between the schools' expectations of them and the agencies' own perception of their roles. In general, liaison between the external agencies and the schools could be improved:

— agents were frequently involved with the same pupil without working together;
— opportunities for consultation and coordination of their efforts were limited;
— communication with the body of staff as a whole in schools was usually not achieved.

In addition, there seemed to be little evidence of accountability or evaluation of the effectiveness of either individual casework or of the whole-service input. There was some contracting of support but performance targets were seldom explicit.

5 *Attitude survey*

The results of our survey suggested that teachers' attitudes and philosophies were generally positive:

— regarding rewards as more effective than punishment;
— believing that support for pupils who are 'difficult to teach' in mainstream schooling is more effective than off-site provision for their education;
— accepting their own responsibility for discipline in the classroom.

The survey also produced clear evidence that:

— schools' policies on rewards and sanctions were not clearly understood;
— insufficient time was made available for monitoring pupils' progress;
— classroom teachers frequently needed more support from senior colleagues.

What we did with what we found

The data gained in these early days were not encouraging. All of our schools had policies for the management of pupils' behaviour. All regarded themselves as meeting the needs of the majority of their pupils. Most of the teachers expressed what we would see as desirable, child-centred, positive teaching attitudes, preferring to see pupils in mainstream rather than segregated education wherever possible. Nevertheless many of the schools appeared unable to limit sufficiently the numbers of pupils considered difficult to teach, and their resources were not adequate to meet the needs of the many identified.

Having gained some insight into the working of the project schools, we developed the view that a small but significant proportion of teachers in some of these schools *were* unable, or *felt* unable, to perform the minimum functions of their task: adequate planning and preparation for a range of performance levels and the consistent enforcement of school rules. It seems that for many teachers in these schools the support and discipline systems are not proving effective, and their schools seem constantly to be responding to frequently occurring crises that overwhelm their resources. As a result, there is no time to consider preventive strategies. This pattern may be evident in other schools.

So, how were we to progress? We felt that we could not expect welcoming receptions in schools with messages of this type. Nor, having delivered the message, could we expect teachers to engage positively with us in the task of developing better preventive strategies.

In short, however sound the data that we had collected, we felt we could not present them to the teachers in the project schools. Fortunately, we were able to draw on other work undertaken as a part of the county-wide training event. This showed that the same data could be collected by teachers themselves. Using teachers to collect and present the evidence, then, as a staff, highlighting the issues and moving onto policy development would seem more likely to be productive. We also found that it was preferable to reframe the evidence gathered into statements of good practice and then query the extent to which the school felt that these standards were universally met.

Having undertaken the studies described, we were led to conclude that support for the difficult to teach can be provided most effectively in schools where whole-school provision ensures that the needs of the overwhelming majority of pupils are met through sound curricular, disciplinary and pastoral provision.

Developing effective whole-school provision

Observation of effective and ineffective processes in schools has led us to conclude that there is at least one way forward in promoting lasting and successful change.

It seemed from our work that the initial impetus for change should come

either from significant individual teachers or from a group of teachers who
have a shared concern and the power to place the concern as an important
item on the school's agenda. Of these significant members of staff the head
teacher is the most powerful and it seems that no whole-school policy or
practice development can occur without the support, even passive, of the
head. In the fields of discipline and unacceptable pupil behaviour it
appears that the active support of the head needs to be engaged particularly early; the nature of the changes required in policy and practice is
likely to be so profound that only by being made the highest priority within
the school will progress in their implementation be maintained in the face
of the other pressures affecting schools at the present time.

Having established on the agenda the concern about the school's
responses to the most difficult to teach, we have found that a three-stage
process of 'introspection', 'consultation' and 'definition' offers schools an
approach that is likely to result in beneficial changes.

Introspection

Before embarking on development planning, our experience has shown
that a school's most effective initial step should be to look carefully at its
current position. Asking questions such as: What, if any policies exist?
Who knows about them? Are they effective? is likely to yield a range of
documents. Our experience suggests that these are likely to be several
years old, highly complex, expressed largely in negative terms, reactive in
describing responses to incidents rather than how to avoid their occurring,
little known of and even less used. The issue of the effectiveness of such
policies will indicate the importance of monitoring and reviewing; both of
these processes are unlikely to be routinely occurring and may well not
have been part of the policies and practices originally. If the process of
introspection is then taken into the classrooms and corridors of the school
by teachers observing one another's lessons and all other aspects of the
school's provision, a picture similar to the one that we found is likely to
emerge. The outcomes of this introspective process, however predictable
they may be, should be empirically derived by each school and should also
be mediated by a positive approach in their presentation. The findings of
the staff and the subsequent proposals depend for their success upon
maximum staff support and not alienating or being seen to 'blame' staff for
all of the difficulties. Thus, for example, if teachers are frequently seen to
ignore misbehaviour in the corridor, feedback might take the form:
'Teachers contribute significantly to the good order of the school by
recognising and appropriately responding to corridor misbehaviour.' It is
helpful if such remarks can be derived directly from observation of good
practice, however infrequently it may be presented.

The feeding back of the results of this introspective process will offer teachers an opportunity to identify the significant issues to be addressed. These issues are likely to include some of the following:

— development of a code of conduct or clear set of rules;
— school policies on the use of rewards and sanctions;
— provision for pupils with special needs;
— clear definition of the roles of different staff;
— the availability of support for staff;
— guidance and advice on classroom management.

Since many of these are interdependent it may be that some of them are seen as issues to be addressed together. There is some danger of attempting to do too many things at once, but experience has shown us that it is possible to start several separate strands at once and then weave them together. A school might identify developing a code of conduct, a policy for rewards and sanctions, and the role of the pastoral staff as priority issues. Work might proceed on all three simultaneously, with the code of conduct offering a framework within which the principles and practice of using rewards and sanctions will operate; both policies could develop at the same time. Meanwhile the role and functioning of the pastoral teams could be reviewed and redefined, with reference to the emerging policy on rewards and sanctions as necessary. Alternatively, a school might decide that there is a logical order in which to tackle these issues and proceed sequentially, perhaps: code of conduct, rewards and sanctions policy, pastoral system. There cannot be a prescribed approach, but we believe that it is essential that a plan which details areas for work, objectives and timelines is produced and adhered to. It is at this stage that detailed consultation should be undertaken.

Consultation

What do we mean by consultation and with whom should we consult? There are some who regard consultation as a matter of producing a detailed policy and implementation plan, asking for comments from a select few without allowing time for careful reading, and then presenting it to all concerned as the agreed consensus.

We have seen that in order to answer fully the question, 'With whom should we consult?', the school should ask another question, 'Who can help us resolve this problem or influence the course of events?' The answer to the latter will be the answer to the former. If the task is to develop a whole-school code of conduct, for example, the list of people who have been found able to help resolve behaviour problems or influence the course of events regarding behaviour has included: bus drivers, local shopkeepers, parents/carers and all members of the school community.

Consultation itself needs careful handling. Are *we* telling others what *they* should be concerned about? We might assume that others share our concerns, but we must not proceed on that assumption; we should ask others what their concerns are and how they feel they can best contribute to the process. Asking midday supervisors what they are concerned about, what they feel they can do and what they need in order to be able to support the school, can yield some surprising solutions, such as a football-referee style of cards in response to offences (Imich and Jefferies 1987).

From the process of consultation, which schools have successfully accomplished by using methods such as guided interviews, questionnaires and working parties, issues will have been identified, views will have been sought and a consensus may have been developed that will form the basis of a school policy. That policy should apply to all and should be intended to enable the whole school to function better. It should lead to the definition of specific practices and structures that are intended to make the policy work.

Definition

We have seen that schools often have highly complex policies that are sometimes not operating effectively. This may be because those required to perform specific tasks are not given the necessary resources, which usually means time, or because the policies simply do not have the support and understanding of the staff. We have found that what is required is a clarity of roles and the provision of the resources necessary for their performance.

We believe that effective school policies for promoting good behaviour should make clear the normal expectations of all members of the school community. These expectations, possibly expressed in the form of a code of conduct, might also indicate the possible rewards and sanctions that should result from desirable or undesirable behaviour. Within the constraints of the school policy, it should be made clear where individual members of the community are free to adopt their own rules. For example, in a school where there is a stated policy of not chewing, a teacher who condones chewing will be undermining the whole-school approach. If, however, no school policy exists regarding chewing, each teacher will need to establish his or her own rules/expectations and should then be internally consistent.

Where a pupil frequently fails to meet the normal expectations, there may be a need to offer support and possibly guidance in addition to any discipline. We believe that it is essential, if both are to be effective, to distinguish clearly between the disciplinary structures in the school and the support structures. If it is to be the responsibility of the subject teacher, supported by the head of department, to maintain discipline, this should be clearly stated. If the form tutor is to be informed of difficulties, it should be

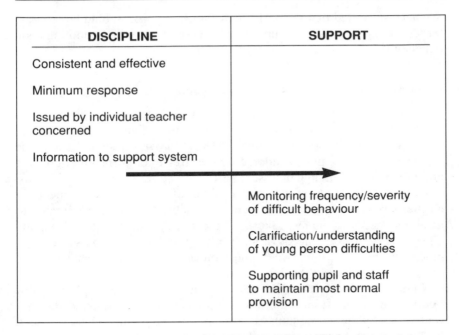

DISCIPLINE	SUPPORT
Consistent and effective	
Minimum response	
Issued by individual teacher concerned	
Information to support system	
	Monitoring frequency/severity of difficult behaviour
	Clarification/understanding of young person difficulties
	Supporting pupil and staff to maintain most normal provision

Figure 19.1 A clear distinction must be drawn between support and discipline

clear that this passage of information is to enable an overall picture to be built up so that coordinated action and effective support is possible, and that it is not intended to involve the tutor in delivering the sanctions. We believe that the links between the disciplinary and the support structure need to be strong but should not confuse the roles (Figure 19.1). Having defined the roles of the various teams within the school, there should be equal clarity regarding the allocation of necessary resources.

If the role requires liaison with external agencies, home visiting and consultation with other teachers, consideration should be given regarding time and skills. It may be necessary to consider who should offer support and what time-allocation and skills they will require.

When all the details have been worked out, the school should have laid the foundations of a whole-school approach to behaviour, affecting all, involving all and owned by all.

MEETING THE NEEDS OF INDIVIDUAL PUPILS

In the ordinary routine of a school, when a pupil does not meet the normal expectations in some respect, discipline may be considered appropriate. Alongside discipline there is usually some support, perhaps in the form of guidance or simply listening, though this may not be formally arranged.

We have suggested that the performance of these tasks should be separate but operating in concert within a whole-school policy for promoting good behaviour.

Every whole-school system will fail some pupils

While the vast majority of pupils routinely get adequate motivation, reward and support through normal classroom interaction with their teachers and parents/carers, so the normal pastoral provision should meet the predictable needs of pupils undergoing the stresses of normal life: growing up, moving house, failing in lessons, etc.

We believe that no pastoral system will be adequate to meet the needs of all the pupils who come to its attention if subject teachers are unable to meet the needs of many. Likewise, the pastoral system must respond effectively to meet the needs of most of the pupils coming to its attention, otherwise the more intensive support on offer will be overwhelmed and consequently will meet the needs of none.

No matter how effectively the school policies have been developed, how clearly defined the responsibilities or how generously resourced the preventive arm of the school support, some pupils and their teachers will need further support. Such support will depend upon a coherent system for the identification of those in need and the adequate provision of necessary resources.

Identifying those in greatest need

One of the most surprising discoveries we made was that schools are not very effective in the interpretation of the mass of data available to them. This might be partly because of the allocation of time to the people who have access to the data, but we believe that it may reflect assumptions which teachers seem to make about who the most difficult pupils are. It seems to us, and to the teachers when they observed lessons, that the pupils they expected to see causing the most disruption were often not the ones observed doing so. This general finding suggests that school systems are not very sensitive to feedback about what is *actually* happening in lessons. Detailed questioning of teachers in schools and examination of their policy documents show that responsibility for the collation of concern forms, if specifically anyone's responsibility, is often the responsibility of someone without sufficient time to do it effectively. We found that time is not usually provided for teachers to share their concerns, even if a teacher, whether tutor or head of year, is well-informed. In some cases, it seems, information about domestic difficulties, which some believe to be vital for all teachers, is limited to those in the pastoral system furthest removed from teaching the pupil.

In a few cases we found schools where there is an established pattern of 'concern meetings' in which those directly involved in teaching a pupil can share their concerns in non-directed time outside the teaching day. In one case a school has developed a within-the-day meeting opportunity for form tutors and year heads to discuss individuals and to develop, with outside agencies if necessary, a specific action plan. In another school a weekly meeting is held involving: pastoral deputy, learning support co-ordinator, EWO, EPS, special needs support service personnel and heads of year/ tutors as appropriate. These meetings are supported by a regular pro- gramme of pastoral team meetings. In another geographical area of the county there is a practice of regular multi-agency meetings involving, in addition, police and social services; this is considered highly effective.

It is our view that, unless specific responsibility and time is given for the identification of the pupils in greatest need of intensive support, this process is unlikely to be effective. We believe that the process of identifi- cation is the most important step towards describing needs. Learning support co-ordinators and their colleagues from the internal and external support services are usually then able, in a positive school environment, to find problem-solving approaches that suit them and help them suggest hypotheses and develop action plans accordingly.

Making special provision within the mainstream school

Identification alone is not enough. The school system should aim, not only to identify those pupils successfully and recognise their needs, but also to meet those needs *from within the available resources*.

Within the project schools, it quickly became clear that decisions are made about allocation of resources – staff time, class sizes and rooms, for example – often without the conscious knowledge of the majority of the staff. While overall teacher:pupil ratios are fairly constant within the county (approximately 15.5:1 in Nottinghamshire secondary schools), average class sizes vary widely, from as small as eighteen to as large as twenty-five; and *actual* class sizes vary even more widely. These variations sometimes seem not to reflect the apparent needs.

The provision of support made by schools for pupils who have special needs can vary, in terms of staff time, from none to more than the equivalent of four full-time teachers (4 FTEs) in a school of 700 pupils. Schools allocate rooms to specific subjects or functions according to criteria that are not always made clear. So, a suite of rooms might be allocated to TVEI and another to commerce, while there are no rooms for the support coordinator or heads of year to provide a space for calm intervention when a classroom crisis occurs.

The distinction between pupils 'with learning difficulties' and those 'with behavioural difficulties' is strengthened in some schools where the role of the support coordinator is seen as being concerned with remedial educational functions and curriculum differentiation *for* departments rather than *with* departments. The responsibility for support in cases where behaviour is perceived to be the problem is here given to the form tutors, who, as we found in some schools, may do no more than punish again!

Schools have the freedom to decide how they attempt to meet the needs of their most demanding pupils. We believe that, as the level of difficulty increases, it becomes more and more important that the functions of discipline and support are constructed separately. It is difficult for both parties, in cases of complex or long-term difficulties over behaviour, when the form tutor, for example, takes on the roles of befriender and disciplinarian simultaneously. Further, the role of supporter should be defined (Figure 19.2) and the supporters themselves should be supported. Support for the supportive tutor is unlikely to be provided by a system which escalates pupils into the exclusion system by involving the senior management team unless it is in a containing, problem-solving role (Figure 19.3).

To perform the role of a supportive tutor, a certain allocation of time is required. Time will also be required for the senior pastoral staff to support the tutors and so on. Alternatively, support might be viewed as the job of the support coordinator and the allocation of time might be made through that person. Before crying, '*But we haven't enough time now!*', let us look at the present ways in which time may be used in schools.

A model of school staffing

As our work took us into a large number of schools we quickly realised that there are enormous variations in the ways in which schools of similar sizes and serving similar catchment areas are organised. We found that, when encouraged to examine critically the way in which classes, timetables and responsibilities are organised, highly imaginative approaches can develop to meet the needs of specific institutions. This section explores the potential for development in a typical secondary school. Two different approaches will be described. The initial position and both developments are based on project schools and work actually undertaken with rolls and staffing equalised for numbers and slightly simplified to give a basic arithmetical model.

Let us take a typical secondary school of seven hundred and fifty pupils with a pupil:teacher ratio of 17:1. In this model the teaching week comprises twenty-five periods. Staffing establishment is forty-four, with a head and three deputies. What follows is a very crude staffing model, used to demonstrate the effect of certain choices.

The senior management team's teaching load is fairly typical, teaching fifty-five periods per week between them (2.2 FTE). (We found that wide variations exist in the extent of timetabled teaching done by senior management teams, with the four most senior teachers contributing anywhere between less than 2 FTEs and over 3 FTEs to the timetable.) Minimum non-contact time is set at three periods each week, thirteen other staff have additional non-contact time as heads of department (one or two periods weekly) or heads of year (two periods weekly).

At the beginning of the development the school's policy is to keep class sizes as low as possible in order to meet the needs of all pupils most efficiently. Average class size is twenty-one and this allows just 1 FTE (the support coordinator) to be released from the timetable for other duties, such as learning support. There is no further flexibility and nobody has really got time to follow up the pastoral support needs of pupils when things go wrong, except for the senior management team, who have fewer options as we have seen. Heads of all departments are also tutors.

After some staff discussions, average teaching groups might be increased to twenty-five. One of the project schools made just such a decision after

---

SUPPORT IS . . .

A   **Collecting and Collating Information**

   a) receiving teacher concerns
   b) pupil interview
   c) classroom observation
   d) parent/carer information
   e) curriculum access

B   **Interventions**

   Pupil –   a) befriending
             b) parent/carer involvement
             c) guidance/counselling
             d) behavioural strategies
             e) planned timetable alterations

   Teacher –

             a) peer support
             b) problem-solving strategies
             c) curriculum differentiation
             d) classroom management skills

   External agency liaison –

             a) involvement
             b) coordination

C   **Review**

Figure 19.2 The role of the supporter is defined

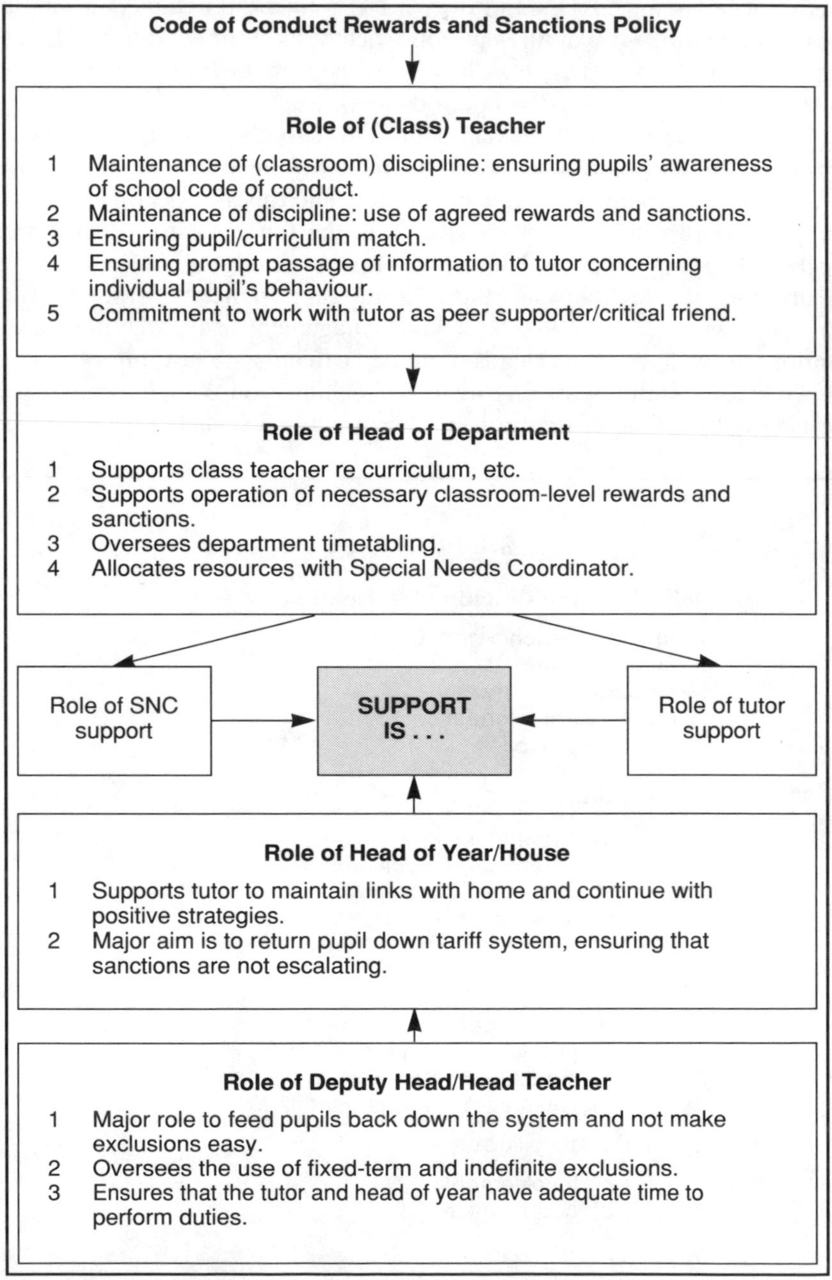

Figure 19.3 The supporter is supported

prolonged whole-staff consultation in the early days of the project. In our model school this releases a further one hundred and forty-three teacher-periods for learning support, pastoral support, etc. Now the school has some flexibility in staffing, a total of one hundred and sixty-five teacher-periods weekly, and has also freed five additional classrooms at any time. Only three heads of departments need now be tutors.

It is now possible to make arrangements for extensive support provision. This support may be channelled through the support coordinator, through the pastoral system, through curriculum departments, or through a combination.

Organising support to come through the pastoral system (Figure 19.4, Model A) tutors could be allocated a further five periods each week for tutorial duties: three periods of curricular support through department heads and two periods of pastoral support. In negotiation between heads of department and the 0.5 special needs coordinator, the ninety periods of learning support can be allocated according to need. Where possible it might be hoped to use tutors to support their own classes. The pastoral support now would have two periods weekly from each tutor, in addition to the contact during form times and PSE sessions. Heads of year could release tutors from these duties in exceptional circumstances for further pastoral work. Such a system should provide very effective support for the vast majority of pupils and their teachers. There would have been an increase in group size, but there would now be time to undertake the important duties necessary to offer effective support when behaviour causes problems and there would be significant support available within the classroom when learning becomes difficult. The role of the tutor would have been considerably enhanced and all become teachers of pupils with special needs. In one of the project schools just such a reorganisation took place.

Alternatively, our typical school might channel most support through an expanded Support Centre provision (Figure 19.5, Model B). Here the distinctions between learning and pastoral support would become blurred. In addition to the, now full-time, support coordinator, there could be two more full-time staff working from the Centre and a further 2 FTEs released for liaison and preparation with staff from the Support Centre. Another project school had established such a provision shortly before the project began. In our model school tutors might be given one extra non-contact period for their pastoral work, in particular to liaise with the Support Centre. Fifteen periods not allocated could, for example, be timetabled to Science for year 7 classes to help with practical work. Now individual pupils can be supported intensively and the pupils with the greatest need can be allocated full-time 1:1 support if needed. The Support Centre staff would have time to coordinate external support staff, liaise with pastoral staff and even undertake home visits. The role of the tutor is reduced and the skills required are fewer. Expertise is seen to be located, however, in *others*, potentially de-skilling the class teacher, who is also a tutor.

Balancing whole-school and individual approaches

Schools allocate resources according to their own priorities. The descriptions above show how schools can vary those allocations. It is clear that the tutor-led support provision allows less intensive support for individuals but should enhance the whole-school provision dramatically. The Support Centre model allows very intensive support for individuals, as well as a range of departmental support approaches, but it does emphasise the separate nature of support and, if the normal provision of the school is not good, is liable to be overwhelmed (Figure 19.6).

Allocation of teachers' time (A)

Average teaching group = 25   Week = 25 periods

Learning support

3 periods per week from all tutors
Allocation to 0.5 support coordinator and head of department for flexible usage
Most effectively, tutor supports own tutor group by:

      (a) Team teaching
      (b) In-class support to pupil
      (c) Small group withdrawal
      (d) Individual withdrawal

Pastoral support

30 mins. daily (tutor period) + 2 periods per week
Allocated by tutor to:

      (a) Individual pupil/group observation
      (b) Learning support
      (c) Individual guidance/counselling/target-setting, etc.
      (d) Parent/carer contact
      (e) External agency liaison
      (f) Support from head of year

PSE

1 period per week with tutor group

Non-contact time

3 periods per week

Figure 19.4 Organising support (Model A)

Allocation of teachers' time (B)

Average teaching group = 25   Week = 25 periods

Learning support

Full-time support coordinator +
2 full-time staff, based in Support Centre +
44 periods per week (selected staff) allocated to head of lower school
and heads of departments for flexible usage, e.g.:

    (a) Team teaching
    (b) In-class support to pupil
    (c) Small group withdrawal
    (d) Individual withdrawal
    (e) Programmed materials preparation

Pastoral support

20 mins. daily (tutor period) + 1 period per week
Allocated by tutor to:

    (a) Individual pupil/group observation
    (b) Learning support
    (c) Individual guidance/counselling/target-setting, etc.
    (d) Parent/carer contact
    (e) External agency liaison
    (f) Support from head of year

PSE

1 period per week with tutor group

Non-contact time

3 periods per week

Figure 19.5 Organising support (Model B)

A balance has to be found – an effective system that enables the maximum number of pupils to maximise their achievement will need to offer different levels of support, from the normal support of caring classroom teachers and tutors within their routine contact with pupils, to the intensive, full-time 1:1 support, delivered on-site to a pupil in the moment of crisis that makes normal classroom provision impossible. The balance appropriate to one school will be different in another and it will change as the school's and pupils' needs change.

CONCLUSION

We have not advocated a right way to support pupils in school. We have not indicated a correct balance between school and individual approaches. We have suggested an approach to development and we have suggested a range of options that schools might consider. It is our view that schools can satisfactorily meet the needs of the most difficult to teach for much more of the time than many now do. What is needed is a strong commitment to maintaining these young people in mainstream schools, rather than resorting to offloading and looking for alternatives outside school. Our experience has shown that, with the firm commitment of the senior management and within an effective whole-school supportive approach, it is possible to improve significantly the support available for the most difficult to teach. Where effective support *is* available within mainstream schools, the need to expand off-site provision should be significantly reduced. Experience in project schools has shown us that in such schools the teaching or learning experience is improved for all.

MODEL A	MODEL B
ADVANTAGES	
Support for all pupils	Support for the most difficult pupils
Early identification of problems	Teachers teach own specialism
Tutor maintains ownership	Breathing space for teachers
More home contact possible	Effective coordination of external agencies
Pupil kept down tariff system	Increase in work differentiation
Tutor skills developed	Calm environment for pupils
Roles and expectations defined	Teachers feel supported
Reduction in class teaching	Allows flexible response
Peer support	
Proper time allocation	
DISADVANTAGES	
No full-time withdrawal	Teachers disown problems
Potential increase in exclusions	Lack of tutor involvement
No 'expertise' in learning support	Home/school liaison difficult
Time delay in tutor skill acquisition	Less support for most pupils
Difficulty in coordinating external support	Skills stay with few people
Larger teaching/tutor groups	Early response less likely

Figure 19.6 Each model has its merits and problems

REFERENCES

Department of Education and Science (1989) *Discipline in Schools* (The Report of the Elton Committee). London: HMSO.

Hanko, G. (1989) 'After Elton – How to "Manage" Disruption?', *British Journal of Special Education*, 16,4, December 1989.

Hargreaves, D.H. (1967) *Social Relations in a Secondary School*. London: Routledge & Kegan Paul.

Hargreaves, D. (1972) *Interpersonal Relations and Education*. London: Routledge & Kegan Paul.

Imich, A. and Jefferies, K. (1987) 'Showing the yellow card', *Times Educational Supplement*, 6 November 1987.

Johnson, D., Ransom, E., Packwood, T., Bowden, K. and Kogan, M. (1980) *Secondary Schools and the Welfare Network*. London: Allen and Unwin.

Mortimore, P., Sammons, P., Stoll, L., Lewis, D. and Ecob, R. (1984) *School Matters*. Wells: Open Books.

Rutter, M., Maughan, B., Mortimore, P. and Ouston, J. (1979) *Fifteen Thousand Hours*. Wells: Open Books.

Author index

Subject index

action plan approach 159
activity analysis 213–22
adjudication 179, 180
adolescence 184–5
advisory support teachers (AST) 121, 126, 127
aggression 14–15
analytical tradition 7–8
ancillary staff 201–12; conditions of service 206; job description, roles and interpersonal factors 204; LEA responsibilities 207–9; nature of work 202–3; poor communication 204–5; qualifications and experience 206–7; role in schools 201–2; school responsibilities 209–11; status 207; support 204–5, 208–9, 209–11; training 205, 206, 208–9, 209–11
apprenticeship training model 134
arbitration: between school and parents 39–40, 102–3; pupil conflict 179, 180
assertive discipline 160, 169
assertiveness training 116
assessment: community-based 73; models 17–18
Association for Behavioural Approaches with Children 6

BATPAC 9, 160
Behaviour Support Conference 6
Behaviour Support Group (parents) 45, 46, 48
behaviour support teachers *see* support teachers
behaviour support team (BST) 120–32; consumer expectations 122–4; evaluation 127–32; initial phase of working 126–7; process for involvement with school 126–7, 128; training and induction 124–6
behavioural approaches 9; classroom management 210–11; successful behaviour support 33–4
boredom, playground 191, 194, 198
brain wave activity 15–16
BS 5750 19
Building a Better Behaved School (BABBS) 145–50, 160; contents 149–50; Positive Behaviour Project *see* Positive Behaviour Project; research background 145–9; using in schools 150
bullying 176, 189

case closure systems 85–6
cause attribution 94–8, 99
checking information 85
child guidance movement 7–8, 10
child protection procedures 71
Child Psychology Service (CPS) 120–1, 123, 127
Children Act (1989) 17
circular causality 96–8, 99
class rules 47
classroom management 146–7; ancillary staff 210–11; teacher peer support 170
clients' rights 18–20
close units 121
codes of conduct 57, 57–8, 249
cognitive dissonance 182
communication: ancillary staff 204–5; home-school 44–5, 59; self-management 233

R.